Coaching Psychology f
Health

Traditionally, coaching psychologists have worked with people who aren't experiencing significant mental distress or have diagnosed mental illness. This book describes an innovative and challenging project of bringing coaching psychology to the lived experience of individuals with a diagnosed mental illness, Borderline Personality Disorder (BPD).

The authors present a case for why coaching psychology needs to be constructively challenged to broaden its base and be more inclusive and of service to people experiencing BPD in particular. The book describes a coaching interaction involving coaching psychologists and a number of individuals with BPD who had completed a behavioural skills programme (Dialectical Behaviour Therapy; DBT). It explores the epistemological and practice tensions involving the dominance of clinical recovery (elimination of symptoms) in mental health services and personal or psychological recovery (originating in the narratives of people with a diagnosis of mental illness who yearn to live a life worth living).

This book, written amidst the COVID-19 pandemic, makes a compelling case for coaching psychologists to engage with the philosophy and practice implications of personal recovery, at both professional and personal levels. It will be vital reading for those engaged in coaching psychology and for the education, training and continuous professional development of coaches, and coaching psychologists.

Martin O'Connor works independently as a coaching and clinical psychologist, is a chartered psychologist (PSI) and is a registered analytic-network coach. He teaches and provides coach mentoring in the Masters in Positive and Coaching Psychology, University College Cork and teaches in Mary Immaculate College of Education (University of Limerick). He provides training, coaching, supervision, and mentoring to individuals working in statutory and voluntary health and disability services in Ireland.

Hugh O'Donovan is a chartered psychologist, teacher, author of *Mindful Walking*, conference speaker, and principal practitioner with Hugh O'Donovan and Associates. He is co-founder of the 1st Masters in Coaching Psychology in an Irish University (University College Cork) as well as a founder member of PSI, DWOP, Coaching Psychology Group. He is an honorary vice president of International Society for Coaching Psychology.

Coaching Psychology
Series Editor: Stephen Palmer

Coaching psychology is a distinct branch of academic and applied psychology that focuses on enhancement of performance, development, and wellbeing in the broader population. Written by leading experts, the **Coaching Psychology** series will highlight innovations in the field, linking theory, research and practice. These books will interest professionals from psychology, coaching, mentoring, business, health, human resources, and management as well as those interested in the psychology underpinning their coaching and mentoring practice.

https://www.routledge.com/Coaching-Psychology/book-series/COACHPSYCH

Coaching Psychology for Mental Health

Borderline Personality Disorder and Personal Psychological Recovery

Martin O'Connor and Hugh O'Donovan

Routledge
Taylor & Francis Group

LONDON AND NEW YORK

First published 2022
by Routledge
2 Park Square, Milton Park, Abingdon, Oxon OX14 4RN

and by Routledge
605 Third Avenue, New York, NY 10158

Routledge is an imprint of the Taylor & Francis Group, an informa business

British Library Cataloguing-in-Publication Data
A catalogue record for this book is available from the British Library

Library of Congress Cataloging-in-Publication Data
A catalog record has been requested for this book

ISBN: 978-0-367-50144-0 (hbk)
ISBN: 978-0-367-50145-7 (pbk)
ISBN: 978-1-003-04897-8 (ebk)

DOI: 10.4324/9781003048978

Typeset in Times New Roman
by MPS Limited, Dehradun

Contents

Preface

The genesis of this book has multiple sources. The main source is the coaching interactions that the authors and two other colleagues had with a number of individuals with a diagnosis of Borderline Personality Disorder (BPD). We owe each of these courageous and resilient individuals a debt of appreciation and gratitude. A further important source is our own personal journeys in negotiating the rapids of mental health and wellbeing. This experience of course is not unique to us. However, we declare this experience because many professional helpers may seek refuge in their professional identities only, often at great emotional cost to themselves.

We want to sincerely thank Daniel Flynn (Principal Psychology Manager, HSE Adult and Child/Adolescent Mental Health Services, Cork, Ireland) and Dr. Mary Kells (Principal Clinical Psychologist, HSE Adult and Child/Adolescent Mental Health Services, Cork, Ireland) with whom we had the opportunity and pleasure to collaborate with in order to bring the GLOW11 coaching interaction to fruition. Their support was steadfast and important. The project also demonstrated how interactions involving coaching psychology and clinical psychology can be fruitful in the service of enhancing the lived experience of individuals with BPD. We also want to thank in particular our GLOW11 coaching psychology colleagues, Sueanne Byford and Niamh Gaffney, for their invaluable contributions to GLOW11 preparation, planning, and implementation.

We hope that the book will help to open out for the reader the broad, interesting, and challenging landscape of mental health and mental distress in particular. While the book is primarily aimed towards coaching psychology (coaching), we hope it will also be of interest to all professions and disciplines working in mental health services, in Ireland and internationally. It will be evident in the book that we drew from multiple sources for our content. We hope that we have adequately and fairly represented all perspectives mentioned.

As authors and practitioners, we spent valuable time in mutual sharing and discussion in order to try to discern a foundation motivation, both regarding our participation in GLOW11 and in writing this book. In the end we were in agreement. To be of service is the energy at work. We hope that the book will stand as an act of service to each person we sat with and walked with in GLOW11 and who shared and trusted us with what each cared about, their values, hopes, dreams, and struggles. We hope that they, too, will find something of value in this book that assists each person towards a clear view of a life worth living.

Chapter 1

Introduction and background review

Guiding purpose

The overall guiding purpose of this book is to present to the reader a doable, flexible, adaptive, and integrated coaching psychology approach that has the potential to assist our understanding of how coaching psychology might be of service to the unique lived experience of individuals with a diagnosis of mental illness in our society, in particular Borderline Personality Disorder (BPD). GLOW 11 (goals for living, options for wellness) refers to a recent coaching psychology interaction in an Irish context with individuals with a diagnosis of BPD (who had previously participated in a Dialectical Behaviour Therapy (DBT) programme facilitated by a Clinical Psychology team in an Adult Mental Health service, and who had been behaviourally stable for the previous 12 months). It will no doubt be evident as the reader travels through this book that the actual coaching interactions with participants in GLOW11 as coachees did not overly if at all, focus on strategies for goal-formulation and became much more concerned with supporting individuals towards clarity about what a life worth living meant to each.

We (the authors) also want to draw attention to and explore concepts of mental health, in particular mental illness, not only in the traditional clinical context of the psychiatric service system, but in the broader and more primary context of societal and corporate assumptions expectations, pressures, and demands regarding the 'good life.'

We also want to invite, if not challenge, the world of coaching psychology to reflect on our ethical and professional responsibilities in the context of a world where certainty and knowing is fast becoming past tense. Einzig (2017) writes that coaches would do well to follow our own advice to pause, step back, take stock and reflect on the role of coaching at this time, where we face into 'a perfect storm of crises – ecological, economic, social, and psycho-spiritual – is affecting us all on a global level' and that 'coaches need to develop the depth, mindset and skills founded in strong values that will help reset the moral compass' (p. 6).

DOI: 10.4324/9781003048978-1

In our challenge, we include traditional normative thinking and psychiatric 'certainties' about BPD and other forms of diagnosed mental illness. The stigmas about mental ill-health remain firmly ensconced within many aspects of contemporary culture. Einzig (2017) writes that 'with an emphasis on performance, positivity and strengths, coaches may deliberately or inadvertently deter their clients from appearing down.' Talking about states of depressed mood, loss of interest or pleasure in life, and generalised anxiety is not welcomed in the workplace, so we dissemble – 'fine' is the expected response to 'how are you?' (pp. 121/1220). In the GLOW 11 coaching psychology intervention, when participants were asked at the beginning of a session 'how are you?' happily but not without challenge to the coaching psychologist, the response was always honest, courageous and real! Consequently, when Einzig (2017) states that 'we live now in a world that favours the light over the dark, upbeat optimism over scepticism, extroverts over introverts and action over reflection' with little patience 'with sadness, doubt, failure, ambivalence or despair' (p. 122), we can invite you, the reader, to suspend your assumptions and beliefs if you have an interest in bringing coaching psychology to the lived subjective experience of persons with BPD.

Beginnings

The genesis of this book emerged in the course of reflective conversations over time between the authors. These conversations, several of them recorded, occurred in the context of developing ideas that eventually translated into GLOW11 and later into this book.

As each author began to experience a sense of trust, psychological safety, and emotional containment with the other, our conversations 'strayed' into a mutual sharing about our own struggles with mental health at various points in life. Implicit in this was sharing and reflecting on the narratives, assumptions, expectations, and beliefs about self that each of us carried forward from childhood families and communities of origin in Ireland. This sharing helped to open up a reflective interpersonal space where we helped one another to linger and go deeper into subjective lived experience, memories, impact and 'muddling through' the fog and sometimes darkness arising from mental health challenges along the way. Stelter (2019) writes 'To be able to linger in dialogue, one has to move away from a narrow goal focus by exploring meaning and values and thus seek a deeper understanding of oneself and one's world' (p. 44). As we lingered in our dialogue about our own lived experiences, we also discovered an energising curiosity about the importance of understanding the lived experience of the individuals with BPD participating in GLOW11. The idea of writing this book thus emerged as something like the right thing to do. The reader can decide for her- or himself whether writing the book was indeed the right thing to do, at this time!

In the context of this book and our coaching psychology work with individuals with BPD, the authors identify with a definition of coaching psychology as being by its nature 'relational and dialogic, where two or more people discover new meaning and co-create new thinking and ways of being and doing in the world between them' (Hawkins & Turner, 2020, p. 1). This definition in being neither limiting nor prescriptive, helps to open a space for considering and reflecting on some of the ways in which the subjective experience of mental illness and our current society are in our view interdependent. In the context of the lived experience of individuals with a diagnosis of BPD, the authors have a particular interest in and concerns about the impacts of the fast-evolving nature of change in current society, the anxiety-provoking threats implicit in climate change and the insidious nature of structural economic and social inequality which pushes increasing numbers of individuals towards marginalisation and alienation. People experiencing mental distress and BPD are likely to be especially vulnerable in this context. In building coaching relationships with individuals with BPD, we frequently had direct experience of and felt challenged by their 'dance' between hope and despair (Wright, 2016) and admiration for their courage and resilience.

The book describes and explores some of the current constructive and energising tensions in thinking, research and approach with regard to our understanding of the lived experience of mental illness and BPD, in particular the paradigm shift from the concept of clinical recovery towards a personal or psychological recovery.

Every new development in the application of coaching psychology asks important questions about the current assumptions underpinning practice. GLOW11 is a new development in the field of coaching/coaching psychology and therefore challenges coaching practitioners, academics, and trainers to develop a critical reflective stance to question the norms and assumptions of coaching (Western, 2012). We believe that this is particularly important as regards assumptions about coaching and people experiencing significant mental distress.

A coaching psychology approach to mental illness and BPD

Cavicchia and Gilbert (2019) write that while existing definitions of coaching tend to be quite general and conceptual, this offers opportunities for coaches 'to develop a unique approach to coaching based on their own personalities, training, histories and life experience, all interacting with these corresponding aspects and unique requirements in their different clients and their contexts' (p. 6). Having participated in the planning and implementation of GLOW11 and engaged in ongoing critical reflection and learning subsequently, this book is an attempt to describe a unique experience of bringing coaching psychology to people with a diagnosis of BPD. In the book, we offer reflection and learning from GLOW11 in the hope of contributing to constructive conversation about the possibilities and challenges of coaching psychology interacting with the lived experience of people with BPD in particular. Here we are also cognisant of the impact of words and language that can be distinctive of different disciplines and professions. Rhodes (2020), writing about the language that tends to be the norm in clinical psychology, states 'these forms of language seek to differentiate the clinician from the client, amplifying polarities. The clinician is objective, the client is the object. The clinician is mentally healthy, the client mentally ill. We both become objects' (p. 2). When considering mental illness/mental distress, coaching psychology is not immune to what might be called the pitfalls of normative thinking and uses of normative language, namely an 'us' and 'them' silo approach of 'non-clinical' and 'clinical' groupings. As coaching psychology diversifies, drawing from rich multiple sources to create new genres, our conviction arising from GLOW11 is that it is timely to critically reflect on our assumptions and beliefs about mental illness/mental distress. Einzig (2017) asks 'but suppose we allowed ourselves to entertain a different view of depression, sadness and anxiety from the polarised and pathologized view held by the Western medical model?' (p. 123). Coaching psychology, if it is to be and remain culturally and socially relevant needs to offer something more to people suffering from significant mental distress, such as BPD, than taking refuge in the ever-increasing classifications of DSM that is resulting in an ever-increasing pathologizing of human experience in a volatile, uncertain, complex, and ambiguous world (VUCA).

While in this book we lean away from adherence to universal or all-embracing definitions of coaching psychology, there are particular 'definitions' that resonate with us in the context of our experience of GLOW11 and which we view as helpful to discussion. For example, Hawkins and Turner (2020) in the context of systemic coaching describe coaching as a collaborative and dialogical inquiry between two people, 'exploring how the coachee can learn and develop in relation to the worlds they are embedded within, in a way that creates positive benefit for them and all the nested systems of which they are part' (p. 28). Einzig (2017) refers to coaches taking a view of people, elements, and actions 'as not only interconnected but interdependent and are willing to engage with the extreme complexity of our age' (p. 46). Western (2012) refers to four critical frames to analyse coaching – emancipation (ethics, liberation, autonomy, and justice: coaching to help create the 'good society'; depth analysis (revealing hidden dynamics in individuals, organisations and the social field); looking awry (bringing desire and disruption to observation and understanding); and network analysis (network coaching, connectivity, interdependence, emergence) (pp. 34/35). Stelter (2019) refers to an increasing realisation in his work how important it is for the coach 'to be a fellow human being and a co-creative partner in the dialogue' and that 'coaching should not be limited to a performance-oriented and goal-driven agenda' (p. 3). In particular, Cavicchia and Gilbert's (2019) reference to an integrative-relational orientation speaks in important ways to the necessity of taking a moment-by-moment perspective in the GLOW11 one-to-one coaching sessions. They highlight also that coaching boundaries are expanding to allow for greater appreciation of the importance of meaning making, wellbeing, complexity, and systemic perspectives. At the same time, just as every new or novel perspective appears in coaching psychology and enters the discourse to become normative, there is the need to continue to playfully experiment. Marsha Linehan (2020) the developer of Dialectical Behaviour Therapy (DBT) as a behavioural skills programme for people with BPD refers to a Zen phrase – beginner's mind – meaning 'that every single moment is the very first experience you have had of that moment. Every new moment is a beginning … Beginner's mind is the recognition of this' (pp. 275/276). Linehan (2020) adds that initially in her deliberations on BPD she analysed everything, seeking the meaning of everything, rather than a radical acceptance that 'everything just is' (p. 276). Certainly, for us GLOW11 required an attitude and approach of beginner's mind! There were no coaching models to guide us on the way. In this book we do not present a coaching model. We present a jigsaw of reflections, insights, discoveries about the self in coaching psychology, and appreciation and gratitude for the people we were privileged to meet, from whom we learned the necessary coexistence of suffering and hope. We are also struck that the vast majority of attempts to define coaching/coaching psychology, including those referenced above, are specific to organisational, executive and leadership contexts. To date, there appears to be very little discussion of coaching psychology in non-organisational contexts. GLOW11 operated in a transitional space of individuals with BPD seeking to emerge from mental health services and build connections with community life.

Given the very particular life experiences of each participant in GLOW11, with a preponderance of emotional pain and trauma experiences implicit in their respective 'recovery' journeys, the importance of creating and sustaining a 'holding environment' in coaching sessions was of critical importance. Lee (2018), citing Winnicott, 1965), refers to the 'holding environment' as a physical and in particular a psychological space 'in which coachees feel safe enough to be open with their thoughts and feelings; to be able to share their anxieties, frustrations, aspirations and deepest hopes' (p. 4/5). The importance of coaching psychologists having both the inclination and capacity to provide a 'holding environment' in coaching sessions is perhaps self-evident generally, however its importance in the work of GLOW11 was critical. Western (2012) draws upon psychoanalytic theory and practice in applying the concepts of 'paternal' and 'maternal' containment to the coaching process, adding that these concepts provide a psycho-social framework for the coaching process and also the education and training of coaches. In a related context, Vaughan Smith (2019) provides a very useful framework in this context about the impact of trauma (which is common in people with BPD). The impacts of trauma include hypervigilance, toxic stress, lowered capacity for self-regulation, high anxiety, insecure attachment patterns, loss of ability to trust self and others, feeling unsafe, loss of good contact with body and felt experience, loss of self-compassion, fragmented and disorganised memory, low self-esteem and self-confidence, and dissociation as a defence against feeling (Vaughan Smith. 2019, p. 34).

From a coaching psychology perspective, the lack of pre-existing and proven coaching psychology frameworks that might be applicable to GLOW11, did open up interesting and exciting spaces of opportunity for engaging with and learning from our coaching interactions. Ultimately, the one non-negotiable attitude necessary was and is that of respect and respectful behaviour. Egan (2014) refers to respect as the foundation value of the helping relationship, a fundamental way of seeing and viewing oneself and others, and which if it is to make a real difference cannot remain simply an attitude – ideally the helping relationship is built on and around two persons who matter to one another (p. 34).

Background

The authors are cognisant of the up-to-now normative assumptions, beliefs and thinking about whether coaching psychology can bring something of value to the lived experience of individuals with a diagnosis of mental illness and/or BPD. For example, Cavanagh and Buckley (2018), citing Buckley (2007) and Grant (2005), write that the 'dominant position among coaches maintains that coaching is targeted towards working with clients from non-clinical populations, whereas therapy is designed to address the needs of people suffering from diagnosable conditions, such as personality disorders, substance abuse, depression, anxiety and other mood disorders' (p. 451). However, Cavanagh and Buckley (2018), citing both the Australian Bureau of Statistics (2008) and Svrakic et al. (2002), also write that this simple distinction between clinical and non-clinical is problematic, based on experience and a growing body of research and that coaches are likely to be 'regularly faced with coachees exhibiting some form of mental health difficulty. Epidemiological studies suggest that up to 45% of people in the general population will suffer some diagnosable mental health problem at some point in their life' and 'that 10–15% of the population suffer from some form of personality disorder' (p. 451). In a similar vein, Einzig (2017), citing the Mental Health Foundation (2016), writes that mental health challenges are responsible for the 'largest burden of dis-ease' (p. 119) in the UK: 28% compared to 16% for cancer or heart disease. Estimates of the prevalence of Borderline Personality Disorder (BPD) vary, however most studies estimate it affects 1–2% of the population (Paris, 2020).

The individuals who participated in GLOW11 had previously been given a diagnosis of Borderline Personality Disorder (BPD). Each had also previously participated in and completed a Dialectical Behaviour Therapy (DBT) intervention programme, organised and facilitated by the relevant Adult Mental Health Psychology Department. In the co-working and planning for GLOW11 between the Adult Mental Health Psychology team and the Coaching Psychologists concerned, it was agreed that each prospective participant would have been 'behaviourally stable' (absence of self-harming) for a period of at least one year, in order to be accepted into GLOW11. Each prospective GLOW11 participant was also interviewed by a coaching psychologist, with their DBT therapist present, to ascertain their interest in, motivation, and readiness for such a coaching psychology interaction. The consultant psychiatrist concerned with each prospective GLOW11 participant was also in agreement with their participation. The process of decision-making involved leaning strongly towards a consideration of each individual's suitability from a perspective of known vulnerabilities as well as their written hopes for personal growth and quality of life.

GLOW11 was comprised of 5 one-to-one coaching sessions with each participant (12 participants) and five group coaching sessions with all participants invited to attend. Both participants and coaching psychologists also spent a full day in a rural-based ecological centre, which proved to be both a mindful and energising individual and group experience for all concerned.

GLOW11 was accompanied by a mixed methods research study. We do not have access as yet to the research data, the gathering and collating of which has been significantly impacted by COVID-19 and related issues. We have included in the book a good deal of qualitative and anecdotal data gathered from GLOW11 participants and from our own notes, which are reported in anonymised form and which we hope will give the reader a solid sense of the coaching process and experience.

In the context of whether coaching psychology and mental illness, the authors note and are in agreement with a key context and question referenced by Cavanagh and Buckley (2018) – 'Coaches whose background is in psychology or the psychological therapies may have the skills, training and experience to be able to come to an informed decision as to what is wrong and may be well placed to offer effective therapy, but should still ask the question, can my coaching help? rather than can I help?' (p. 453). The authors and their coaching psychologist colleagues in GLOW11 considered this question in great detail and depth in a context of a journey into a largely previously unknown coaching space, as to whether coaching psychology might be of genuine service to individuals with BPD.

Coaching psychology and searching for a unifying coaching framework in GLOW11

The co-working and planning between the Adult Mental Health Psychology team and coaching psychologists was central and pivotal to the setting up and sustaining of GLOW11. Each coaching psychologist, in addition to a professional coaching qualification, also had a professional qualification with a primary psychology degree. This was a necessary pre-condition set by Adult Mental Health Psychology and their employer, the Health Service Executive (Ireland), given the inherent challenges and opportunities of GLOW11.

In the context of the question 'can my coaching help?' the four coaching psychologists involved in GLOW11 came together for a series of planning days as preparation. These sessions were essential towards identifying a doable, integrative relational coaching psychology approach, with a core unifying framework, while also allowing for and receptive to individual differences across personality, temperament, experience, gender, and life/ work background. Through detailed discussion and reflection, the core unifying framework agreed was a focus on the clarification of participant's individual values and working with these values in both one-to-one and group settings. We felt that working with values would provide each participant with a direction for their struggles and hopes that would be both supportive and challenging, as well as providing a containing focus and point of reference for discussion in coaching sessions.

Hill and Oliver (2019), from an acceptance and commitment perspective, refer to particular guiding questions regarding working with values, which we found helpful in GLOW11 – 'in simplest terms, one could see values as the answer to the question "why?" Why would someone willingly open up to and accept difficult feelings? Why would someone consciously observe and come into contact with uncomfortable thoughts? Why would someone mindfully connect with a present moment that might be challenging or scary? Why would someone invest the time and energy that it takes to develop these skills?' (p. 37). Hill and Oliver (2019) define values as personally chosen, which when acted on, bring an internal sense of meaning, vitality or fulfilment, and as consisting of a life direction rather than a destination. Hill and Oliver (2019) use a helpful metaphor to illuminate this difference between a life direction and destination – 'to think of values as being like a compass guiding you through the journey of life. Taking conscious action on your values is like heading west – it's a direction you can head in, rather than a destination you will actually reach' (p. 39).

In a coaching context, Stelter (2012) writes – 'often the coachee is not fully aware of the values that are such an essential guide for his or her actions. They lie dormant under the surface of action. The coach's questions about the value base of an act may serve to wake them up, activating them and initiating a process of reflection and development' (p. 131).

The critical importance of values has also been described across the broad literature on psychological recovery in the context of diagnosed mental illness. Andresen, Oades, and Caputi (2011) write that values relate more to the quality of action brought to bear by an individual in any given particular situation, rather than being linked explicitly to achieving particular out-comes, a moving towards one's preferred identity. These author–researchers further write that 'relevant to mental health recovery, values can provide a powerful motivational force in directing purposeful action during times of adversity' (p. 141) and citing Twohig, Hayes, and Masuda (2006) and Gregg, Callaghan, Hayes, and Glenn-Lawson (2007) 'research indicates that in-dividuals who engage in more values-consistent behaviour experience higher quality of life and reduced physical and psychological pain than other in-dividuals' (pp. 143/144). In the context of a values-based approach to practice in mental health services, which has implications for coaching psychology practice in mental health, Slade (2009) writes that being aware of and engaging in discussion about implicit values is critical and that 'a mental health service using a values-based practice approach necessarily places great emphasis on the dreams, aspirations and goals of the person. This approach therefore promotes a focus on personal recovery' (pp. 140/141). In the context of GLOW11 each participant was supported to reflect on and identify personally chosen core values in individually selected life domains and subsequently to identify key life goals underpinned and guided by their chosen values. This emphasis on values, in particular the process of values guiding behaviour and decision-making, proved to be a critical life-giving element of GLOW11 for each participant, based on their regular anecdotal and qualitative feedback throughout and following the completed coaching interaction.

Central to the coaching psychologists' preparation for GLOW11 was our preparatory work on clarification, questioning and application regarding our own values. The process understandably revealed both some shared values and uniquely personal values, though no values conflict. This process also helped to identify and solidify a shared sense of commitment to our coaching, not only informed by values in GLOW11, but also cognisant of the very human tendency towards viewing and communicating with others through a filter of one's own values. A further and interesting perspective on the importance of trying to help others, in particular persons who have experienced emotional pain and trauma, is that written by Walser (2019) – 'are we guiding ourselves and our clients to be explicitly in contact with the two different ways of knowing the world – with the mind and with experi-ence? Are we and our clients working to find a place where the stance taken in relationship to our experience is such that painful thoughts, feelings, sensations, and memories are encountered in a non-judgmental and open way? Are we and our clients finding the freedom to live by our values and not just the literal content of emotions and thoughts?' (p. 7). In the authors' experience from GLOW11, this important emphasis on the importance of engaging and connecting with participants in a non-judgemental and open way brought into view what turned out to be a critical issue – does the coachee 'matter' to the coach and how does the capacity to demonstrate this quality constitute something important in bringing coaching psychology to mental illness and BPD? Is this a core necessary and required capacity for the coaching psychologist in all coaching contexts? How can this quality be nurtured and sustained? Is it essential to the coaching relationship? Does mattering really matter? Simply, the authors say yes to these questions.

Borderline Personality Disorder (BPD)

Paris (2020) presents a compelling overview of the nature and symptoms associated with Borderline Personality Disorder (BPD), including that 'the most frightening symptoms of BPD are chronic suicidal ideation, repeated suicide attempts, and self-harm' (p. 1). Paris (2020) goes on to list several other symptom domains also associated with a diagnosis of BPD, each of which can present with very difficult life challenges for the person concerned and for the helping professional involved – emotional dysregulation (difficult to manage and showing only a weak response to medication); impulsive behaviours (both in and out of therapy); interpersonal sensitivity (relationships often chaotic, marked by dependency and anger, a pattern that can also occur in disrupting the therapeutic alliance); and cognitive symptoms (paranoid ideas, depersonalization, auditory hallucinations); with an onset early in life. In a similar vein, Stanghellini and Mancini (2019) highlight general agreement about the fact that the main features of BPD are '1) emotions tend to be intense and rapidly shifting; 2) relationships tend to be conflicted and stormy; 3) there may be impulsive, self-destructive, or self-defeating behaviours; 4) there is a lack of a clear and coherent sense of identity' (p. 665).

There have been and continue to be many criticisms of the term 'borderline.' Kulkarni and Walker (2019) refer to BPD as a highly stigmatised and misunderstood disorder, better understood as a complex response to a history of major trauma, often experienced in childhood (includes sexual and physical abuse, extreme neglect, and separation from parents or loved ones). From a coaching perspective, Vaughan Smith (2019) states that the understanding in the trauma field is that most forms of undiagnosed or diagnosed mental ill health, including personality disorder, 'have their roots in early childhood trauma and are forms of trauma survival' (p. 14). Paris (2020) agrees that the term 'borderline' is a misnomer and fails to capture the most essential features of the condition – unstable mood, impulsivity, and unstable relationships. However, Paris (2020) argues that to date a better term than 'borderline' has not been identified, with most suggestions focusing on only one of the salient features and thereby not doing justice to the full complexity of the condition.

DSM-5 (2013) describes BPD as having nine essential criteria – fear of abandonment, unstable relationships, unstable self-image, impulsivity, self-damaging behaviours, affective instability, emptiness, excessive anger, and paranoid ideas or dissociation. Kulkarni and Walker (2019) note that BPD is referenced in the DSM-5 text section devoted to personality disorders rather than in the section on trauma and stressor-related disorders.

Resonant with our experience of coaching psychology in GLOW11 regarding the mental health challenges of persons with Borderline Personality Disorder, Fuchs (2007) captures something important about the lived experience of people with BPD – 'this fragmentation of life results in the loss of a coherent personal identity, leaving the individual at the mercy of momentary impulses and mood states, unable to integrate the pieces of his life into a coherent narrative, and thus also unable to, at least, attach a meaning to his suffering itself' (p. 386).

Mattering

During a particular individual coaching session, a GLOW11 participant, in giving feedback to the coaching psychologist concerned, said 'at the start of our coaching sessions, you said that I mattered to you and that the work we did together mattered to you … you said that to me at a time when I felt that I didn't really matter to myself. At the time and even more so now, what you said to me, it mattered!' The concept and the felt emotional experience of 'mattering' during the course of GLOW11 and endeavouring to build a working relationship, constituted a strong element of the anecdotal feedback by participants at the conclusion of coaching. The authors have included this reference to 'mattering' here because they consider it to be a critical component of bring coaching psychology to individuals with a diagnosed mental illness, in particular BPD. The authors are also of the view that 'mattering' to others and its implications for the coaching relationship should be a key consideration in coach training, supervision, continuing professional development and coaching research. Flett 2018) writes that mattering is essential to wellbeing and unfortunately has been largely neglected by the academic and research community. In a counselling context, Rayle (2006) writes that 'this powerful experience is needed by all people, including clients and counsellors, and thus has promising prospects for strengthening the counselling relationship' (p. 486). Thomas (2011) writes that mattering intuitively matters to mental health and that it makes sense to mental health professionals that individuals who believe that they do not matter would be vulnerable to depression, possibly suicide or perhaps acting–out to compel the attention of someone. Elliott, Kao, and Grant (2004) pose the following scenario – 'if people do not share themselves meaningfully with us, if no one listens to what we have to say, if we are interesting to no one, then we must cope with the realisation that we do not matter. The world not only can but does get along without us, and we are truly irrelevant' (p. 339). Is there a human being who cannot identify somewhat or strongly with this scenario?

The authors propose that the concept of 'mattering' in order for it to 'matter' to coaching psychology practice, needs to be viewed essentially as a relational process, rather than a quality residing only in one individual in a helping relationship. In the context of positive psychology, Peterson (2009) comments 'let's assume that mattering matters. The obvious question is how can we matter? I suggest that one good strategy for cultivating mattering is indirect, allowing other people to matter to you. Mattering is usually discussed as a feature of the individual, but it is likely as well a feature of one's relationship with others. And I suspect mattering is highly contagious' (p. 2). In this context, Stanghellini's (2017) comments about individuals who experience mental illness and trauma are significant – 'trauma is part and piece of everyday existence', an experience we live by that is one with our need and desire to establish relationships, and that 'the kind of teleology at play in human relationships is *the desire for reciprocal recognition*' (p. 3), with our deepest need and desire being 'to be loved *as we are*, notwithstanding our limitations, weaknesses, faults, and culpabilities' (p. 3).

Conclusion

Drawing from the statement by Fuchs (2007) above about the lived experience of people with BPD, it is possible that one of the benefits of GLOW11 is that a number of individuals with BPD were supported on their journey of trying to bring some meaning that mattered to their experiences of trauma, suffering, and fragmenting identities. This perspective may be at odds with much of the normative commentary and research on coaching psychology; however, it does reflect what Western (2012) refers to (albeit primarily in the context of organisational and executive coaching) as the need to bridge the 'Wounded Self' (a self that is damaged, fragmented or emotionally hurt) and the 'Celebrated Self' (a more positive view of the individual where 'in contemporary society we face the imperative to discover and then celebrate our true selves; this is our only refuge in an uncertain world' (p. 9).

Arising from our individual and shared experiences of and learnings from GLOW11, the authors of this book strongly advocate for a renewal in cultivating a critical reflective and reflexive practice regarding coaching psychology and the various definitions, perspectives, and understandings of mental illness, mental disorder and/or mental distress. Gardiner (2019) describes reflective practice as a looking back to learn from past situations and actions and reflexive practice as 'a responsivity that comes from attending, with acute awareness, to what is current and calling for attention in the present moment' (p. 110). The authors can attest to the humanising, ethical, and emancipatory impacts of engaging with both reflective and reflexive practice, as we struggled enthusiastically with our colleagues in preparing for GLOW11, in experiencing new dimensions and perspectives in coaching psychology, and not least, endeavouring to make sense and find meaning in our respective mental health struggles.

In conclusion here, from a perspective of progressive psychiatry, Stanghellini (2017) states that the basis of working with individuals with a mental illness is based on two pillars – a dialectic, person-centred understanding of mental disorders, and values-based practice. Our work in GLOW11 and in the writing of this book has been informed and influenced by several disciplines and ways of knowing. We consider that coaching psychology, with the hybrid nature of coaching practice reflecting the hybrid nature of post-modern society (Western, 2012), has much to learn and much to offer in the cross-fertilisation energies of a globalised world. We agree with Western (2012) that the 'call for professionalizing and institutionalizing coaching into a homogenous body of knowledge carries with it great dangers...' because 'any move towards professionalization or unity of coaching practice has to be tempered by the knowledge that coaching is at its strongest when it can be fluid, adaptive, entrepreneurial and reads the contemporary social times' (p. 112).

GLOW11, as a process of endeavouring to understand how coaching psychology might be of service to the lived experience of individuals with BPD, intentionally adopted and committed to the unifying energy of values and mattering as a shared coaching practice framework and a shared orientation point for coaching psychologist review sessions and peer support.

Discussion points

1. What are your current assumptions about the role of coaching psychology in the context of working with people experiencing significant mental distress?
2. What knowledge gap do you have about Borderline Personality Disorder (BPD) and other forms of significant mental distress?
3. Do you/how do you incorporate clarifying and working with values into your work as a coaching practitioner?
4. Have you considered the importance of 'mattering' in your reflections on coaching practice?

Suggested reading

Cavicchia, S., & Gilbert, M. (2019). *The theory and practice of relational coaching: Complexity, paradox and integration.* London, UK: Routledge. (Chapter 1 has a very interesting overview of an integrative relational approach to coaching in challenging times).

Einzig, H. (2017). *The future of coaching; Vision, leadership and responsibility in a transforming world.* London, UK: Routledge. (While the book itself is recommended reading, the section on mental health issues and implications for coaching makes for interesting reading pp. 119–24, pp. 129–30).

Hill, J., & Oliver, J. (2019). *Acceptance and commitment coaching: Distinctive features*. London, UK: Routledge. (Chapters 10, 22, and 23 provide concise overviews about working with values).

Paris, J. (2020). *Treatment of borderline personality disorder: A guide to evidence-based practice* (2nd ed.). New York: Guilford Press. (Chapter 1 provides a good overview of the diagnosis of Borderline Personality Disorder).

Western, S. (2012). *Coaching and mentoring: A critical text*. London, UK: Sage Publications. (Chapter 13 (pp. 264–271) outlines the concepts of 'paternal' and 'maternal' containment in coaching).

References

Andresen, R., Oades, L. G., & Caputi, P. (2011). *Psychological recovery: Beyond mental illness*. Chichester, UK: Wiley-Blackwell.

Australian Bureau of Statistics. (2008). *National survey of mental health and well-being: Summary of results, 2007*. Retrieved April 2013 from www.abs.gov.au/ausstats/abs

Buckley, A. (2007). The mental health boundary in relationship to coaching and other activities. *International Journal of Evidence Based Coaching and Mentoring*, Special Issue, Summer: 17–23.

Cavanagh, M., & Buckley, A. (2018). Coaching and mental health. In E. Cox, T. Bachkirova, & D. Clutterbuck (Eds.), *The Complete Handbook of Coaching* (3rd ed., pp. 451–464). London, UK: Sage Publications.

Cavicchia, S., & Gilbert, M. (2019). *The theory and practice of relational coaching: Complexity, paradox and integration*. London, UK: Routledge.

DSM-5. (2013). *Diagnostic and statistical manual of mental disorders* (5th ed.). Washington, DC: American Psychiatric Publishing.

Egan, G. (2014). *The skilled helper: A client-centred approach*. Andover, UK: Cengage Learning.

Einzig, H. (2017). *The future of coaching; Vision, leadership and responsibility in a transforming world*. London, UK: Routledge.

Elliott, G., Kao, S., & Grant, A. M. (2004). Mattering: Empirical validation of a social-psychological concept. *Self and Identity*, *3*(4), 339–354.

Flett, G. L. (2018). *The psychology of mattering: Understanding the human need to be significant*. London, UK: Academic Press.

Fuchs, T. (2007). Fragmented selves: Temporality and identity in borderline personality disorder. *Psychopathology*, *40*, 379–387.

Gardiner, L. J. N. (2019). Attending, daring, becoming: Making boundary-play conscious. In J. Birch, & P. Welch (Eds.), *Coaching supervision: Advancing practice, changing landscapes*. London, UK: Routledge.

Grant, A. M. (2005). A model of goal striving and mental health for coaching populations. *International Coaching Psychology Review*, *2*(3), 248–262.

Gregg, G. A., Callaghan, G. M., Hayes, S. C., & Glenn-Lawson, J. L. (2007). Improved diabetes self-management through acceptance, mindfulness and values:

A randomised controlled trial. *Journal of Consulting and Clinical Psychology*, *75*(2), 336–343.

Hawkins, P., & Turner, E. (2020). *Systemic coaching: Delivering value beyond the individual*. London, UK: Routledge.

Hill, J., & Oliver, J. (2019). *Acceptance and commitment coaching: Distinctive features.* London, UK: Routledge.

Kulkarni, J., & Walker, P. (2019). Retrieved 11th February, 2020 from https://theconversation.com

Lee, G. (2018). The psychodynamic approach to coaching. In E. Cox, T. Bachkirova, & D. Clutterbuck (Eds.), *The complete handbook of coaching* (pp. 3–16). London, UK: Sage.

Linehan, M. (2020). *Building a life worth living: A memoir*. New York: Random House.

Mental Health Foundation. (2016). *Fundamental facts about mental health*. Mental Health Foundation. https://www.mentalhealth.Org.uk/sites/default/files/fundamental-facts-15.pdf

Paris, J. (2020). *Treatment of borderline personality disorder: A guide to evidence-based practice* (2nd ed.). New York: Guilford Press.

Peterson, C. (2009). *The good life. Some muttering on mattering*. Retrieved 11th February, 2020 from https://www.psychologytoday.com/blog/the-good-life/200912/some-muttering-mattering

Rayle, A. D. (2006). Mattering to others: Implications for the counselling relationship. *Journal of Counselling and Development*, *84*, 483–487.

Rhodes, P. (Ed.) (2020). *Beyond the psychology industry: How else might we heal?* Cham, Switzerland: Springer.

Slade, M. (2009). *Personal recovery and mental illness: A guide for mental health professionals*. Cambridge, UK: Cambridge University Press.

Stanghellini, G. (2017). *The therapeutic interview in mental health: A values-based and person-centred approach*. Cambridge, UK: Cambridge University Press.

Stanghellini, G., & Mancini, M. (2019). The life-world of persons with borderline personality disorder. In G. Stanghellini, M. Broome, A. Raballo, A. V. Fernandez, P. Fusar-Poli, & R. Rosfort (Eds.), *The Oxford handbook of phenomenological psychopathology* (pp. 665–681). Oxford, UK: Oxford University Press.

Stelter, R. (2012). *A guide to third generation coaching: Narrative - collaborative theory and practice*. London, UK: Springer.

Stelter, R. (2019). *The art of dialogue in coaching: Towards transformative exchange*. London, UK: Routledge.

Svrakic, D. M., Draganic, S., Hill, K., Bayon, C., Przybeck, T. R., & Cloninger, C. R. (2002). Temperament, character, and personality disorders; etiologic, diagnostic, treatment issues. *Acta Psychiatrica Scandinavica*, *106*(3), 189–195.

Thomas, S. (2011). What is mattering and how does it relate to mental health? *Issues in Mental Health Nursing*, *32*, 485.

Twohig, M. P., Hayes, S. C., & Masuda, A. (2006). A preliminary investigation of acceptance and commitment therapy as a treatment for chronic skin picking. *Behaviour Research and Therapy*, *44*, 1513–1522.

Vaughan Smith, J. (2019). *Coaching and trauma*. London, UK: Open University Press.

Walser, R. (2019). *The heart of act: Developing a flexible, process-based & client-centred practice using acceptance & commitment therapy*. Oakland, CA: Harbinger.

Western, S. (2012). *Coaching and mentoring: A critical text*. London, UK: Sage Publications.

Winnicott, D. W. (1965). *The maturational processes and the facilitating environment: Studies in the theory of emotional development*. International Universities Press.

Wright, S. (2016). *Dancing between hope and despair: Trauma, attachment and the therapeutic relationship*. London, UK: Palgrave.

Chapter 2

Mental health policy and recovery: The challenge of moving from rhetoric to reality

An overview

The concept of recovery is currently the guiding principle underpinning mental health policy in several Western and English-speaking countries, including Ireland (Department of Health, 2006), Department of Health, Social Services and Public Safety (Northern Ireland) (2010), England (Department of Health, 2001), Scotland (Scottish Government, 2012), Australia (2003), New Zealand (Mental Health Commission, 1998), Mental Health Commission of Canada (2012), and the United States (President's New Freedom Commission on Mental Health, 2003). The American Psychiatric Association (2005) has signed up to the concept of recovery.

As authors and coaching psychologists in Ireland we will focus here on relevant Irish government mental health policy document publications. We think such an overview provides a useful flavour of the challenges involved in moving from policy statements to implementation.

In 2006 'A Vision for Change: Report of the Expert Group on Mental Health Policy' identified recovery as underlining Irish mental health policy, but did not have any implementation plan. In 2017, a framework document 'A National Framework for Recovery in Mental Health' (2018–2020) was published. The purpose of this document is to provide mental health service providers with a framework for the delivery of quality, person-centred mental health services. The document identifies four main recovery principles: the centrality of the service – user lived experience; the co-production of recovery – promoting services involving all stakeholders; an organisational commitment to the development of recovery-oriented mental health services; and supporting recovery-oriented learning and recovery-oriented practice across all stakeholder groups. The document refers to the recovery expertise of 'service users,' family members and carers having three core elements: lived experience – having a unique insight into the experience of having a mental health condition, using mental health services, and the impact of each on their lives; recovery experience – 'as people come to an understanding, acceptance and ownership of their mental health condition,

DOI: 10.4324/9781003048978-2

they begin to reclaim their lives from illness' (p. 10), which can involve strategies, techniques and skills that help to achieve self-determined goals that are important to them; and experts by experience – the knowledge and insights gained on the road to recovery from a mental health condition makes the lived and recovery experience valuable as a resource in a recovery-oriented mental health service.

Mental health services professional staff are described as having a fund of practice wisdom, as well as their own experiences of mental health challenges, which can be of assistance to 'service-users' in their efforts towards recovery.

The Irish document refers to what is recognised as the traditional view of mental health recovery where the person has 'full symptom remission, full/part-time work/education, independent living without supervision by informal carers, having friends with whom activities can be shared and sustained for a period of two years' (Libermann & Kopelowicz, 2002). This definition is referred to as clinical recovery in the literature. The document also refers to a systematic literature review (Leamy, Bird, Le Boutillier, Williams, & Slade, 2011) which identified five processes that people with mental health challenges considered essential for recovery to happen: connectedness – having social connectedness in one's life; feeling a part of one's community, rather than feeling isolated from it through illness; hope: having a hope that life can and will get better; identity – having identities in life beyond that of service – user; meaningful role-building on strengths and skills to have fulfilling and esteem-building activities in life; and empowerment – having the information, choices and confidence to make informed decisions on one's life. In the literature, frameworks of this nature are described as constituting a personal (or psychological) recovery. Both clinical recovery and personal recovery will be explored in greater detail later in the book.

In 2020, a policy document 'Sharing the Vision: A Mental Health Policy for Everyone' was published in Ireland (during the COVID-19 pandemic) as a refreshing of the 2006 policy document 'A Vision for Change.'

The core values central to 'Sharing the Vision: A Mental Health Policy for Everyone' (2020) are stated as respect; compassion; equity and hope. The vision underpinning this policy is 'to create a mental health system that addresses the needs of the population through a focus on the requirements of the individual. This mental health system should deliver a range of integrated activities to promote positive mental health in the community; it should intervene early when problems develop; and it should enhance the inclusion and recovery of people who have complex mental health difficulties. Service providers should work in partnership with service users and their families to facilitate recovery and reintegration through the provision of accessible, comprehensive and community-based mental health services' (p. 16).

The service delivery principles underpinning 'Sharing the Vision: A Mental Health Policy for Everyone' (2020) are as follows:

1. **Recovery**: 'Recovery means people experiencing and living with mental health issues while pursuing the personal goals they want to achieve in life, regardless of the presence or severity of those mental health difficulties. This understanding of recovery is best achieved through the primacy of personal decision-making, supported by informed clinical best practice and lived mental health experience. In line with the National Recovery Framework*, recovery-oriented services empower and facilitate the process of a person's self-determined recovery. Such services offer hope and choice, work in partnership with service users and FCS** and are outward-looking. They engage with all the aspects and supports that will constitute and sustain recovery in a person's life' (p. 17).

2. **Trauma-informed:** 'Trauma-informed service delivery means that everyone at all levels of the mental health services and wider mental health provision has a basic understanding of trauma and how it can affect families, groups, organisations, communities and individuals. People delivering services recognise the signs of trauma, which may be gender-, age-, or setting-specific. Services respond by applying the principles of a trauma-informed care. Staff in every part of the organisation change their language, behaviour and policies to take into consideration the experiences of those who have trauma histories, including staff members themselves. A trauma-informed approach resists traumatising or re-traumatising service users and staff. Staff are taught to recognise how organisational practices may trigger painful memories for service users with trauma histories. Applying a trauma-informed approach does not mean that everyone with a mental health difficulty or everyone using mental health services has experienced trauma. It simply means that the service system needs to be aware of and respond to the presence of trauma in people who may be using a wide variety of supports' (p. 17).

3. **Human rights:** 'Human rights treaties recognise the right of everyone to the highest attainable standard of physical and mental health. At the core of Ireland's human rights treaty commitments is a range of principles that underpin the fulfilment of all civil and political, social and economic rights for all people. Service users and their FCS as appropriate should lead in the planning and delivery of their care. Partnership should exist in the planning, development, delivery, evaluation and monitoring of mental health services and supports, and include all stakeholders. Partnership will build trust for all involved' (p. 17).

4. **Valuing and learning:** 'Everyone accessing and delivering mental health services should be valued and respected as human beings in their own

right, and for the experience, expertise and skills they bring. Staff and all those involved also need to be valued and respected. Reflective practice and openness to learning are essential qualities for staff, people using mental health services and for the service system itself. All need to be open to continuous learning and development' (p. 17).

*Health Services Executive (Ireland) (2017). A National Framework for Recovery in Mental Health 2018–2020
  ****FCS**: Family, Carers & Supporters.

Implementation of 'A Shared Vision: A Mental Health Policy for Everyone' (2020)

Regarding implementation, the document states that the implementation of government policy is a challenging process – 'The literature on what determines a successful transition from policy thinking into reality emphasises that implementation is complex, contextual and as much a bottom-up as - a top-down imperative. This is particularly the case since the strategic ambition of Sharing the Vision is characterised by its being:

- **Long-term** – a 10-year framework with some returns measurable only over several years
- **Whole-system** – covers all aspects of the mental health domain and beyond
- **Dispersed governance** – multiple actors with distinct mandates and accountability
- **High requirement for collaboration** – working through partnership is a core value

Regarding the implementation of the Irish government policy, the document states that a recurring theme 'in the process of consultation, review and validation which underpinned the review process was the need to do everything possible to ensure effective implementation of the next phase of the national plan' (p. 20). The policy document lists the key factors underpinning implementation as leadership; implementation structures; planning; resourcing; communication; and data and research evaluation (p. 20) and places a strong emphasis on continuous monitoring and performance management (p. 84).

Challenges of implementation of a policy for recovery internationally

Slade (2014) refers to two challenging realities regarding governments signing up to the recovery ethos – firstly, policy is often inconsistent in that 'an emphasis on recovery can and does simultaneously co-occur with policy encouraging a focus on risk, deficit and segregation' (p. 76), and secondly, policy is not practice, meaning that the clinical model of recovery is still dominant in mental health services.

Slade (2014) states that a clinical model provides just one of multiple ways to make sense of human experience, and should be treated as a hypothesis rather than revealed truth. Similar to Bracken and Thomas (2009), Slade (2014) further states that human experience cannot be grasped by using a technical/scientific model of knowing. Bracken and Thomas (2009) state that while causal explanations of human experience and distress cannot always be ruled out, 'a hermeneutic exploration of (i) meaning; (ii) significance; and (iii) value should always precede the move to causal explanation' and that 'more than any other branch of medicine, psychiatry is *primarily* concerned with the meaningful reality of the patient's distress' (p. 133), namely there is always context to human distress. Slade (2014) rejects claims of any theory to be universally valid and advocates a partnership relationship – where the clinician is modest regarding the universality of their theory and places emphasis on listening and negotiation, asking 'do you want help?' and if so, 'what kind?' (p. 117). Such an approach would appear to be valid and helpful in many fields of professional practice, including coaching/coaching psychology!

Conclusion

This chapter has presented a brief overview of current mental health policy and concepts of recovery in mental health/mental illness, with particular emphasis on the challenge of moving from policy rhetoric to practical implementation. This issue will be explored in greater detail later in the book, with particular reference to how different 'ways of knowing' and knowledge bases inform radically different understandings of human experience and distress, with significant implications for practice. We believe that this is also a very important topic for serious consideration in coaching psychology education/training and practice, in the context of engagement with people experiencing significant mental distress/illness, and in particular the importance of bringing critical reflection to coaching psychologists' assumptions, beliefs, and values in this regard.

Discussion points

1. How familiar are you with the concept of recovery in mental health?
2. How familiar are you with the implementation gap between recovery as government policy and recovery as mental health practice?

Recommended reading

Bracken, P., & Thomas, P. (2009). *Post-psychiatry: Mental health in a post-modern world*. Oxford, UK. Oxford University Press. (Introduction provides a clear overview of current tensions in thinking and practice of psychiatry).

Leamy, M., Bird, V., Le Boutillier, C., Williams, J., & Slade, M. (2011). Conceptual framework for personal recovery in mental health: Systematic review and narrative synthesis. *The British Journal of Psychiatry*, *199*, 445–452. (Very comprehensive research article that identifies key elements of personal recovery in the context of mental health).

References

American Psychiatric Association. (2005). *Position statement on the use of the concept of recovery*. Washington, DC: American Psychiatric Association.

Australian Health Ministers. (2001). *National mental health plan 2003–2008*. Canberra: Australian Government.

Bracken, P., & Thomas, P. (2009). *Post-psychiatry: Mental health in a post-modern world*. Oxford, UK. Oxford University Press.

Department of Health. (2001). *The journey to recovery: The government's vision for mental health care*. London: Department of Health.

Department of Health. (2006). *From values to action: The chief nursing officer's review of mental health nursing*. London, UK: HMSO.

Department of Health & Children. (2006). *A vision for change: Report of the expert group on mental health policy*. Dublin: Stationary Office.

Department of Health, Social Services and Public Safety (Northern Ireland). (2010). *Service framework for mental health and wellbeing*. Belfast, UK: DHSSPS (NI).

Health Services Executive (Ireland). (2017). *A National Framework for Recovery in Mental Health: A national framework for mental health service providers to support the delivery of a quality, person-centred service (2018–2020)*. HSE.

Leamy, M., Bird, V., Le Boutillier, C., Williams, J., & Slade, M. (2011). Conceptual framework for personal recovery in mental health: Systematic review and narrative synthesis. *The British Journal of Psychiatry*, *199*, 445–452.

Libermann, R. P., & Kopelowicz, A. (2002). Recovery from schizophrenia: A challenge for the 21st century. *International Review of Psychiatry*, *14*, 242–255.

Mental Health Commission (New Zealand). (1998). *Blueprint for mental health services in New Zealand: How things need to be*. Wellington: Mental Health Commission.

Mental Health Commission of Canada. (2012). *Changing directions, changing lives: The mental health strategy for Canada*. Calgary, Alberta: Mental Health Commission of Canada.

President's New Freedom Commission on Mental Health. (2003). *Achieving the promise: Transforming mental health care in America*. Rockville, MD: DHHS.

Scottish Government. (2012). *Mental health strategy for Scotland 2012–2015*. Edinburgh: Scottish Government.

Slade, M. (2014). *Personal Recovery and Mental Illness: A Guide for Mental Health Professionals*. Cambridge, UK: Cambridge University Press.

Chapter 3

Whether coaching psychology and Borderline Personality Disorder?

The focus of this chapter is to explore the current state of coaching psychology, nationally and internationally; current research and practise issues that have particular relevance to a discussion of the role of coaching psychology in interacting with persons with a diagnosed mental illness, in particular Borderline Personality Disorder (BPD). Our (coaching psychologists) preparation for GLOW11 is also outlined.

International spread and diversity of coaching psychology

The development of coaching/coaching psychology theory and practise is now global (Palmer & Whybrow, 2019). As a measure of the international spread and diversity of coaching, there are formal coaching/coaching psychology interest groups in Australia (2002), United Kingdom (2004), Switzerland (2006), South Africa (2006), Denmark (2007), Spain (2008), Ireland (2008), Hungary (2008), New Zealand (2009), Sweden (2009), Israel (2010), Netherlands (2010), Japan (2011), Italy (2011), South Korea (2011), USA (2012), Hungary (2014), Singapore (2016), Serbia (2018), and growing. The coaching/coaching psychology interest groups are attached to their national professional psychological bodies in the main and their activities are organised around accreditation/certification routes for coaching psychologists; accreditation systems for coaching/coaching psychology supervisors; journals/publications; workshops and conferences; and hosting of events (O'Riordan & Palmer, 2019).

In tandem with the global development and spread of coaching/coaching psychology, several university-based coaching/coaching psychology units (CPUs) have been established – University of Sydney, Australia (2002); City University London, United Kingdom (2005); University of East London, United Kingdom (2008); University of Copenhagen, Denmark (2008); Aalborg University, Denmark (2010), Federal University of Rio de Janeiro, Brazil (2011); Herriot Watt University Edinburgh, Scotland (2013) (O'Riordan &

DOI: 10.4324/9781003048978-3

Palmer, 2019); and the School of Applied Psychology, University College Cork, Ireland (2013).

Coaching/coaching psychology is practised across both traditional and diverse areas such as work, health and wellbeing, personal life, education and performance, and growing, with coaches/coaching psychologists drawing from multiple approaches, theories, and evidence sources (O'Riordan & Palmer, 2019), and from varied and different knowledge bases and ways of knowing.

Whether a coaching psychology definition for interacting with individuals with BPD?

The ongoing development and diversity of coaching/coaching psychology approaches and their knowledge bases is echoed in debates about definitions and whether it is possible or even desirable at this point to seek for a unifying definition.

Palmer and Whybrow (2019) state that there is no one definition of coaching psychology and that similar to consulting psychology, counselling psychology and clinical psychology, definitions of coaching psychology have been developed by national professional bodies, based on policies, committees and expert inputs, within the context of relevant legislation. For example, they (Palmer & Whybrow, 2019) cite the Australian Psychological Society definition, which makes a link between positive psychology and coaching psychology – 'Coaching Psychology; as an applied positive psychology, draws on and develops established psychological approaches, and can be understood as being the systematic application of behavioural science in the enhancement of life experience, work performance and well-being, for individuals, groups and organisations who do not have clinically significant mental health (sic) or abnormal levels of distress' (APS, 2016). We mention this definition here, both as information about a common type of definition of coaching psychology, but also to highlight that GLOW11 was a coaching psychology intervention with individuals who *do* 'have clinically significant mental health and/or abnormal levels of distress.'

Lai, Stopforth, and Passmore (2018) refer to the fact that definitions of coaching have been intrinsic to the debate in coaching for the past 30 years or more, with different authors adopting different perspectives and emphasising different aspects of coaching in their definitions. Lai et al. (2018) argue that a clear definition of coaching is necessary to mark the boundaries of practise, stating it is essential for practise that clients are clear about what to expect from coaches, vital for research so that coaching interventions can be differentiated from other interventions, and vital for teaching in terms of asking the question 'what distinct body of knowledge marks 'coaching psychology' out from 'coaching,' 'mentoring,' 'change conversations,' or even just 'purposeful conversations' (p. 121).

However, the fact that different authors and practitioners adopt different perspectives and emphasise different aspects of coaching in their definitions surely points towards the impossibility of trying to devise one definition for coaching psychology, not to mention possible differences of emphasis depending on whether one practices as a coach or as a coaching psychologist? Bachkirova, Spence, and Drake (2017) state that while almost every text on coaching starts with an attempt to define the concept and practice of coaching and this is an understandable endeavour, given the number of authors in the world of coaching/coaching psychology it is highly likely there will be a wide range of significantly different positions.

Bachkirova et al. (2017) ask a number of questions relevant to the discussion about definition, for example, as to whether a unified definition of coaching is necessary?, why coaching is so difficult to define?, and what are the implications of not achieving a unified definition? Citing Cavanagh (2009), Bachkirova et al. (2017) conclude that trying to establish coaching as a discrete domain of practice is likely to 'be problematic and unnecessarily restrictive, as the commonalities with counselling and other related professions enrich the practice of coaching' (p. 5); that the criteria of universality (elements common to all the various types, genres and approaches to coaching) and uniqueness (elements of coaching that would clearly differentiate it from other forms of professional assistance) are especially important for a definition of practice, and that none of the definitions focused on purpose (what coaching is for); process (what coaching involves); context (where coaching is carried out); and clientele (what population(s) coaching serves) could satisfy the criteria for universality and uniqueness.

We (the authors) have discussed at length whether to offer a working definition of coaching psychology in the context of working with individuals with 'clinically significant mental health or abnormal levels of distress' and whether this might be helpful. Again, similar to the burgeoning diversity of knowledge bases, theoretical models and practice approaches in coaching psychology, the mental health system is also experiencing a diversity of interpretations and perspectives, for example, regarding differing concepts of recovery and different underpinning knowledge-bases, that makes it impossible to create a definition that would satisfy the criteria of universality and uniqueness. We explore the concept of 'recovery' in a further chapter, in particular 'clinical recovery' and personal recovery.'

Consequently, we echo Bachkirova et al. (2017) leaning towards the need to highlight the inherent diversity and flexibility of coaching psychology, rather than aiming for clear definitions (citing Cavanagh, 2009). This diversity and flexibility is reflected in the growing emphasis on complexity theories in coaching (Stacey, 2003, 2012; Cavanagh & Lane, 2012; Bachkirova & Lawton Smith, 2015); in the emergence of more pragmatic, postmodern perspectives on coaching that advocate for diversity in coaching and 'also provide a substantial critique of the desire to apply fixed rules and regulations to the coaching industry (citing Garvey, Stokes, & Megginson, 2009; Western, 2012; Bachkirova & Lawton Smith, 2015). Given that an application of coaching psychology to the lived experience of persons with BPD is certainly somewhat askew of current normative thinking about coaching psychology and mental illness, we view GLOW11 as leaning towards a more pragmatic, postmodern perspective and will expand on this later in the book.

Bringing coaching psychology to mental illness

Overview of current position

First, we will briefly refer to our understanding of the current normative thinking regarding coaching psychology and non–clinical/clinical mental health distinctions. Cavanagh and Buckley (2018) citing Buckley (2007) and Grant (2005) point out that historically, the normative thinking among coaching psychologists has been that coaching is targeted towards working with individuals from non-clinical populations, with therapy aiming to meet the needs of individuals with diagnosable clinical conditions, such as personality disorders, substance abuse, depression, anxiety, and other mood disorders. However, these authors also state that this distinction poses problems because the boundary between clinical and non-clinical is both fluid and imprecise. Cavanagh and Buckley (2018) state that in reality coaches are likely to regularly find themselves faced with individuals showing some form of mental health difficulty. Szymanska (2019) refers to the UK Mental Health Foundation (2015) report that one in four people will experience a mental health problem in any given year. In her brief overview of more common mental health disorders, Szymanska (2019) includes BPD and states that assessment and treatment of personality disorders are solely within the remit of psychiatrists and other clinical practitioners, while coaching psychologists may work with coachees who show personality traits that impact on the process of coaching. Szymanska (2019) suggests that in the context of personality disorders, two areas that coaching might focus on are the interpersonal process within the coaching relationship, and, if necessary, skills acquisition and practise. More typically, Dialectical Behaviour Therapy (DBT) is an evidence-based approach for BPD that addresses issue of interpersonal process, skill acquisition, practise, and other relevant aspects. As mentioned in this book, GLOW11 coachees had participated in a DBT programme prior to GLOW11.

Regarding the bigger picture of coaching psychology and individuals with clinical mental health difficulties, Szymanska (2019) usefully suggests that in the context of working with coachees presenting with mental health issues, coaching psychologists can benefit from gaining an overview of the key psychological disorders and the symptoms that coachees may present with;

improving their familiarity with helpful questions to ask that may uncover mental health problems; developing knowledge of some generic evidence-based strategies to support coachees; and consider the benefit of a thorough assessment and regular supervision in their work. Cavanagh and Buckley (2018) advise taking an ethical approach based around non-malfeasance, a commitment to taking actions that do not harm the person. In the final analysis, these authors state that as most coaches are not trained diagnosticians, the primary question for the coach needs to be *'Is my coaching in the best interest of the coachee?'* and if not *'Is referral to another professional indicated?'*

The question about whether coaching might be in the best interests of GLOW11 participants was addressed and explored in discussion involving the clinical psychologists working in the relevant Adult & Child/Adolescent Mental Health Service and the coaching psychologists involved in GLOW11. The question was also discussed in face-to-face interviews with each prospective participant in GLOW11. Regarding the question about referral to another professional, it was also agreed that if during GLOW11 any participant reported suicidal ideation/self-harm or the respective coaching psychologist felt it necessary to ask questions if concerned, an immediate contact/referral would be made to the relevant mental health team.

Borderline Personality Disorder: Issues for consideration in preparing for GLOW11

We want to give a brief, and hopefully fair overview of some of the issues and challenges reported in the literature associated with BPD, both for individuals with the diagnosis and for clinicians/therapists, and some implications for coaching psychology. The issues and challenges we include were also among factors that we considered and reflected upon in our preparations for GLOW11 as a coaching psychology interaction.

Individuals with BPD typically experience significant difficulties in regulating their emotions, unstable relationship patterns, mood swings, feelings of emptiness, frequently chaotic lifestyles, with suicide and/or self-harming common in up to 80% of situations (Katsakou et al., 2012).

Paris (2020) reports that BPD is associated with several symptom domains, each of which can present significant difficulties both in daily life and in therapeutic work–emotional dysregulation and impulsive behaviours can be very disruptive and difficult to manage; interpersonal sensitivity contributes to relationships being often chaotic, marked by dependency and anger, disrupting efforts to build a therapeutic alliance; and cognitive symptoms, such as paranoid ideas and depersonalisation, also presenting management challenges. Up to 20% of psychiatric inpatients are estimated to have BPD and it is diagnosed mainly (75%) in females (APA, 2000).

In the context of therapeutic work, the literature in general tends to highlight difficulties and challenges associated in working with individuals with BPD. For example, individuals with BPD can require significant therapeutic resources (Higgitt & Fonagy, 1992); therapists and other professionals involved can experience significant feelings of distress, overwhelm and that negative perceptions of persons with BPD can impact the building of therapeutic relationships (Markham & Trower, 2003; Skegg, 2005; Monti & D'Agostino, 2015); therapists/clinicians have to deal with behavioural problems that disrupt the structure of the treatment approach (Paris, 2020); and that there has been no systematic research to identify whether individuals with BPD benefit from more frequent or less frequent sessions (Paris, 2020).

In terms of the dynamic of engagement in therapeutic activity, Monti and D'Agostino (2015) report that 'in brief, one cannot be a borderline person all by oneself and that those who interact with a borderline personality are inevitably at risk to being drawn into borderland territory. Thus, being a borderline means disturbing someone; that is, it means to force the other to bear and share one's own subjective states (especially when the other is a clinician who adopts a therapeutic point of view)' (p. 452). In a related context, Paris (2020) advises against a higher frequency of therapy sessions, as persons with BPD do not use what he calls high-level, mature defences and their intimate relationships are already overly dependent. Ultimately, Paris (2020) states that persons with BPD 'need to get a life, not to centre life around therapy or a therapist' (p. 224) and that 'not having a life can be the cause of serious unhappiness' (p. 31). In this context, Paris (2020), from the perspective of psychiatry, helpfully states that helping individuals with BPD to control emotions, avoid impulsive behaviours, and get along better with other people is far more effective that any current medication.

Linehan (2020), whose pioneering work led to the development of DBT, writes that it is not possible to develop a therapy for a disorder unless one understands the basis of the disorder and that she had developed her understanding 'by listening carefully to my clients as they talked about their lives' and that she came to realize that 'one of the things clients need most is validation, an understanding of why they behave the way they do,' adding that she realised that her clients 'very probably had experienced an invalidating environment for much of their lives, and probably a *traumatic* invalidating environment' (p. 301). Tellingly, Linehan (2020) states she has never been interested in BPD as a 'disorder' in itself, that her focus is on out-of-control and suicidal behaviour.

Dialectical Behaviour Therapy (DBT)

A number of therapeutic interventions have been identified as having positive effects for individuals with BPD, in particular the reduction of symptoms. Citing Linehan (1987, 1993), Flynn et al. (2017) write that Dialectical Behaviour Therapy (DBT) is one of the most researched interventions for treating BPD, with a growing body of evidence demonstrating its efficacy in treating individuals diagnosed with BPD. Flynn et al. (2017) also provide a helpful and succinct capture of perhaps the core issue to be understood about BPD – that 'biosocial theory posits that certain biological and temperamental vulnerabilities coupled with a perceived invalidating environment result in emotional and behavioural dysregulation' (p. 5). In a similar vein, Paris (2020) writes that DBT is based on a specific theory about BPD which hypothesises that emotional dysregulation is the core developmental and temperamental problem behind the disorder, and that it involves delivery of a complex package of interventions whose main elements are – validation of emotional experiences and understanding past invalidating environments; a dialectical balance between acceptance and change; problem – solving and change strategies to improve interpersonal relationships and overall psychological functioning; linking analysis of events leading to parasuicidal episodes; strategies for attaining greater interpersonal effectiveness; and the use of mindfulness to increase distress tolerance, leading to better emotion regulation and control of impulsivity. DBT also 'emphasises empathic responses by therapists that provide validation for patients' inner experiences' (Paris, 2020, p. 158).

Linehan (2020) writes that at the core of DBT 'is the dynamic balance between opposing therapeutic goals: acceptance of oneself and one's situation in life, on the one hand, and embracing change towards a better life, on the other. That is what 'dialectics' means: the balance of opposites and the coming to a synthesis of two opposites' (p. 167). Linehan (2020) emphasises that DBT is a behavioural treatment programme and not so much an individual psychotherapy approach per se.

Linehan (2020) presents a compelling overview of what is regarded as the uniqueness of DBT. Firstly, there is a very real, egalitarian relationship between therapist and client, 'embracing the fact that both people are equal human beings outside of the specific roles of therapist and client, and should view each other as such' (p. 168). The anchoring nature and importance of the relationship in DBT is exemplified by Linehan (2020) as the therapist's task of trying to give clients 'skills that will help them navigate their turbulent lives is like trying to teach an individual how to build a house that will not fall down in a tornado – just as the tornado hits' (p. 171).

Factors that can make a big difference are therapists being open to talking about themselves to some degree and being willing to take phone calls at any time when a client desperately needs to talk and that 'with a highly suicidal client, the relationship with the therapist is sometimes what keeps her alive when all else fails' (p. 168). Secondly, the learning of a set of DBT skills has a central role that helps clients to more effectively navigate what are frequently 'unbelievably stressful lives' (p. 168).

DBT skills fall into four categories each designed to solve a different set of problems – firstly, mindfulness skills (to help reduce pain and increase happiness) and secondly, distress tolerance skills (which teach how to tolerate crisis situations in order to effectively find a solution to whatever is causing stress) – mindfulness skills and distress tolerance skills offer a path towards *acceptance* of reality as it is (Linehan, 2020). Thirdly, emotion regulation skills (teach how to control emotions so the person doesn't react to what is happening without reflection and doesn't say things or do things that make a situation worse) and fourthly, interpersonal effectiveness skills (help the person to be effective in relationships with others) – emotion regulation skills and interpersonal effectiveness skills taken together, are *change* skills that help clients to embrace the changes needed in their lives (Linehan, 2020).

Linehan (2020) writes that her core rationale at the beginning was her 'unshakable conviction that I would develop a behaviour therapy that would help highly suicidal people live lives worth living' (p. 7). Learning the identified skills is essential to the effectiveness of DBT with the emphasis on being effective in the social and practical domains of one's life. Interestingly, in terms of how DBT differs from other therapeutic approaches, Linehan (2020) makes the comparison that in psychodynamic therapy, 'therapists never tell a client what to do. I tell clients what to do all the time' (p. 7). So, DBT is a very directive, teaching – based behaviour skills programme. Linehan (2020) states that in essence, as a behaviourist the core of DBT is to figure out ways to replace negative and unwanted behaviours with positive or effective behaviours by focusing on the context of the behaviour, and that 'DBT is a very pragmatic therapy, helping people to be effective in all aspects of their lives. DBT is a very problem-solving, focused, action-oriented treatment' (p. 172).

It is important to state here that given the presenting symptoms associated with BPD, without the DBT intervention that GLOW11 participants had completed, there would not have been a GLOW11 coaching psychology intervention. So, a key operational, planning and strategic context for GLOW11 was the reality of the DBT programme happening and being effective in different ways for the different individuals with BPD who participated in GLOW11.

Brief operational background to GLOW11

Preparation for GLOW11 included an orientation session on BPD and the standard Dialectical Behaviour Therapy (DBT) programme, given by the clinical psychologists who manage and lead delivery of that programme to individuals diagnosed with BPD in the area concerned. The orientation session comprised shared content and question-and-answer format.

As mentioned, each GLOW11 participant had previously completed a 12-month standard DBT programme provided by the Adult & Child/Adolescent Mental Health Services (Health Service Executive/HSE) in Cork city and county (Ireland). A requirement for participation in GLOW11 was that each participant had not self-harmed in the previous 12 months. A significant degree of joint planning was critical to enabling GLOW11 to occur. Joint planning involved key personnel from the Adult & Child/Adolescent Mental Health Services and GLOW11 Coaching Psychologists meeting for discussion and planning purposes on a regular basis.

The initiative for GLOW11 emerged from an earlier iteration, GLOW1, carried out by Hugh O' Donovan, one of the authors. GLOW1 resulted from initially informal discussion between Daniel Flynn (Clinical Psychologist/Principal Psychology Manager, Adult & Child/Adolescent Mental Health Services, HSE, Cork, Ireland) and Hugh O'Donovan (Consultant Coaching Psychologist) regarding how coaching psychology might bring value to individuals diagnosed with BPD who had previously completed a standard DBT programme. The impetus for the initial discussion regarding GLOW11 came from feedback by a number of participants in the DBT programme, who while generally satisfied with progress made in their lives, were seeking to further personal development, learning, and life opportunities.

Through consultation within the mental health services a number of individuals with BPD who had completed the DBT programme were invited to apply to participate in GLOW 11. Applicants made a written application on a prepared form. Each applicant was invited to a meeting where they met with one of the GLOW11 coaching psychologists and a familiar DBT therapist. A brief overview of coaching was shared with each applicant. At this meeting the contents of their application were discussed with each individual. Ultimately twelve individuals were invited to participate in GLOW11.

Each participant identified in the application the issues they wanted to explore in GLOW 11

Among these were:

- 'To be able to break big life goals down into smaller, more manageable steps, for example in trying to get a satisfying job.'
- 'To be less self-critical and judgmental and be more kind to myself.'
- 'To build up greater resilience in stressful situations, in particular to cope better with disappointment.'
- 'To learn how to have more effective personal boundaries in my relationships, family and personal.'
- 'To have a more structured daily routine to feel more productive and increase feelings of self-worth.'
- 'To feel less physically and emotionally isolated in myself and spend more quality time with my family members.'
- 'To be able to speak to other people with some confidence and make eye contact without feeling so much anxiety.'

- 'To have some sense of personal purpose in my life.'
- 'To try to find an identity beyond the diagnosis of BPD, as I feel that it has taken over how others view me also.'
- 'To regain a sense of having an important role in the family again and in particular regain a sense of loss of respect from my children.'
- 'I feel that I am on a recovery path already and that it would be good to have another person to help me stay 'on track' with my goals.'
- 'I want to return to my previous business of salvaging and restoring furniture.'
- 'I want to increase my physical and mental wellbeing by spending more time with family and friends.'
- 'I want to develop the talents that I have as a writer, singer, and artist, because I want to believe more in myself and put my work out there.'
- 'I need to widen my social circle for my mental wellbeing.'

Each participant also identified barriers she/he felt were stopping them from making progress in their life

Among these were:

- 'I feel like I'm just about getting by day by day, without the energy or expertise to change things.'
- 'I have intrusive thoughts and a lack of focus about where I want to be in life.'
- 'I feel demoralised when I think about doing everyday things, especially trying to get on better with family members and then feeling less motivated, a vicious cycle.'
- 'I feel afraid about the future and have a lack of self -belief and regret about the past, feeling like I am stuck there in my thinking.'
- 'I have thoughts about not being worthy of kindness from others, I judge myself negatively a lot and worry about being judged negatively by others.'
- 'I feel vulnerable because I experience a lot of pain, tiredness and high stress every day and this makes it more difficult to check the facts about situations, not just react, and reach wise mind.'
- 'Due to my own negativity, I feel nervous about pushing for what I want, because things that have happened in the past have hit me very hard emotionally.'
- 'I have a lot of self – blaming thoughts, especially all-or-nothing thinking that really gets me down.'
- 'I have feelings of fear and anxiety that BPD will take over my life again.'
- 'I am trying to stay clear of the old mindset and feel afraid that history will repeat itself and I will be unwell again.'

- 'I am loving what I do and what I'm good at, but I feel really fearful of criticism from others – it just hits any self-belief I have.'
- 'I enjoy my own company a lot but I know I need to have some friends at the same time, for my mental health.'

It can be noted and is important to mention that the hopes, aspirations and perceived obstacles identified by GLOW11 participants are intrinsic to the very human need for having a life that is experienced as worth living.

An introductory group workshop was arranged to which each applicant was invited, and attended. The four GLOW11 coaching psychologists also attended. An information booklet was distributed and discussed with the group. The booklet contained brief information overviews on GLOW11, coaching psychology, positive psychology, the recovery philosophy, and personal recovery in mental health. The workshop also had a strong focus on the importance of reflection on personal values as a springboard for positive change.

The programme structure of GLOW11 was outlined – to run over 22 weeks, comprising five individual and five group coaching sessions. Each participant was invited to read through a coaching psychology agreement, with a proviso that a participant could withdraw from the process at any point, and a confidentiality clause. Each coaching psychologist was assigned to a smaller group of participants for individual coaching purposes. Group coaching sessions were attended by all of the GLOW11 participants and the four coaching psychologists. The individual coaching psychology agreement was signed by both parties, coachee and coaching psychologist.

Critical reflection as important preparation for GLOW11: What mattered?

In preparing for GLOW11 we (coaching psychologists) engaged in group discussions and critical self – reflection to examine our existing assumptions and values about coaching psychology and mental illness, with particular focus given to the application and possible value of coaching psychology in working with individuals with a diagnosis of BPD. Exploring such assumptions and values helped to surface particular bedrock questions, for example, what exactly is coaching psychology that makes it different to other forms of professional helping?; what is the possible relevance of coaching psychology to the lived experience of individuals with a diagnosis of BPD?; is there a definition of coaching psychology that is relevant here?; are there particular personal qualities, areas of professional expertise and qualifications that are required to work in this area as coaching psychologists?; are we personally and professionally competent to carry out this work?, to mention but a few! We did not come up with nor necessarily set out to come up with clear answers to these questions, however it was very helpful and important to have such questions identified, not least because they helped to highlight some of the apprehension that was felt about the relatively unknown space that we were entering, both personally and professionally with little or no existing roadmap. In its own way, the latter turned out to be a blessing!

Among the topics that surfaced during our 'thinking time' sessions were stigma as a phenomenon frequently identified as endemic to the experience of mental illness, certainly in Ireland; the importance of respect as a value demonstrated by respectful behaviours in helping to create an emotionally validating environment for GLOW11 participants; relational empathy; professional humility; the importance of ethical maturity; and values (again!).

i. **Stigma**

Regarding stigma, Jackson (2019) writes, that 'mentally ill individuals most often feel at odds with society at large…that this sense of alienation and estrangement only worsens when the mentally ill person then faces social stigma' (p. 989). Watts and Higgins (2017) writing about narratives of recovery by persons with a diagnosed mental illness, state that the internalisation of stigma associated with being labelled 'mentally ill' 'has the potential not only to undermine self-esteem, self-efficacy and self-confidence, but may result in the person withdrawing from social interaction and contact as a stigma-resistance or -reduction strategy' (p. 22). Paris (2020) writes that all mental disorders carry a stigma, a term that 'can be defined as shame associated with being unacceptable or defective as a person' (p. 203). Paris (2020) states that stigma associated with BPD may be stronger than the shame associated with other mental disorders and implicit here is that mental health professionals often continue to view BPD in negative terms. He adds that such views are frequently based on mistaken ideas about the treatability of BPD and its outcomes, and the fact that many mental health professionals have not read the relevant research literature. Interestingly, Paris (2020) concludes that one way to view the stigma associated with mental disorder 'is that we are all afraid of losing our minds, and look down on people who seem to have lost theirs' (p. 203).

Of particular relevance to coaching psychology in the context of stigma/shame is the work of Cavicchia and Gilbert (2019). They write that the 'direct experience of shame is characterised by feelings of exposure, self-consciousness, inner torment, judgment, comparison with others and often vicious self-criticism' (p. 144). These feelings are among the feelings identified and sometimes expressed by a number of participants in GLOW11. The fact that coachees felt safe enough to voice such feelings in coaching sessions affirms the value of DBT in enabling individuals to gain emotion regulation skills and interpersonal effectiveness skills. The associated sense of vulnerability and limitation that diagnosed mental illness might trigger in an individual is captured well by Cavicchia and Gilbert (2019) in the context of relational coaching. These authors write that 'one of the reasons why vulnerability and limitation are so difficult to bear is that we, as coaches and our coachees, are under enormous social pressure from the happiness imperative (citing Western, 2012) to be permanently positive and attain images and ideals of success and achievement' (p. 151).

Consideration of the experience and impacts of stigma, shame and vulnerability are very important in the context of bringing coaching psychology to the lived experience of BPD. These are phenomena that were triggered and surfaced on several occasions during GLOW11. It is important that the coaching psychologist can sit with, hold and help coachees to regulate their anxiety and make sense of their experience, 'think about their situation, their emotional responses and identify new strategies for action ... this requires that coaches be sufficiently aware of themselves and practiced in managing their own anxiety and reactivity' (Cavicchia & Gilbert, 2019, p. 125).

The issue of stigma and its possible meanings in GLOW11, also has meaning for one of the authors, related to some months as a client in the Irish mental health system, when younger. Reflection on this experience helped to surface how stigma can have an almost contagious aspect, at personal, familial and community levels simultaneously, whereby it can be difficult to speak about such experiences as a 'helping professional.' It may well be that the experience of mental health challenges and of personal recovery can indeed greatly assist 'helping professionals' to actually be of real help to others. How does this sit currently in the field of coaching psychology? In our experience it is extremely rare for coaching psychologists to speak about mental health struggles in public discourse. Then again, perhaps we each find our own ways of speaking about such experiences when we find trustworthy colleagues.

However, we think there is a risk that coaching psychology is not sufficiently challenging publicly the frenetic, fictional and mindless world of goal-directed hyperactivity and multitasking, which may be contributing to the triggering of mental health crises in organisations and more widely. The human brain was not designed to move at the speed the globalised hyper-capitalist 'developed' world seems to currently demand, without consequences for mental health. In the world of constant doing, there is little time to stand and stare, and simply be.

Without recourse to standing and staring as being normal and necessary for human wellbeing, are we coaching psychologists, in trying to find a relevant carriage for ourselves in the runaway train of globalization, accelerating change and greed capitalism, in danger of not crying out – 'enough!' Are we fearful of becoming stained by the stigma of irrelevancy should we cry out 'enough!'? Perhaps COVID-19, in its multilingual messages to the 'developed world' is telling us (coaching psychologists) to reopen Pandora's box 'and in so doing 'do something that causes a lot of problems to appear that did not exist or were not known about before' (www.collinsdictionary.com).

ii. **Respect**

We gave considerable time to reflecting on respect as the foundation ethical value in the helping relationship (Egan, 2014) and the importance of respectful behaviours in creating an emotionally validating and safe relational coaching environment in GLOW11. The importance of respectful behaviours, in the contexts of both supporting and challenging coachees should not be underestimated, given the prevalence of invalidating environments in the life stories of persons with BPD (Linehan, 2020).

In the context of prizing the building of an egalitarian coaching relationship with each GLOW11 participant, we think it important the reader take a moment to consider the value of respect as a challenge. We say as a challenge, simply because we have never come across in training workshops or networked conferences anybody who does not nod their head in apparent agreement when a speaker refers to the importance of interpersonal respect as both a value and desired behaviour. And yet it seems that we are often unaware of the values that underpin and guide our behaviours. Argyris and Schon (1974) held that our behaviour does not happen randomly in the main, but is guided by the theories of action we hold, for example, espoused theory and theory-in-use. Our espoused theory is based on the values we believe guide our behaviours. Our theory-in-use refers to the values reflected in the behaviours that actually occur. We may not be aware of our theory-in-use or that it may not always be the same as the theory we espouse. This is not merely the difference between what we say and do. It is more that we have a theory consistent with what we say and a theory consistent with what we do. Hence the distinction between espoused theory and theory-in-use. Egan (2014) cites Argyris and Schon (1974) in stating that our values can be seen as 'mental maps' which define how to act in situations and that 'often enough there is a split between espoused values and action on the part of either helper or client that adds a note of uncertainty to the helping process…and some values-in-use lead to life-limiting rather than life-enhancing outcomes' (p. 33). Carroll and Shaw (2013) state that 'at times, I seem to have two sets of values. there are values I think and say I believe in, and another invisible set that inform my decisions and actions. The two sets of values do not talk to each other and often seem to have no connecting links' (p. 15).

We hope this highlights the importance of both reflection-in-action and reflection-on-action (Schon, 1991) regarding both our espoused values *and* values-in-action. Egan (2014) states that professional helpers without a set of working values are adrift and consequently 'reviewing the values that drive your behaviours as a helper is not optional' (p. 34).

Respect as the foundation value in the helping relationship eludes definition, but is a particular way of viewing and *seeing* oneself and others and that if it is to make a difference, it cannot remain just an attitude or a way of viewing others (Egan, 2014). Citing Rayle (2006) Egan (2014) states that ideally professional helpers and their clients must 'matter to one another.' As mentioned elsewhere in this book, this idea of 'mattering' came to the fore frequently in coachee observations about the coaching process in GLOW11. This is an important element, we believe, for consideration in the training, development and supervision of coaching psychologists generally, in particular regarding self, and certainly if one is interested in the type of work under consideration here. Again, as mentioned previously, the importance of communicating respect through respectful behaviours as a positive factor in GLOW11 resonates with Linehan's (2020) concept of the egalitarian relationship in which each party views the other as a fellow human being first and foremost, as more fundamental than role and upon which an ethical anchor for role depends.

iii. Relational empathy

A critical way of demonstrating respect is empathy, which involves an understanding and feeling for the mental states and emotions of another person, and how the person's context influences their thinking and feeling (Egan, 2014). However, Egan (2014) asks whether empathy is even possible, whether a helper can really understand another person who is very different from him/her – and answers his question by saying it is possible, providing the helper who espouses the value of empathy has the communicative competence so that the client feels understood.

In the context of this communicative competence, Egan (2014) refers to the importance of empathic presence, so that 'during some of the more dramatic moments of life, simply being with another person is extremely important' (p. 57) and empathy at its best is relationship oriented. Egan (2014) also refers to a two-way relational empathy which we outline in full, since it provides a very helpful framework not only for empathic communication, but seeing its importance in recognising and responding to the fullness of the other person's life and contexts. Capacity for demonstrating relational empathy was a critical factor in interactions with individuals with BPD, hence we outline its meaning in some detail here.

Egan (2014) writes that relational empathy posits that 'while the client's reality is knowable, the helper's understanding is always partial and fallible; helpers need to be attuned not only to underlying mental states and feelings but also to the cultural meaning of the client's words; relationship-empathy is not just person-centred but encompasses the key contexts of the client's life; the complex socio-political environment and status of the client ('social location') is often a key part of context; when it comes to the client's cultural uniqueness, the helper is not an expert but a learner; the client's deductive understandings of self and the world are more important than the helper's deductive understandings, from theory, research and practise, about the client; empathy is not something unilaterally offered by the helper, rather something that is mutually produced through dialogue; and self-awareness of such things as cultural bias on the part of the helper is not sufficient; ongoing introspection or self-reflexivity regarding ideas, fears, mistakes, confusion, breakthroughs, and obstacles that arise in the helping sessions is essential' (Egan, 2014, pp. 37–38). This perspective on relational empathy is we believe critical to an understanding of how coaching psychology may bring something of value to the lived experience of persons with BPD, and perhaps more broadly, because it emphasises the importance of listening for understanding the meaning of the person's own words; views the person in a relational/systemic perspective; stresses the importance of curiosity in order to honour a 'not-knowing' and a 'letting go' orientation regarding one's own theoretical understanding in order to stand side-by-side with the other person. Stelter (2019) expresses it as follows: '…I have increasingly realised how important it is for the coach to be a fellow human being and a co-creative partner in the dialogue. Coaching should not be limited to a performance-oriented and goal-driven agenda' (p. 3).

Ultimately, Egan (2014) posits empathy as a value that involves a radical commitment on the part of the helper to try to understand the client as fully as possible, and that respectful empathy 'is very important when interacting with clients who are different from you in any respect – personally, socially, and culturally. There is often something profoundly important that occurs in the moments before a coaching session 'formally' begins. For example, on one occasion, a coachee said to the coaching psychologist, 'from the moment we meet before each session, I feel welcomed. You open the door into the meeting room and you hold it open until I come into the room. You close the door and outside it says 'occupied.' Inside the room, you wait until I am sitting in a way that is comfortable for me. I can see you waiting. Thank you. It matters to me.'

iv.   **Professional humility**

We believe that the coaching psychology process that emerged in GLOW11 contributes to working in 'good faith' towards a 'good society' (Western, 2012) for persons with BPD. We also believe that professional and personal humility is a requirement in working with persons with BPD and more generally. We do not claim to have this virtue ourselves, however, we do recognise its intrinsic importance for helping professionals who desire to practise from ethical maturity with individuals who, while having strengths, are also vulnerable to unethical influence, persuasion and imposition of power. Akhtar (2019) offers some very telling insights on humility as a relational phenomenon, which while written from the perspective of a practicing psychoanalyst, we think is eminently applicable to coaching psychology and indeed any form of skilled helping. Akhtar (2019) writes that humility plays or should play an important role in the way we 'select' individuals with whom we work (we delude ourselves if we hold on to the idea that we can work with anybody who shows up); work ethically vis a vis matters of importance in individual's lives; how we listen to and speak with those individuals. He refers to listening as itself an act of humility, involving the creation of internal space for another person, and that to listen in only one way and from only a theoretical perspective narrows one's receptive capacities and pushes one towards arrogance (Akhtar, 2019). He adds that it is clear that humility exists in both normal and pathological (e.g., excessive, deficient, false and compartmentalised) forms and that ultimately true humility is shown by regarding and relating to the other individual as a full human being who is capable of moral and therapeutic reciprocity (Akhtar, 2019). This view of professional humility resonates strongly with Linehan's (2020) perspective on the necessity of an egalitarian relationship (in the context of DBT), where at a level deeper than roles, each views the other as an equal human being.

v. **Ethical maturity**

A reflective consideration of ethics and ethical behaviour also underpinned our psychological preparation for GLOW11. Ethics and ethical behaviour must be a fundamental issue for coaching psychology that should underpin knowledge base, theoretical model and approach to practise. A concern is that the term 'ethics' usually gets a peremptory nod as it lands into our internal 'inbox' without perhaps feeling any great need to 'open' it up and examine it at some depth. Ethical codes are certainly important, though limited, regarding standards of conduct that define the essentials of appropriate behaviour within a particular area or organisation (Brennan & Wildflower, 2018). Common themes across various disciplines include – do no harm; duty of care; knowing limits of competence; respecting the interests of the client (Brennan & Wildflower, 2018). These authors, citing Clutterbuck (2013), point out how subtle ethical transgressions, such as issues of coaching competence can manifest where coaches make promises about unrealistic outcomes (Brennan & Wildflower, 2018).

The issue of coaching competence was certainly a consideration for GLOW11. A diverse range of personal and professional factors were considered. Ultimately we found ourselves leaning towards the work of Bachkirova (2015, 2016) regarding the importance of considering capabilities more than competencies (in the assessment and accreditation of coaches); the nature of and contextual influences on self-deception in coaching practise; and critically, a professional-practice view of the self as the primary instrument of coaching (we explore this later in the book). Regarding the latter, Bachkirova (2016) uses the metaphor of instrument to discuss the conditions for making good use of self in coaching practise – 'understanding the instrument, looking after it, and checking for quality and sensitivity' (p. 153). Bachkirova (2011) also emphasises that 'it is the coach as a person, rather than the application of particular techniques or methods, that makes a difference in coaching practise. Therefore, coaches have to be aware of their own stages of development in order to reflect on their own role in the coaching process and the dynamics of the coaching relationship' (pp. 54–55).

We collectively arrived at a conclusion that each of us had sufficiently met the 'conditions' to warrant considering ourselves as professionally competent, with the proviso that we would be on-guard regarding individual or collective self-deception! In addition, when considering our professional competency, individually and collectively, to implement GLOW11 ethically, we were also cognisant of our own mental health experiences and learning.

In the need to move through and beyond an over-reliance on ethical codes and competencies, Carroll and Shaw (2013) provide a helpful contextual concept that translates ethics from an overreliance on ethical 'rules' to a consideration of ethical maturity – having ethical antennae of sensitivity and watchfulness that keep us alert to when ethical issues/ dilemmas are present/having a moral compass; ability to make ethical decisions aligned to one's ethical values; ability to apply ethical decisions once decided upon; ability to express and justify to others reasons why particular ethical decisions were made and implemented; ability to live peacefully with the consequences of ethical decision-making as critical to ongoing wellbeing; and to learn from has occurred through reflection. Hawkins and Turner (2020) refer to the importance also of developing a systemic ethical maturity whereby there is the need to 'cultivate several key capacities that counteract the human tendency to privilege the individual that is present, the local, the tribal and human-centricity' (pp. 179–180). They recommend cultural awareness – to become more aware of one's inherent biases, assumptions and the lens through which one sees the world, arising from family, community and culture, which then inform one's personal philosophy; listening not only to what is in the room, but what is not in the room – how one needs to listen deeply to the individual person, their issues, feelings and concerns, but also listening through the individual to their world, what they bring to the coaching session alongside what they fail to see, hear or mention; a wide-angled empathy – not only having empathy and compassion for the coachee, but for every individual, group and system. This also has interesting linkages with Egan (2014) regarding how the values of respect and relationship empathy are demonstrated in the helping context.

We have referred to coaching ethics in some detail here in consideration of the particularity of the individuals we had the honour of working with in GLOW11. We attached particular importance to the hope that each individual would find us to be respectful, trustworthy and empathic and therefore experience support as validation and challenge as affirmation.

vi. **Working with values mattered in GLOW11**

It is interesting at this juncture that initially we considered that GLOW11 might be a more directive and goal-focused coaching psychology approach. There was a sense of wanting to keep the coaching approach 'simple' and 'focused' with a desire for 'results.' There was an early draft of a possible GLOW11 coaching manual, with set exercises built around strengths, gratitude, self-compassion, and mindfulness. Each of these coaching concepts are known to have value and research evidence in their own right.

It is difficult to pinpoint whether there was an exact moment where we felt enabled to 'let go' of any leanings towards over-structure and control. There was perhaps an understandable apprehension about entering a previously unknown coaching space. Some of this sentiment was undoubtedly influenced by over-exposure to some of the 'negative press' around persons with BPD. Potter (2009) writes that the fact that individuals with BPD *do* evoke negative responses is unquestionable, but the reasons are more complex than that such individuals just *are* particularly difficult. The main issue here appears to centre around some professional's attribution of choice and responsibility, in that 'studies have found that clinicians tend to impute the ability to have self-control to BPD patients in comparison with other diagnoses and, then, blame them for their behaviour' (Potter, p. 162). Potter (2009) cites Hacking's (1994) description of 'the looping effect of human kinds' (p. 34) which posits that when individuals are aware of how they are categorised, stereotyped (or diagnosed), it can lead them to experience themselves differently and even change their behaviour, emotions, attitudes, and beliefs in response to such awareness.

While aware of this clinical scenario, our desire was to engage with GLOW11 participants in ways that did not reproduce unintentionally the invalidating emotional environments that many of them had experienced. In reality, the source of our initial apprehension was simply our own sense of vulnerability. Orange (2011), citing Levinas (1981), writes that the vulnerability of the other (person) 'makes me vulnerable, traumatizes me, takes me hostage, puts me in a state of suffering where the most I can do is offer my crust of bread, my hope from empty hands' (p. 63). In reading about BPD and learning through the previous experience of one of our number in GLOW1, we also discerned how the individuals we would meet in GLOW11 would likely come to that space feeling quite vulnerable, and hopeful. Our acknowledgement of the importance of accepting vulnerability and limitation paradoxically helped to create a new space of greater psychological flexibility and freedom to practise our coaching from a relational anchoring of hope and possibility.

In the end, our main guiding orientation was the expressed desires of the GLOW11 participants and the 'inner' barriers they identified. We decided to proceed with a broadly values-based coaching approach. It was felt that this approach would also allow each coaching psychologist more freedom to show up, notice, and experience comfort and discomfort while exploring the edges of both coachee and coach comfort and discomfort.

LeJeune and Luoma (2019) refer to values as 'how you are living when you are living a meaningful life' (p. 10). These authors also provide a delineated framework which we found very useful in working with GLOW11 coachees:

- Values are behaviours. They are ways of living, not just words.
- Values are freely chosen. They are not the result of reasoning, outside pressure, or moral rules. Freely chosen, also means that choice of values is not limited in any way, including by one's current circumstances, life events or personal histories.
- Values are life directions, not goals to achieve. They are always immediately accessible, but you'll never complete them.
- Values are about things you want to move toward, not what you want to get away from (LeJeune & Luoma, 2019, p. 11).

Ultimately in working with values, it is about developing an inner, integrated and guiding sense of 'the lived pattern of behaviour that would be most meaningful and vital to them, in other words, what they would do if they were living compassionately and committedly' (p. 11), without allowing chosen words, metaphors or images replace the actual journey – 'the *process* of valuing is what is important' (LeJeune & Luoma, 2019, p. 11).

A very helpful and important distinction made by LeJeune & Luoma (2019) is that around values being the life directions, like a compass, and goals being markers or milestones along the way. While goals are helpful as an orientation point, they are not the point or purpose of the life journey, as it is values that enable greater flexibility than goals (LeJeune & Luoma, 2019). In our coaching, the values – based process also proved to be most helpful in enabling coachees learn to remain focused on the chosen value behind a particular decision or action and thereby developing flexibility needed 'to stay on course if one route gets blocked…' (LeJeune & Luoma, 2019). An important point made by these authors regarding values being freely chosen, is the acknowledgment that if values are behaviour, then they will of course be influenced by personal history, current context, and one's biology – however, a values-based approach is intent on creating a context 'in which the individual experiences their values as having been freely chosen, because that is useful when our aim is to help people consistently live lives that are aligned with their values in a sustainable way' (LeJeune & Luoma, 2019, p. 17).

The focus on values in GROW11 also facilitated a broader and deeper coaching conversation with coachees, in which what might be called more resonating value-based goals emerged. In reality, GLOW11 participants preferred to talk about taking steps towards something of value, rather than goals per se. A broader and deeper coaching conversation with values as a fulcrum for exploring what each participant cared most about and what mattered most, also helped to highlight issues around identity (BPD/psychiatric identity; desired identities) and life purpose and meaning (having a sense of mattering to self, to others and to the world at large). Our trustworthiness and empathy as coaching psychologists, but more fundamentally person-to-person, were critical elements in this conversational process. In a coaching and mentoring context, Clutterbuck (2013) advises that instead of pinning the individual immediately to a specific goal, to which they may or may not be committed, 'the effective coach/mentor in this scenario facilitates an exploration from a much wider horizon' in which key areas might include identity, values, resources and purpose, exploring questions like who are you?, what do you care about?, how well supported are you?, and what do you want to contribute/ what do you want to achieve for yourself? GLOW11 coachees aspired to and desired to move beyond the BPD/psychiatric sense of defining identity to a variety of identities around relationships, intimacy, creativity, spirituality, meaningful work, self-expression through the arts, and further education.

Regarding what matters (values) to persons with BPD, Stanghellini and Mancini (2019), from a psychiatry perspective, offer a view that 'the values that are at play in the interpersonal world of borderline persons are directed to achieve life goals like:

- to belong
- to be accepted
- to draw close and enjoyably reciprocate with another

- to converse in a friendly manner, to tell stories, exchange sentiments, ideas, secrets
- to communicate, to converse
- to laugh and make jokes' (citing Kane, 2001: pp. 234–235).and add, 'but these aspirations are often unrealistic and almost unattainable' (p. 679).

From the coaching process of GLOW11 we recognise the validity and importance each value mentioned above. Participants spoke about how life experiences and their relationship with the diagnosis of BPD impacted on desires to belong, to be accepted, to enjoy the company of family or friends and have this reciprocated, and not least, to experience the joy of humour and laughing. Some participants spoke in this context about learning to live honourably in dark times. In this sense, it was evident that working with values was a critical core component of GLOW11.

A reason why Stanghellini and Mancini (2019) refer to the above values often being unrealistic and almost unattainable for individuals with BPD appears to be a perspective that for persons with BPD their emotional intensity does not allow them 'to distance themselves from what they feel here and now, and therefore they are not able to understand their feelings in the light of the values that constitute their life-world' (p. 678). While we recognise the validity of the reference to emotional intensity as broadly valid in our experience of working with GLOW11 participants, we also have a sense that in their leaning into the work on values, participants actually brought a strong feeling edge which may have helped in what emerged as a strong liking for working with values. In addition, a factor which helped some participants to internalise more their working with personal values as an orientation point for making decisions and taking actions in different life domains, was a strong identification with the metaphor of an inner North Star. While technically the North Star is not the brightest star in the solar system it can be located relatively quickly. Also, the North Star appears to stay steady in a more or less fixed point while other stars circle round it. It is also almost exactly aligned with the earth's axis, making it a well-known navigation tool. For several participants, it emerged that the process of identifying, clarifying and reflecting on their personal values was a comforting and humanizing experience in itself.

vii. Welcoming the other

At the conclusion of the GLOW11 coaching psychology process, we held a group meeting with coachees, intended as an opportunity to share reflections about the process experienced along the way. We regret that we did not ask coachees permission to record this meeting.

Coachees reflections both delighted us and shocked us, if one can be positively shocked. What they shared about their experiences helped us discover perhaps something almost intangible as regards what really mattered to each of them, but when it was shared by each person from their perspective, we recognised it immediately as the truth. What each coachee shared affirmed that the relational and dialogical person-to-person engagement had been a critical anchor point in their journey in GLOW11. They valued greatly being valued, as exemplified in the behaviour of each coaching psychologist who interacted with them. They observed and noticed and appreciated respectful behaviours. They valued moments when a coaching psychologist waited and waited further while the coachee struggled to find a word or words. They valued what happened when they found it difficult to make or maintain eye contact, often a brief checking in, asking 'are you okay?' They appreciated that when a coachee gave vent to an angry frustration with her/himself or with the world, there was an acceptance and an empathic response. They valued that there was no pressure to 'get somewhere' by being busy about goal-setting, rather a slower, cautious and checking-in approach, which in reality could often be more challenging, since it asked for a sharing of feelings in the moment. They valued the space made available to reflect on their emotions in the moment and to find a word or words to identify what was experienced. And they valued that they were given this opportunity to reflect on what a life worth living actually meant to each. In these moments, we could also discern ways in which the DBT programme has been of benefit to each coachee, in various ways that mattered to their capacity to self-regulate and relate interpersonally. They also valued the professional and ethical boundaries that were applied, within which each felt psychologically safe enough and motivated to think seriously about and share their hopes, desires and dreams.

Perhaps a sense of what coachees shared is captured in the following: 'the critical importance of 'welcoming the Other,' not just as a corollary to practise, but its very essence (Cooper and Hermans, 2007, citing Levinas, 1969) – 'the road from mental illness to mental health is...to regain one's obligations, one's responsibilities to and for the other' – the gentleness of the word 'welcoming' belies its capacity to profoundly challenge clients. It is a deep, radical welcoming, with the potential to evoke dramatic transformation in clients' lives' – 'through a welcoming of our clients, the hope is that they will come to feel more welcoming of themselves and their self-otherness and to feel more integrated into the human community' (Cooper, 2009; Cooper & Hermans, 2007).

In essence, it seems that the nature of the interpersonal dynamic experienced, around 'mattering' and 'radical welcome' was a springboard for each participant to envision their particular version of 'building a life worth living' (Linehan, 2020) during the GLOW11 sessions

Whether coaching psychology and mental illness/BPD?

Jackson (2019) writes that our understanding of mental illness is informed by different discipline practises and attitudes and that 'faced with a cacophony of different competing disciplinary approaches to mental health, those with mental disorders who try to navigate their own self-care and self-knowledge become epistemically adrift' (p. 989). Here, Jackson (2019) is advocating for the critical importance of taking into full consideration the fact that at best, the contributions of different disciplines can fill out a partial understanding of human phenomena and lived experience – 'each discipline provides a perspective of the world of mental phenomena, but we cannot reduce the phenomena to any one approach' (p. 1000).

Consequently, we have no wish to add to the existing panoply of the different and often competing discipline approaches and theoretical models regarding mental health, from a coaching psychology perspective. However, based on our experience of and learning from GLOW11, it may be useful to outline some perspectives that we think may be helpful to coaching psychologists considering work of this nature. We think that the following perspectives are important and provide a brief orientation to each:

i.   Values as an essential orientation for a coaching psychologist
ii. Helpful character traits in working with persons with BPD towards personal recovery
iii. Coaching psychology as a 'bridge-builder' towards personal recovery
iv. The self of the coaching psychologist (this is addressed in chapter)

i.   **Values as an essential orientation for a coaching psychologist**
     In the context of coaching, Stelter (2017) proposes values as a central aspect of one's identity and therefore an essential point of reference for coaching, for both coaches and coachees, providing a primary orientation for meaning making in work and life, given the hyper-complexity and challenges of modern life. Helpfully, Stelter (2017) states that values can be included in coaching regardless of one's preferred knowledge – bases, theoretical models, or practises.

     For a coaching psychologist interested in this work, it will mean leaning into significant diversity of different life histories, experience of trauma and dislocation. Making and taking – time for thinking and reflecting on values is critical to locating oneself, both at a personal and professional level. Stelter (2017) writes that values have a meaning closely related to thinking and taking action, reflecting one's ethical-interpersonal foundation, and giving purpose and legitimacy to goal-directed actions. Such thinking and reflection on values is essential in bringing coaching psychology into any GLOW11 type context. As Western (2019) states, 'we all carry personal, social and historical culture/baggage within us, and however PC (politically correct) we are, however progressive or liberal, we all belong to social groups, which exclude others, and we all make value judgments on a daily basis, often at unconscious levels' (p. 89).

Our experience of working on and trying to act from particular core values, while challenging, what with the ongoing promptings of internal voices, biases, assumptions, judgments and beliefs, gave us an anchor-point for making choices, decisions and ultimately a reliable basis for action. This dynamic around values also played out in the respective coaching relationships in GLOW11 and became central to how coaching conversations located to things that really mattered to coachees.

ii.   Some helpful character traits in working with persons with BPD

The Oxford Dictionary of English (2011) refers to a 'character trait' as a distinguishing characteristic of a person, or the distinct qualities that a person possesses. At first glance, it may appear strange that we advocate for particular character traits in coaching psychologists with an interest in working with persons with BPD. It should be evident from the references so far in this book to persons with BPD, that we approached and viewed each individual as being much more than the diagnosed disorder. And that we endeavoured to communicate this conviction to each individual. It is difficult to relate to another human being with this mind if one is perennially struggling to view oneself kindly and accept oneself as one is, moment by moment.

Linehan (2020) builds on her reference to 'beginner's mind' by commenting on 'wise mind' as a synthesis of emotion mind (when emotions are in control and are not balanced by reason) and reasonable mind (when reason is in control and is not balanced by emotions and values). Linehan (2020) states that wise mind 'adds intuitive knowing to emotional experience and logical analysis. Intuition eludes easy definition, but each of us knows what it is. It is that sense of knowing something in a particular situation, without knowing exactly how you know. You meet someone, and within seconds you feel somehow you can't quite trust this person' (p. 282). Linehan advocates the practise of mindfulness skills to help to balance emotion mind with reasonable mind, with the intention of making wise decisions. Again, as with so much of what this book describes, wise mind is equally important to both coaching psychologist and to coachee.

Potter (2009) advocates that trustworthiness is especially important in working with persons with BPD. She writes in a context mainly of clinicians working with persons with BPD. We want to make her comments here also relevant to coaching psychologists doing this work. Potter (2009) refers to the need to be critically self-reflective about the assumptions and knowledge one is committed to professionally and the importance of self-awareness that one's training, theoretical model/s and professional status can function as a barrier to progress being made. She posits this issue as both an ethical issue and an epistemic issue in that there is an ethical responsibility to be a certain kind of knower, a knower who seeks to engage the other person become a reliable knower of self and come to see herself as so. This is consistent with several themes in this book relevant to Linehan's (2020) advocacy of an egalitarian relationship between professional and client. Potter (2009) argues that trust has a relational nature, there is an expectation or belief that the trusted person has good intentions and the ability to carry through with what is expected of them. She goes on to say that the trusting relationship is one of vulnerability – it changes power positions – 'trusting others involves depending on them, being vulnerable to the possibility of disappointment or betrayal, and risking harm to self' (p. 121). Being trustworthy, worthy of another's trust, points to an ethical requirement of taking care to ensure that one does not exploit the power potential one has to do harm. The first rule of the helper is do no harm – helping is not a neutral process, it is for better or for worse – an unprincipled or incompetent helper will do harm, a fundamental disrespect to the other person (Egan, 2014). The issue of trustworthiness was an important consideration in GLOW11. As previously mentioned, it was agreed at the planning stage that should any participant show evidence of self-harming or suicidal ideation, a referral back to their mental health team would be made. In this context, which did occur for one participant, being trustworthy would involve clarifying limits and caring properly for the person entrusted to us (Potter, 2009).

Potter (2009) makes an important point about being trustworthy involves 'seeing others in their particularity…sensing what others are counting on when they place their trust in us, and having a fairly good idea of who they are, independent of our needs, projections, stereotypes, and fantasies…' (p. 130). In a context of coaching psychology, this requires an ethically mature understanding of self as a coaching psychologist, an issue we explore further in chapter seven of the book. In conclusion here we refer again to Linehan (2020) who developed a set of six rules to guide therapists working with persons with DBT. She writes that her favourite is the 'fallibility agreement' – that no one therapist is perfect, or can be, there must be an acceptance 'that all therapists are fallible and can make mistakes that cause pain and suffering (p. 225). For 'therapist' substitute coaching psychologist!

iii Coaching psychology as a 'bridge-builder' towards personal recovery

The title of this book makes reference to coaching psychology in a context of working with persons with BPD towards personal recovery. The next chapter explores the concept of recovery in some detail. Here, we want to underscore that rather than trying to come up with a working definition of coaching psychology in the context of mental health, we instead bridge to what has become a cornerstone definition of personal recovery, devised by a person in recovery.

Personal recovery is 'a deeply personal, unique process of changing one's attitudes, values, feelings, goals, skills, and/or roles. It is a way of living a satisfying, hopeful, and contributing life even within the limitations caused by illness' (Anthony, 1993).

Personal recovery is a direction and not a destination. Leamy et al. (2011) in a systematic review into published descriptions and models of personal recovery, used narrative synthesis to identify a conceptual framework for personal recovery. Recovery is described as gradual, non-linear, a struggle, and multidimensional, with key psychological processes – *connectedness; hope and optimism; identity; meaning and purpose; and empowerment.* Slade (2012) comments that this is quite different from clinical preoccupations with symptom reduction, risk management, and crisis containment – 'it is all positive and forward-looking – not at all about getting rid of things like symptoms or social disability. In psychological terminology, it relates to approach motivation rather than avoidance motivation. It points to a completely different way of constructing the job of a mental health professional' (p. 86). The next chapter explores the concept of recovery and associated issues in more detail and will outline how coaching psychology, as reflected upon in this book, has a real value in supporting individuals with BPD, and perhaps other mental health diagnoses, on the journey of recovery.

Vignette overview

The vignettes in the book are informed by the following brief outline sequence that characterised GLOW11 coaching psychology approach:

At the initial GLOW11 group meeting, participants were informed that:

a. Individual coaching would begin by putting an agreed coaching structure in place with each individual, for example, clear contracting and expectations; frequency, timing and coaching venues agreed; clarification about confidentiality and record-keeping, and the critical importance for all concerned of creating a safe space for coaching. (the costs associated with GLOW11 were covered by the Health Services Executive (HSE), Ireland).

b. Clarifying, working with and ongoing review of participants' personal values in their life domains would form an important starting point for coaching sessions. Personal values were defined as 'what is important to us and gives us a sense of purpose; the person we want to be and the things we want to stand for' (Hill & Oliver, 2019, p. 37). This was followed by an invitation to open discussion and question-and-answer to tease out participants' familiarity with and understanding of personal values as ultimately what was important to each person in different life domains.

c. A GLOW11 life domains questionnaire loosely modelled on the Valued Living Questionnaire (Wilson et al., 2010) and a values list (Harris, 2019) was distributed to each participant, with information-sharing on how the questionnaire might be helpful in preparation for individual coaching. Life domains included in the questionnaire were: personal growth and learning; health and wellbeing; money and finance; partner and love; fun and recreation; work and career; family and friends; and community and environment.

d. Participants were asked to take time to think about 'which life domains are really important to you at the moment?' in order of importance (1–5), and within each important life domain, 'what really matters most to you/what do you care most about?'

e. The values list (Harris, 2019) was referred to in order to assist each participant in their thinking about values and to begin the process of clarifying personal values associated with prioritised life domains.

f. This was followed by small-group discussions, each of which was facilitated by a coaching psychologist who was participating in GLOW11 (4), where individuals were invited to share their thoughts thus far, as much as each felt comfortable in so doing.

g. Each participant was requested to bring their life-domains and values materials to their first individual coaching session.

Individual coaching sessions (5) built upon the process begun in the initial group meeting. Group coaching sessions (5) focused on strengthening participants' sense of self as regards feeling safe to speak and be listened to, encouraging reflection and learning about actions being taken in daily life, and importantly, having fun together.

Coaching in GLOW11 while primarily focused on clarifying and working with personal values towards participants taking on valued actions in daily life, was also strongly cognisant of the importance for individuals with BPD of personal validation in the context of:

- 'how the coachee speaks, what he speaks about, and the effect this has on the coach are rich sources of information about the coachee and his constructions of self and reality which may only surface to conscious awareness in the speaking and interaction with the 'other' of the coach' (Cavicchia and Gilbert, 2019, p. 40);
- 'verbalising one's inner thoughts to a professional confidential listener … changes conversation into another form of speech that acts upon us in a different way … speaking in a coaching session is to speak oneself into existence. The speaker is also the listener' (Western, 2012, p. 150);

- 'strengthening the self as knower is crucial in constructing a more coherent self and a life worth living' … unless individuals (with BPD) 'trust their basic feelings and wants, there is no basis for elaborating a sense of who they are and what they want from life' (Livesley, 2017, p. 231); and
- 'Personal recovery means a deeply personal, unique process of changing one's attitudes, values, feelings, goals, skills, and/or roles. It is a way of living a satisfying, hopeful and contributing life even within the limitations caused by illness. Recovery involves the development of new meaning and purpose in one's life as one grows beyond the catastrophic effects of mental illness' (Anthony, 1993).

Vignette

At the start of coaching, Eddie, a man in his late 30s who has a diagnosis of Borderline Personality Disorder (BPD), speaks about his current life situation, in particular, that he has stopped self-harming and has reduced his alcohol consumption. In this context, he says that when he read through the life domains and values questionnaire at the initial group meeting, he felt that he was ready and more motivated to try to have a more structured and productive daily routine and that this would help to increase his feelings of self-worth.

However, Eddie now says that in the meantime he has been thinking more about different areas of his life and what is important to him and that he wants to look at something in the coaching sessions that he has been avoiding for some time. The coaching psychologist asks Eddie what he wants to focus on now in coaching. Eddie tells the coach that since his teenage years, just after he was diagnosed with BPD, his relationship with his older brother had deteriorated badly. As an example, Eddie says that he and his brother frequently argued, that he usually lost his temper and the fallout affected everybody and the atmosphere in the family. Eddie has not spoken to his brother in a number of years, but has learned recently from his sister that his brother would like to patch things up with him. Eddie says that he would like to meet with his brother and hopefully patch things up. However, Eddie is also afraid that if such a meeting goes badly then he might start drinking heavily again and self-harm.

To help bring focus and direction to the conversation, the coaching psychologist asks Eddie to look again at the life domains and values questionnaire and to identify the area of his life that might improve through meeting with his brother. Eddie identifies 'family and friends' as the life domain involved. The coaching psychologist asks Eddie how meeting and speaking with his brother might affect this area of his life if the meeting goes well and if the meeting does not go well. If the meeting goes well, Eddie hopes his brother will accept Eddie as his brother and see that Eddie is trying hard to improve his life. Eddie has some insight into how he has a deep need to be accepted back into his family and consequently if the meeting goes badly, he is afraid of having another angry outburst with his brother, as well as how his behaviour might deteriorate afterwards. The coaching psychologist then asks Eddie to think more about what really matters most to him as he thinks about his relationship with his brother and the wider family, and suggests that Eddie reads slowly through the values words sheet to see if any of the words resonate for him. Eddie queries the word 'resonate.' The coaching psychologist explains that people sometimes choose values they think they 'should' have, but that 'resonate' means that a values word or words speaks to the heart and to feelings. Eddie is encouraged to take his time reading through the values list.

Eddie spends some time reading through the values list and says the word he is looking at and coming back to is 'honesty' and in particular that the word means 'to be honest, truthful and sincere, with myself and others.' Eddie becomes tearful as he speaks. The coaching psychologist waits. Eddie says 'there's a lot there in those words ... especially being honest, truthful and sincere with myself. It's not something I've been good at over the years.' The coaching psychologist asks Eddie to say more about being honest with himself. At the heart of what Eddie speaks about is his sense of having brought pain into the lives of other people in relationships, including his family. The coaching psychologist acknowledges what Eddie is saying and elaborates that there is probably not a human being alive, including the coaching psychologist, who has not brought pain into the lives of other people, usually people they are close to or want to be close to. Eddie is asked if pain is the only thing he has brought into the lives of other people. Eddie speaks about how he is trying to be respectful and kind and more open in his relationship with his partner and that he enjoys seeing the difference this makes. From Eddie's account, this relationship is mainly positive and is important to his wellbeing and sense of self as a person who is able to be in an intimate relationship. Eddie is asked if he feels accepted by his partner. He says that most of the time he does and this brings Eddie back to what is emerging as a core issue for him – being honest with himself about himself – self-acceptance, in particular acceptance of negative emotions, rather than trying to avoid such emotions and becoming dysregulated. The coaching psychologist compliments Eddie on feeling safe enough and courageous enough to speak about his emotions in the session, both positive and negative emotions. Eddie replies that the session is helping him to understand better what being honest with himself means – to actually say what he is feeling, what he is thinking, and what is happening, at the time.

Given the importance of validation for individuals with BPD, the coaching psychologist asks Eddie how he feels their relationship in the coaching sessions is working for him. Eddie says 'I feel like you get me. That I matter to you. It's a good feeling to have.' Eddie is asked why mattering is important to him. He says 'when you have borderline (BPD) there are times when you feel you don't matter to yourself or to others, that nobody really gets you.'

Given the importance of emotional regulation for individuals with BPD, Eddie is asked if he is continuing to practise the emotional regulation skills learned in the DBT programme. Eddie says that he recently showed the emotional regulation exercises from the DBT programme to his partner, when she asked about it. He adds that his partner is now helping him by reminding him about these skills. He says, 'She reminds me in a kind way. I don't feel she's telling me what to do.'

Eddie refers to having negative thoughts as being like in a mental prison and that he finds it very hard to 'let myself off the hook.' The coaching psychologist asks Eddie whether he thinks it is possible to have negative thoughts and at the same time try to focus on behaving in accordance with his values, for example, being honest, truthful and sincere with himself and with others? Eddie asks the coaching psychologist for an example of what he means. The coaching psychologist says, 'Well, you would like to meet with your brother and have an honest, sincere and truthful conversation with him about the relationship you want to have with him and patch things up. As you think about this, as well as what you hope for by meeting him, for example, acceptance, you also have negative thoughts about the worst that might happen.' The coaching psychologist checks that Eddie is following the meaning of the words being spoken. Eddie nods. 'So, you might find yourself getting side-tracked by the negative thoughts and decide you won't go ahead with contacting your brother. Or, even while having negative thoughts about meeting your brother, you choose to move towards what you want – to focus on and move towards what you really want according to your value of honesty – to meet your brother, especially now that you know from your sister that he would like to meet you too.'

The coaching psychologist notices that Eddie is moving about a lot in his chair and asks if he would like a break, to stretch or walk about. Eddie takes the break offered, which helps.

Eddie is visibly interested in and curious about what would be a new way of thinking about the situation and tells the coaching psychologist that he wants to learn more so he can put it to use for himself. At this point, the coaching psychologist decides to introduce Eddie to the idea of the choice point (Ciarrochi et al., 2016) in the belief that it will provide both of them with a road map for working together with Eddie's values in the coaching sessions, as well as helping Eddie to think about the particular situation of speaking again with his brother.

Discussion points

1. What is your perspective as to whether a universal definition of coaching/coaching psychology is desirable or otherwise?
2. How familiar are you with the more recent and ongoing developments in coaching psychology that emphasises pragmatic, postmodern and complexity perspectives?

3. If the boundary between 'clinical' and 'non-clinical' individuals is fluid and imprecise, have you considered the possible implications for your coaching psychology practise?

4. What does 'ethical maturity' mean to you as a practicing coaching psychologist?

Recommended reading

Anthony, W. (1993). Recovery from mental illness: The guiding vision of the mental health system in the 1990s. *Psychosocial Rehabilitation Journal, 16*(4), 11–23.

Bachkirova, T., Spence, G. & Drake, D. (2017). Introduction. In: T.Bachkirova, G. Spence & D. Drake(eds.), The Sage Handbook of Coaching, London, UK: Sage Publications Ltd (pp. 1-7).

Carroll, M., & Shaw, E. (2013). *Ethical maturity in the helping professions: Making difficult life and work decisions.* London, UK: Jessica Kingsley Publishers. (Chapter 2 is a helpful exploration of ethical maturity and unethical behaviour in the helping professions).

Cavanagh, M.J., & Buckley, A. (2018). Coaching and mental health. In E. Cox, T. Bachkirova, & D. Clutterbuck (Eds.), *The complete handbook of coaching* (3rd ed., pp. 451–464). London, UK: Sage Publications Ltd. (A very clear overview of issues arising in considering the role of coaching psychology in mental health).

Deegan, P. (1996). Recovery as a journey of the heart. *Psychiatric Rehabilitation Journal, 19*(3), 91–97. (A testimony of personal recovery).

Flynn, D., Kells, M., Joyce, M., Corcoran, P., Gillespie, C., Suarez, …Cotter, P. (2017). Standard 12 month dialectical behaviour therapy for adults with borderline personality disorder in a public community mental health setting. *Borderline Personality Disorder and Emotional Dysregulation, 4*(19), 1–11. (This research article provides a comprehensive overview of the application of Dialectical Behaviour Therapy (DBT) and individuals with BPD).

LeJeune, J., & Luoma, K. B. (2019). *Values in therapy: A clinician's guide to helping clients explore values, increase psychological flexibility & live a more meaningful life.* Oakland, CA: Context Press. (Chapter 1 provides an interesting perspective on 'The What and Why of Values').

Palmer, S., & Whybrow, A. (2019). *Handbook of coaching psychology: A guide for practitioners* (2nd ed). London, UK: Routledge. (Chapter 1 provides a concise overview of the historical roots of coaching psychology and key aspects of the current state of play, including issues arising in the debate about defining coaching psychology).

Paris, J. (2020). *Treatment of borderline personality disorder: A guide to evidence-based practice* (2nd ed.). New York: Guilford Press. (pp. 189–191 focuses on the importance of helping individuals with BPD in 'getting a life').

References

Akhtar, S. (2019). *Silent virtues: Patience, curiosity, privacy, intimacy, humility, and dignity.* London, UK: Routledge.

Anthony, W. A. (1993). Recovery from mental illness: The guiding vision of the mental health service system in the 1990s. *Psychosocial Rehabilitation Journal,* *16*(4), 11–23.

American Psychiatric Association. (2000). *Diagnostic and statistical manual of mental disorders* (4th ed.). Washington, DC: American Psychiatric Association.

Argyris, C., & Schon, D. (1974). *Theory in practice: Increasing professional effectiveness.* San Francisco, CA: Jossey Bass.

Australian Psychological Society (APS). www.org.au

Australian Psychological Society (n.d.). Definition of coaching psychology. Retrieved on 5/9/2018 from www.groups.psychology.org.au/igcp/

Bachkirova, T. (2011). *Developmental coaching: Working with the self.* Maidenhead, UK: Open University Press.

Bachkirova, T. (2015). Self-deception in coaches: An issue in principle and a challenge for supervision. *Coaching: An International Journal of Theory, Research and Practice, 8*(1), 4–19.

Bachkirova, T. (2016). A new perspective on self-deception for applied purposes. *New Ideas in Psychology, 43,* 1–9.

Bachkirova, T. (2016). The self of the coach: Conceptualisation, issues, and opportunities for practitioner development. *Consulting Psychology Journal: Practice and Research, 68*(2), 143–156.

Bachkirova, T. (2017). Developing a knowledge base of coaching: Questions to explore. In T. Bachkirova, G. Spence, & D. Drake (Eds.), *The SAGE handbook of Coaching* (pp. 23–41). London, UK: Sage Publications.

Bachkirova, T., & Lawton Smith, C. (2015). From competencies to capabilities in the assessment and accreditation of coaches. *International Journal of Evidence Based Coaching and Mentoring, 13*(2), 123–140.

Bachkirova, T., Cox, E., & Clutterbuck, D. (2018). Introduction. In E. Cox, T. Bachkirova, & D. Clutterbuck (Eds.), *The complete handbook of coaching* (xxix). London, UK: Sage Publications.

Bachkirova, T., Spence, G., & Drake, D. (Eds.). (2017). *The SAGE handbook of coaching.* London, UK: Sage Publications.

Brennan, D., & Wildflower, L. (2018). Ethics and coaching. In E. Cox, T. Bachkirova, & D. Clutterbuck (Eds.), *The complete handbook of coaching* (3rd ed., pp. 500–517). London, UK: Sage Publications Ltd.

Buckley, A. (2007). The mental health boundary in relationship to coaching and other activities. *International Journal of Evidence-Based Coaching and Mentoring,* Special Issue, Summer: 17–23.

Carroll, M., & Shaw, E. (2013). *Ethical maturity in the helping professions: Making difficult life and work decisions.* London, UK: Jessica Kingsley Publishers.

Cavanagh, M. (2009). Coaching as a method for joining up the dots: An interview by T. Bachkirova & C. Kauffman. *Coaching: An International Journal of Theory, Research and Practice, 2*(2), 106–116.

Cavanagh, M. & Lane, D. (2012). Coaching psychology coming of age: The challenges we face in the messy world of complexity. *International Coaching Psychology Review, 7,* 75–90.

Cavanagh, M.J., & Buckley, A. (2018). Coaching and mental health. In E. Cox, T. Bachkirova, & D. Clutterbuck (Eds.), *The complete handbook of coaching* (3rd ed., pp. 451–464). London, UK: Sage.

Cavicchia, S., & Gilbert, M. (2019). *The theory and practice of relational coaching: Complexity, paradox and integration.* London, UK: Routledge.

Ciarrochi, J., Zettle, R.D., Brockman, R. et al. (2016). Measures that Make a Difference: A functional contextualistic approach to optimizing psychological measurement in clinical research and practice. In: R.D. Zettle, S.C. Hayes, D. Barnes-Holmes & A. Biglan (eds.), *The Wiley Handbook of Contextual Behavioural Science* (pp. 320–346). Chichester, UK: Wiley.

Clutterbuck, D. (2013). *Step forward the ethical mentor.*www.davidclutterbuckpartner ship.com/step-forward-the-ethical-mentor/

Cox, E., Bachkirova, T., & Clutterbuck, D. (2014). Theoretical traditions and coaching genres: Mapping the territory. *Advances in Developing Human Resources, 16*(2), 127–138.

Cooper, M. (2009). Welcoming the other: Actualising the humanistic ethic at the core of counselling psychology practice. *Counselling Psychology Review, 24*(3), 119–129.

Cooper, M., & Hermans, H. (2007). Honouring self-otherness: Alterity and the in-trapersonal. In L. M. Simao, & J. Valsiner (Eds.), *Otherness in question: Labyrinths of the Self* (pp. 305–315). Charlotte, NC: Information Age.

David, S., Clutterbuck, D., & Megginson, D. (Eds.). (2013). *Beyond goals: Effective strategies for coaching and mentoring.* Farnham, UK: Gower.

Egan, G. (2014). *The skilled helper: A client-centred approach.* Andover, UK: Cengage Learning.

Flynn, D., Kells, M., Joyce, M., Corcoran, P., Gillespie, C., Suarez, C.,.. .Cotter, P. (2017). Standard 12 month dialectical behaviour therapy for adults with borderline personality disorder in a public community mental health setting. *Borderline Personality Disorder and Emotional Dysregulation, 4*(19), 1–11.

Garvey, B., Stokes, P., & Megginson, D. (2009). *Coaching and mentoring: Theory and practice.* London, UK: Sage.

Grant, A. M. (2005). What is evidence-based executive, workplace and life-coaching? In M. Cavanagh, A. M. Grant, & T. Kemp (Eds.), *Evidence-based coaching. Vol. 1: Theory, research and practice from the behavioural sciences* (pp. 1–12). Bowen Hills, QLD: Australian Academic Press.

Hacking, I. (1999). *The social construction of what?* Cambridge: Harvard University Press.

Harris. (2019). www.actmindfully.com.au

Hawkins, P., & Turner, E. (2020). *Systemic coaching: Delivering value beyond the individual.* London, UK: Routledge.

Higgitt A., & Fonagy P. (1992). Psychotherapy in borderline and narcissistic personality disorder. *British Journal of Psychiatry, 161*, 23–43.

Hill, J. & Oliver, J. (2019). *Acceptance and commitment coaching: Distinctive features.* London, UK: Routledge.

Jackson, J. (2019). Phenomenological psychopathology and America's social life-world. In G. Stanghellini, M. R. Broome, A. V. Fernandez, P. Fusar-Poli, A. Raballo, & R. Rosfort (Eds.), *The Oxford handbook of phenomenological psy-chopathology* (pp. 985–1003). Oxford, UK: Oxford University Press.

Kane, S. (2001). "4.48 psychosis." In S. Kane (Ed.), *Complete plays* (pp. 203–246). London, UK: Methuen.

Katsakou, C., Marougka, S., Barnicott, K., Savill, M., White, H., Lockwood, K., & Priebe, S. (2012). Recovery in borderline personality disorder (BPD): A qualitative study of service users' perspectives. *PLoS ONE, 7*(5), E36517.

Lai, Y.-L., Stopforth., M., & Passmore, J. (2018). Defining coaching psychology: Debating coaching and coaching psychology definitions. *The Coaching Psychologist, 14*(2), 120–123.

Leamy, M., Bird, V., Le Boutillier, C., Williams, J., & Slade, M. (2011). Conceptual framework for personal recovery in mental health: Systematic review and narrative synthesis. *British Journal of Psychiatry, 199*(6), 445–452.

LeJeune, J., & Luoma, K.B. (2019). *Values in therapy: A Clinician's Guide to Helping Clients Explore Values, Increase Psychological Flexibility & Live A More Meaningful Life*. Oakland, CA: Context Press.

Levinas, E. (1969). *Totality and infinity: An essay on exteriority* (A. Lingis, Trans.). Pittsburgh, PA: Duquesne University Press.

Levinas, E. (1981). *Otherwise than being: Or, beyond essence*. The Hague: Netherlands: M. Nijhoff.

Linehan, M.M. (1987). Dialectical behavior therapy for borderline personality disorder. *Theory Method Bulletin of the Menninger Clinic, 51*(3), 261–276.

Linehan, M.M. (1993). *Cognitive behavioral therapy of borderline personality disorder*. New York: Guilford Press.

Linehan, M.M. (1993). *Skills training manual for treating borderline personality disorder*. New York: Guilford Press.

Linehan, M.M. (2020). *Building a life worth living: A memoir*. New York, NY: Random House Books.

Livesley, W.J. (2017). *Integrated modular treatment for borderline personality disorder: A practical guide to combining effective treatment methods*. Cambridge, UK: Cambridge University Press.

Markham, D., & Trower, P. (2003). The effects of the psychiatric label 'borderline personality disorder' on nursing staff's perceptions and causal attributions for challenging behaviours. *Clinical Psychology, 42*(3), 243–256.

Mental Health Foundation. (2015). Fundamental Facts about Mental Health. www.mentalhealth.org.uk

Merriam-Webster Dictionary. (2016). Merriam–webster.com

Monti, M.R., & D'Agostino, A. (2015). Borderline personality disorder from a psychopathological-dynamic perspective. *Journal of Psychopathology, 20*, 451–460.

Orange, D. (2011). *The suffering stranger: Hermeneutics for everyday practice*. London, UK: Routledge.

O'Riordan, S., & Palmer, S. (2019). Global activity in the education and practice of coaching psychology. In S. Palmer, & A. Whybrow (Eds.), *Handbook of coaching psychology: A guide for practitioners* (2nd ed., pp. 573–583). London, UK: Routledge.

Oxford Dictionary of English. (2011). Oxford, UK: Oxford University Press.

Palmer, S., & Whybrow, A. (2019). *Handbook of coaching psychology: A guide for practitioners* (2nd ed). London, UK: Routledge.

Paris, J. (2020). *Treatment of borderline personality disorder: A guide to evidence-based practice* (2nd ed.). New York: Guilford Press.

Potter, N.N. (2009). *Mapping the edges and the in-between: A critical analysis of borderline personality disorder*. Oxford, UK: Oxford University Press.

Rayle, A.D. (2006). Mattering to others: Implications for the counselling relationship. *Journal of Counselling and Development, 84*, 483–487.

Schon, D. (1991). *The reflective practitioner: How professionals think in action*. Farnham UK: Ashgate Publishing.

Skegg K (2005). Self-harm. *The Lancet 366*, 1471–1483.

Slade, M. (2012). The epistemological basis of personal recovery. In: A. Rudnick (Ed.), *Recovery of people with mental illness: Philosophical and related perspectives* (pp. 78–94). Oxford, UK: Oxford University Press.

Stacey, R.D. (2003). *Strategic management and organisational dynamics: The challenge of complexity*. Harlow, UK: Prentice-Hall.

Stacey, R.D. (2012). Comment on debate article: Coaching psychology coming of age: The challenges we face in the messy world of complexity. *International Coaching Psychology Review, 7*(1), 91–95.

Stanghellini, G., & Mancini, M. (2019). The life-world of persons with borderline personality disorder. In G. Stanghellini, M. R. Broome, A. V. Fernandez, P. Fusar-Poli, A. Raballo, & R. Rosfort (Eds.), *The Oxford handbook of phenomenological psychopathology* (pp. 665–681). Oxford, UK: Oxford University Press.

Stelter, R.(2017). Working with values in coaching. In T. Bachkirova, G. Spence, & D. Drake (Eds.), *The Sage handbook of coaching* (pp. 331–345). London, UK: Sage Publications.

Stelter, R. (2019). *The art of dialogue in coaching: Towards transformative exchange*. London, UK: Routledge.

Szymanska, K. (2019). Coachee mental health: Practice implications for coaching psychologists. In S. Palmer, & A. Whybrow (Eds.), *Handbook of coaching psychology: A guide for practitioners* (2nd ed., pp. 537–547). London, UK: Routledge.

Watts, M., & Higgins, A. (2017). *Narratives of recovery from mental illness: The role of peer* support. London, UK: Routledge.

Western, S. (2012). *Coaching and mentoring: A critical text*. London, UK: Sage Publications.

Western, S. (2019). *Leadership: A critical text* (3rd ed). London, UK: Sage.

Wilson, K.G., Sandoz, E.K., & Kitchens, J. (2010). The valued living questionnaire: Defining and measuring valued action within a behavioral framework. *The Psychological Record, 60*, 249–272.

Chapter 4

Recovery – personal or clinical: Implications for coaching psychology

Overview

This chapter is written with the intention of informing coaching psychologists and interested others about the 'landscape of recovery' in the context of mental health/illness. In terms of thinking about the possibilities of bringing coaching psychology to the lived experience of persons with BPD, it is important to be cognisant of the current and historical influences in the field, in particular the different concepts of recovery. For coaching psychologists with an interest in being of service to persons (with BPD) who experience significant mental, emotional, and spiritual suffering as a state of being, the need to be informed about recovery and related issues is necessary for professional and ethical practice.

Historically, the concept of recovery in mental health services has been described as an individual who is assessed as having full remission of symptoms, full- or part-time work/education, independent living without supervision by informal carers, having friends with whom activities can be sustained for at least two years (Libermann & Kopelowicz, 2002). This description approximates to what is referred to in the literature as clinical recovery (Andresen, Oades, & Caputi, 2011; Slade, Amering, & Oades, 2008).

More recently, a broader conceptualisation of recovery has emerged, which emphasises the importance of the individual with mental illness being empowered to discover and live a more meaningful and satisfying life towards outcomes that are personally important (Amering & Schmolke, 2009; Oades, Crowe, & Nguyen, 2009; Slade et al., 2008). This description approximates to what is referred to in the literature as personal recovery (Slade, 2009) or psychological recovery (Andresen et al., 2011), placing emphasis on values that promote hope, autonomy, a positive identity, personal meaning and purpose in life, wellbeing, and a belief that people can and do recover from mental illness (Amering & Schmolke, 2009; Farkas, Gagne, Anthony & Chamberlain, 2005), even when continuing to live with particular symptoms.

DOI: 10.4324/9781003048978-4

Andresen et al. (2011) state that the (personal/psychological) recovery movement emerged in response to increasing evidence that persons with a diagnosis of for example, schizophrenia, could move towards living a meaningful and fulfilling life. This evidence refers to personal narratives by individuals with a diagnosed mental illness, which has been critical of the medical (pathological) model of mental illness and recovery (Andresen et al., 2011). The recovery movement grew out of consumer dissatisfaction with a mental health system that appeared not to hear the voice of consumers, and at worst, was dehumanising in the use of restrictive treatments (Anthony, 2000; Trivedi, 2010).

Mental health services and recovery

Slade et al. (2014) states that a focus 'on personal recovery will require fundamental changes in the values, beliefs and working practices of mental health professionals' (p. 1). Despite the increasing interest at a government policy level, professional training remains largely focused on symptoms and clinical recovery, and many mental health service organisations continue with practices based on traditional clinical models (Oades, 2012).

Within services, when making decisions based around a values-based approach, mental health professionals need to negotiate both the client's and their own personal values, in a context of mental health service delivery where complex and conflicting values are often at play (Petrova, Dale, & Fulford, 2006). The implementation of recovery-oriented practices at service-delivery level has proven to be an enduring challenge (Glover, 2005; Uppal, Oades, Crowe, & Deane, 2010; Oh, Noorsdy, & Robert, 2013). At the heart of the challenge in translating the recovery vision into practice, is that in attempting to build consensus around core principles and values for practice, there is a risk that the essence of personal narratives and individual needs are taken over by services or lost (Trivedi, 2010). Recovery as an attitude or approach is a deeply human process, involving dignity of hope and growth – full risk which emphasises the very individual nature of personal recovery (Deegan, 1996). Trivedi (2010) suggests that in mental health services, day-to-day implementation of recovery is more likely to occur where mental health professionals are enabled to reflect on, identify and live out their personally held values, in what would be a shift in power-relations away from the dominant process of following organisational norms. This might help to increase opportunities for recovery operationalisation as a bottom-up, person-to-person process of change (Trivedi, 2010). While top-down organisation-wide recovery-oriented interventions are important, they may have limited usefulness in directly influencing the daily interactions of mental health staff with consumers, whose day-to-day relational experiences are commonly endorsed as the most critical element of the recovery journey by consumers of services (Deegan, 1996; Kramer & Gagne, 1997;

McGregor, Repper, & Brown, 2014). An additional and fundamental challenge is that the word 'recovery' is used in the literature and in discourse with often quite different meanings, assumptions and understandings, and underpinned by quite different epistemologies (knowledge – bases).

Clinical recovery

Clinical recovery as a medical definition of recovery is the definition that is most commonly understood in discourse (Andresen et al., 2011) and is associated with sustained remission of psychiatric symptoms, which locates recovery in an illness and medical framework of understanding (Libermann & Kopelowicz, 2002; Slade et al., 2008)

Slade and Wallace (2017) state that clinical recovery is a product of professional/psychiatrist-led research and practice, with four key elements:

  (i) It is an outcome or a state, generally dichotomous – a person is either 'in recovery' or 'not in recovery.'
  (ii) It is observable – in clinical language, it is objective, not subjective.
  (iii) It is rated by the expert clinician, not the person concerned.
  (iv) The definition of clinical recovery does not vary between individuals (is invariant).

Clinical recovery (medical model) makes the assumption that mental illness is a physiologically/biologically-based disease with recovery referring to a return to a former state of mental health whereby the person is cured (Andresen et al., 2011). Hence recovery is conceptualised as an outcome (Slade, 2009), unlike personal outcomes which is conceptualised as a process or a personal journey.

A key feature of the clinical recovery definition is that it is invariant across individuals (Slade et al., 2008). Consequently, from a research perspective, it is relatively easy to define, measure and examine in empirical studies (Slade & Wallace, 2017). This kind of research is only possible by looking at recovery in invariant and operational terms only (Slade et al., 2008).

In terms of the knowledge base that underpins clinical recovery, this 'way of knowing' refers to a view of psychiatry as a modernist phenomenon (Bracken & Thomas, 2015; Slade, 2012; Slade et al., 2014). The implications of clinical recovery as a modernist phenomenon are described by Bracken and Thomas (2015) from their perspective as psychiatrists, as:

• States of distress being characterised in terms of 'symptoms' where it is generally assumed that a medical framework and vocabulary can capture the essential nature of such problems.
• Mental problems can be scientifically investigated, modelled, measured, and counted, with experts who can organise treatments and interventions.

- Progress can be understood in terms of new scientific discoveries in neuroscience, cognitive psychology, or psychopharmacology and that such discoveries happen in university departments and research laboratories.
- Non-technical issues such as relationships, meanings, and values are not ignored, but viewed as of secondary importance.
- Service-user organisations are viewed as helpful in terms of fund-raising, identifying individuals for research projects, providing peer support, and witnessing to the benefits of expert interventions.
- The modernist, technological approach works to separate discourse about mental distress from contextual issues, privileging aspects like biological factors as the domain of experts who are trained to understand distress in terms of psychopathology.
- Service users are frequently referred to as 'partners' but ultimately it is the opinions of experts that count.

These authors (Bracken & Thomas, 2015), go on to state that the technological approach has complete dominance across media discussions of mental health issues, government decisions about research and service priorities, and the shaping of mental health policies and legislation. The authors also make the point that many psychological approaches in mental health, while being critical of the 'medical model' nevertheless also engage with mental distress mainly as 'a technical problem to be modelled and measured … organised and presented in a particular vocabulary that is developed over time by experts' (Bracken & Thomas, 2015, p. 124). This is a particularly important point for critical reflection by coaching psychologists regarding one's assumptions and understandings about the nature of mental illness or mental distress and what constitutes an appropriate 'intervention'? What a person assumes they assume is frequently not the case at all! This is because our assumptions, particularly deeply held assumptions, can be particularly difficult to 'hunt,' to surface, become aware of and identify. Brookfield (2012) defines critical thinking as the ability to assess one's assumptions, beliefs and actions and states that critical thinking 'is a way of living that helps you stay intact when any number of organisations (corporate, political, educational, and cultural) are trying to get you to think and act in ways that serve their purposes' (p. 2).

There is as yet a significant gap between the rhetoric of recovery (personal) as the expressed mental health policy of governments and mental health services, nationally and internationally, and its implementation across mental health services. As yet, many individuals do not feel fully met as persons in service cultures increasingly giving priority to narrow and specialised outcomes, targets, technology, audit pathways, and efficiency drives (Galvin & Todres, 2013).

Personal (or psychological) recovery

Definitions of personal or psychological recovery have largely emerged 'from the increasingly coherent voices of individuals who have experienced mental illness and used mental health services' and not from the mental health research literature (Slade et al., 2008, p. 130).

In contrast to clinical recovery, personal recovery is described as:

(i) A process or a continuum.
(ii) Is defined subjectively by the person concerned.
(iii) Is 'rated' by the person experiencing mental health difficulties, regarded as the expert on their own recovery, and
(iv) Means different things to different people, while there are many elements shared in common (Slade & Wallace, 2017).

The main theme from the accounts of individuals who have experienced mental illness is their emphasis on understanding recovery as something significantly different than the absence of symptom illness markers and functional impairment (Slade et al., 2008). Their meaning of recovery goes beyond definitions of illness, emphasising wellbeing or 'living the good life' (Andresen et al., 2011).

Generally speaking, individuals own accounts rarely offer a definition of recovery as such (Andresen et al., 2011). These author/researchers, citing various sources refer to terms used other than recovery, such as 'getting on with life' (Tooth, Kalyanasundaram, Glover, & Momenzadah, 2003); 'healing' (Prior, 2000); 'transformation' (Ralph, 2000). Bracken and Thomas (2005) refer to this growing body of research and narrative as user-led research (ULR). While GLOW11 participants did not use the word 'recovery' and some said they did not find it a helpful term, their expressed life hopes and dreams (Chapter 3) do resonate with the definition below.

Probably the most widely cited definition of personal recovery internationally is:

'Recovery is a deeply personal, unique process of changing one's attitudes, values, feelings, goals, skills, and/or roles. It is a way of living a satisfying, hopeful, and contributing life even within the limitations caused by illness. Recovery involves the development of new meaning and purpose in one's life as one grows beyond the catastrophic effects of mental illness' (Anthony, 1993).

Watts and Higgins (2017) carried out research in an Irish context that challenges the view that recovery from mental illness must happen within a mental health service context, using a narrative approach created the following definition:

'Recovery is a dynamic and ongoing educative process of personal transformation, effected through reciprocal relationships with compassionate but honest others. It involves self-activation, the taking of personal responsibility and the development of personal resources and support systems, which enable people to flourish and have a zest for living, even when life becomes challenging' (p. 136).

There is a clear point of divergence between clinical recovery and personal recovery in that 'recovery (personal) is seen as a journey into life, not an outcome to be arrived at ... seeing people beyond their problems – their abilities, possibilities, interests, and dreams – and recovering social roles and relationships that give life value and meaning' (Slade, 2009, p. 38, citing Repper & Perkins, 2003, p. ix).

Conceptual frameworks of recovery

Conceptual frameworks underpinning personal recovery have been derived from detailed analysis of the narratives and commentaries of individuals who view themselves as being in recovery. Two such important frameworks are the Collaborative Recovery Model (CRM) (Oades, Deane, & Crowe, 2017) and CHIME (Leamy, Bird, Le Boutillier, Williams, & Slade, 2011). CRM (Australia) and CHIME (United Kingdom) are targeted mainly towards mental health professionals and 'service-users' involved in mental health services with a view towards establishing recovery-oriented services.

Collaborative Recovery Model (CRM)

The CRM is one example of a conceptual framework that draws together the key principles of recovery as expressed broadly by consumers, with evidence-based practices that enable the translation of these towards routine practice (Oades et al., 2005).

Andresen et al. (2011) in their examination of the narratives of individuals with diagnosed mental illness (schizophrenia and other forms of enduring mental illness) describing themselves as being in recovery or recovered, found many different ways of understanding personal recovery, with each person's recovery a very subjective experience. However, sufficient common ground was found to formulate a conceptual model of psychological recovery, while also making the point that while 'personal recovery' is similar to 'psychological recovery' psychological recovery differs in a specific emphasis on psychological processes underpinning recovery (Andresen et al., 2011).

The CRM, anchored to psychological recovery, is underpinned by four key processes:

  (i) Finding and maintaining hope
 (ii) Taking personal responsibility for health and wellbeing
(iii) Renewal of the sense of self and building a positive identity
(iv) Finding meaning in life

These four processes are contextualised within a five-stage journey of re-covery (Andresen et al., 2011). The five stages of psychological recovery identified from consumer narratives and qualitative research are:

(i) **moratorium:** characterised by denial of an 'illness' identity, confusion, hopelessness and withdrawal as a self-defensive mechanism, whereby it seems 'life is on hold';

(ii) **awareness:** a first glimmer of hope for a better life and realising that recovery is possible, with an awareness of a possible self that is different to that of 'sick person';

(iii) **preparation:** individual commits to start working on recovery, taking account of the intact self, values, strengths and weaknesses, learning recovery skills, connecting with groups towards building strengths and confidence;

(iv) **rebuilding:** (the difficult work of recovery takes place, working towards personally valued goals, which may involve reassessing previous values and goals, accepting responsibility for managing one's illness – all of which involves taking risks, accepting setbacks and with resilience, coming back again); and

(v) **growth:** viewed as an outcome of the recovery process, whereby the individual feels greater confidence in managing their illness, more resilient in face of setbacks, with a more positive sense of self in the context of living a more meaningful life in terms of ongoing effort towards personal growth and psychological wellbeing.

Andresen et al. (2011) emphasise that the stage model of psychological re-covery is an abstraction, a conceptualisation and a model; that the growth stage is not an endpoint, but a dynamic stage involving ongoing efforts towards purpose and goals in line with core values; and that consequently it is an ongoing direction, qualitatively different from earlier stages.

The CRM is a modularised model that guides both one-to-one and sys-temic interventions and is informed by positive psychology and positive organisational scholarship (citing Cameron, Dutton, & Quinn, 2003), which provide a helpful base on which to build human growth and mental health service reform (Oades, 2012). CRM includes assumptions and practices that emphasise human growth, hope, personal meaning and self-determination – issues that have not been to the forefront of psychiatric practice historically (Oades, 2012).

The CRM has been conceptualised as a values and strengths-based coaching model (Oades et al., 2009), involving front-line mental health professionals and people accessing mental health services. Key elements that operationalise the CRM to be delivered in a coaching style (rather than a counselling or clinical style), primarily intended for delivery by front-line mental health professionals, are the Life Journey Enhancement Tools

(LifeJET), with a strong focus on building relationship as a working alliance and on personal goals (rather than professional-centred clinical goals) (Oades & Crowe, 2008). The CRM is based around the metaphor of a life journey of recovery, with particular protocols:

> **'Camera':** to help individuals identify valued life domains and strengths, assess the extent to which these have been sought and focus attention on areas for potential change;
> **'Compass':** to help individuals to connect their chosen values and their goals, quantify goal importance, and identify different levels of possible attainment of goals;
> **'MAP'** (My Action Plan): an action-planning tool to help individuals to carry out homework on goal-attainment tasks; and
> **'Good Life Album':** to bring together the outputs of the Camera, Compass, and MAP to build a personal album of the recovery journey.

CRM also functions as an organisational intervention and has a broad systemic framework to guide a variety of interventions with individuals, family carers, professional mental health staff, and organisational systems, with the systemic aspect viewed as critical, given the history of psychiatric service provision and associated culture (Oades et al., 2005).

As a coaching-based intervention, the CRM, with its guiding principles (recovery as an individual process alongside collaboration and autonomy support) and the LifeJET protocol can also be used for individual self-development (self-coaching); as part of mental health professional-client coaching (practitioner coaching); for carer recovery (carer coaching); and at an organisational level, can include practitioners coaching other practitioners, towards personal and professional development (Oades, 2012).

CHIME framework

Connectedness; Hope and optimism; Identity; Meaning and purpose in life; Empowerment (Leamy et al., 2011).

To clarify what personal recovery means, Leamy et al. (2011) carried out a systematic review to collate and synthesise published frameworks and models of recovery.

A modified narrative synthesis showed that recovery can be conceptualised as:

> A journey which varies from one person to another,
> Has interlinking sets of processes, and
> Can also be understood through the application of social cognition models of how the recovery journey itself varies over time and within individuals (Slade et al. 2012).

Thirteen ways that individuals described recovery from mental illness experiences were identified, for example, recovery as an active and gradual process, a journey, a struggle, a life-changing experience, is without a cure and unique to the individual, and has stages (Fortune et al., 2015).

Agreement that recovery occurs in stages was identified, although each individual's experience is unique, therefore stages may not be linear:

Stage 1: a crisis period where the individual is overwhelmed yet unaware of the extent of their illness.

Stage 2: an awareness of illness and a turning point where support is accepted.

Stage 3: believing recovery is possible and a determination to recover.

Stage 4: the rebuilding of life and starting on the road to recovery.

Stage 5: involving personal growth, improved quality of life, integration into community, and 'living beyond the disability' (Fortune et al., 2015).

Five over-arching recovery processes were identified (giving the acronym CHIME).

Connectedness: having social connection with others in daily life.

Hope and optimism about the future: having a belief that a meaningful life is possible despite serious mental illness.

Identity: not being defined by mental illness and having other identities in life.

Meaning in life: having a meaningful role in life.

Empowerment: making informed choices and decisions in daily life.

(Leamy et al., 2011)

The author/researchers proposed that 'characteristics of the recovery journey provide conceptual clarity about the philosophy (of personal recovery). Recovery processes can be understood as measurable dimensions of change, which typically occur during recovery and provide a taxonomy of recovery outcomes. Recovery stages provide a framework for guiding stage-specific clinical interventions and evaluation strategies' (Leamy et al., p. 449).

It is also proposed that the CHIME framework contributes to understanding about stages and processes of recovery by enabling available evidence to be more easily identified and providing a structure around which clinical efforts can be oriented, with a recovery orientation having overlap with the literature on well-being, positive psychology and self-management (Leamy et al., 2011; citing Hanlon & Carlisle, 2008; Slade, 2010; Sterling, von Esenwein, Tucker, Fricks, & Druss, 2010). In the context of clinical practice, the CHIME recovery processes are proposed as a framework for supporting mental health professionals in reflective practice in evaluating how their working practices impact on the recovery processes (Leamy et al., 2011).

The CRM framework of psychological recovery (Oades et al., 2017) differs from the CHIME framework of personal recovery (Leamy et al., 2011) insofar as it does not explicitly emphasise social components, for example, connectedness. Oades et al. (2017) in the context of CRM, do acknowledge that positive social relationships have a significant impact on psychological processes and are central to recovery in mental health, however, their focus on 'psychological' recovery is generally more internally derived.

Both CRM and CHIME were very helpful to our preparation for GLOW11 in terms of identifying the broad, systemic scope of recovery-oriented frameworks with a strong coaching relational focus and also a focus on organisational transformation. To date, the majority of research regarding personal/psychological recovery has been targeted towards schizophrenia. Consequently, while both CRM and CHIME offer conceptually compelling frameworks and processes, it remains to be seen whether and/or how either or both can be adapted to the lived experience of recovery for individuals with Borderline Personality Disorder (BPD).

If using the CRM and/or CHIME as guiding frameworks, it is of interest to reflect on how the GLOW11 experience might be examined in terms of the five-stages journeys of recovery (Andresen et al., 2011; Leamy et al., 2011). What possible interaction/s might there be between DBT and coaching psychology as exemplified in GLOW11 as regards how the five-stages journeys of recovery, particularly in terms of understanding participants' experience? How might DBT assist individuals with BPD as regards 'moving' along the stage's continuum? How might coaching psychology vis a vis an interaction such as GLOW11 be of assistance in building further, for example, towards a rebuilding-personal growth phase? Perhaps future research will inquire into these questions and others, so helping to further understand how coaching psychology in particular can contribute to the recovery journeys and quality of life of people with BPD and/or other forms of significant mental distress.

Borderline personality disorder (BPD) and recovery

In this section, we focus on how the experience of recovery regarding people with BPD has featured in the research literature and draw some implications as we see them, for coaching psychology in this regard. As will be evident, much of the existing literature on BPD has a focus on clinical recovery and symptom remission in particular. However, there is also a growing literature, primarily qualitative, with a focus on personal recovery related to the lived experience of people with BPD. As far as can be ascertained, to date there has been no published material regarding coaching psychology and BPD in particular. In a related context, Campone (2014) has published a case study based around a coaching interaction with an individual with a diagnosis of Dissociative Identity Disorder. The literature to date regarding concepts of recovery in BPD is overwhelmingly focused on activities associated with therapy, whether specialist to BPD or otherwise. However, we believe that there is much to be gleaned from even a brief review of the literature that can inform coaching psychologists who have an interest or curiosity about interacting with people with BPD. We have selected a number of studies which hopefully presents a balanced picture.

In the context of BPD and the struggle towards recovery and a life worth living, Gray (2011) writes 'long before I knew I had a personality disorder, I simply knew that my life felt unbearably difficult to live. For me, life has always been an uphill struggle, and at times I have just let myself tumble down the hill I have strived so hard to climb. Fortunately, I now understand how to keep going, and even to avoid falling down in the first place, but this learning process has taken the entire 28 years of my life, and I still feel I have a long way to go' (p. 185). Further on, she writes 'in my adult life, I have struggled a great deal with a sense of identity confusion, and an unsettling feeling that I may not be doing the right job or the right course. I've found it difficult to know myself and to recognise my strengths and weaknesses. My perfectionism compels me to want to be good at everything (and sometimes to convince myself that I live up to this)' (p. 188). And finally, she writes 'I feel I can enjoy life much more than before I went into therapy, as I've worked through many of the difficult feelings I've been carrying around since childhood. Unfortunately, my relationships with men still feel chaotic and painful. However, when I experience relationship problems, I no longer immediately think of harming myself. Instead, I might think about whether I am partly responsible for the problems, as opposed to thinking that the responsibility rests in the main with them. I find it easier now to open up to my friends about problems so I can get support rather than suffering alone' (Gray, 2011, p. 189). This personal narrative captures several aspects of personal recovery that have been identified in qualitative studies by people with BPD. It also resonates with the reported different life experiences of individuals who participated in GLOW11 as coachees.

Donald et al. (2017) state that while the concept of personal recovery is now well established in the literature, its relevance to BPD and other personality disorders, is only beginning to be explored, given that the majority of the recovery literature has focused on mental health diagnoses such as schizophrenia. Donald et al. (2017) acknowledge that CHIME (Leamy et al., 2011) as a recovery framework may be a good fit with the experiences of individuals with BPD but this has yet to be established.

Evidence from epidemiological studies and randomized controlled trials (RCTs) indicates that individuals with a diagnosis of BPD can experience significant symptom improvement through specialist psychotherapies, for example, Dialectical Behaviour Therapy (DBT (Linehan, 1993), Mentalization-Based Therapy (MBT) (Bateman & Fonagy, 2004), and Schema-focused Therapy (Young, 1999). Paris (2020) writes that while each of the evidence-based approaches to BPD looks different, all teach individuals to observe feelings and behaviour. What is less clear is whether people with BPD believe they are supported in making positive changes in their lives, since clinical recovery and risk reduction do not always coincide with individuals' personal evaluations of recovery in their lives (Katsakou & Pistrang, 2018; citing Slade et al., 2008).

Among the more numerous studies examining clinical recovery in BPD, Zanarini, Frankenburg, Reich, and Fitzmaurice (2010) reported that recovery from BPD, with both symptom remission *and* good social and work-based functioning (recovery) seems difficult to achieve for many individuals, though once achieved, such a recovery remains relatively stable over time. Zanarini, Frankenburg, Reich, and Fitzmaurice (2012) in a follow-up study reported that sustained symptom remission is significantly more common than sustained recovery (personal). It is of interest that these researchers concluded that there needs to be greater emphasis on a rehabilitation model of treatment (p. 666) to focus on helping individuals become employed, make friends, take care of physical health, and develop interests that would help to fill leisure time more productively (Zanarini et al., 2010), factors that are more resonant of personal recovery. They further concluded that clearly, as with any group of individuals with a particular diagnosis, there will be individual differences for a variety of reasons, for example, some may be more goal-oriented, others more resilient (Zanarini et al., 2012). However, Zanarini et al. (2012) also comment that other factors may also contribute to differing outcomes for individuals with BPD, for example, family members, friends, or therapists may be concerned that the stress of trying to work might lead to an upsurge in self-harm or suicidal impulses or that work should be ruled out until more serious symptoms of BPD are fully resolved. In the context of GLOW11, several participants identified employment, friendships, health, and hobbies as important, similar to recovery factors identified by Zanarini et al., 2012). In fact, no participant in GLOW 11 identified symptom remission as being of primary importance, though their relationship to their symptoms did sometimes emerge in the context of factors that might support and/or impede their striving towards a life worth living. All participants identified elements of what is commonly called personal recovery as being intrinsic to the life they hoped for and planned. This may also be related to participants in GLOW11 having previously taken part in a DBT programme which had contributed to symptom remission, for example, in episodes of self-harm.

Paris (2020) states that there is strong evidence that childhood sexual abuse makes the prognosis of BPD more severe, citing Soloff, Lynch, and Kelly (2002). Paris (2020) also highlights that many individuals with BPD have difficulty in managing close relationships, finding remaining intimate with another person without conflict particularly difficult, though many in recovery do find satisfaction in less demanding relationships. In this regard, Paris (2020) states that for people with BPD 'learning to be comfortably alone, and finding other, less conflictual ways of establishing social networks and support, may make serious difficulty less likely' (p. 142). In the context of aspiring to create more positive relationships, Donald et al. (2017) echo advice from individuals with BPD that it is not sufficient to aspire towards better relationships, but there is also a need to recognise and acknowledge one's past behaviour that may have negatively affected such relationships. In this context, Donald et al. (2017) advise that professionals 'need to be mindful not only of the sequelae for trauma, but also of their clients' experiences of stigma associated with blame and the re-traumatisation this may create' (p. 358).

Katsakou and Pistrang (2018) carried out a meta-analysis of qualitative studies regarding individuals' experiences of treatment and recovery in BPD. The aim of the review was to synthesise individuals' experiences of treatment and recovery in BPD, as described in 14 qualitative studies. Many of the findings are of interest and have implications for how coaching psychologists might interact with individuals with BPD and resonate with some important themes identified in GLOW11. The meta-synthesis identified 10 themes, grouped into three domains. Themes in the first domain, pertaining to 'areas of change' suggest that clients made positive changes in four main areas, for example, developing self-acceptance and self-confidence; developing new ways of relating to others; developing greater balance of difficult emotions and challenging negative thoughts; and implementing practical life changes and developing hope. Themes in the second domain, pertaining to 'helpful and unhelpful treatment characteristics' highlight aspects of treatment/therapy that clients believed either supported or hindered them in making progress, for example, where a sense of safety and containment was provided in the therapeutic relationship and environment; feeling cared for, accepted and respected and thus having a sense of being valued as opposed to feeling isolated, criticised, and undeserving of support when therapists were distant, judgmental, or not understanding; not being an equal partner in treatment, where for example therapy goals were imposed rather than negotiated, associated with feelings of anger and powerlessness; and treatment focusing on facilitating change, where therapists both supported and challenged and there was a clear focus for change rather than too open-ended. Themes in the third domain, pertaining to 'the nature of change' highlight clients' experience of change as an open-ended journey rather than a dichotomous outcome, with 'full' recovery viewed as an inappropriate way to describe improvement in BPD, because it could reflect a sense of denial about ongoing difficulties; and change as a series of achievements and setbacks, characterised by periods of feeling in control and periods of feeling defeated, while still maintaining a sense of moving forward (Katsakou & Pistrang, 2018). In the latter issue regarding change, the following captures acutely an important dynamic in how people with BPD can experience living a life – 'clients were described as feeling torn between longing for life and longing for death; between feeling hopeless and struggling to make changes;

and between remaining isolated and reaching out to others' (Katsakou & Pistrang, 2018, p. 952). This echoes an earlier study by Katsakou et al. (2012) where, for people with BPD, full recovery was seen as a distant goal, with most participants reporting fluctuations in recovery, where periods of improvement were followed by periods of challenge and struggle. Some participants felt in the context of BPD that trying to separate oneself from the disorder was especially difficult since they had experienced emotional problems for as long as they could remember. Overall, participants in this study felt that a number of challenges were identified which are likely to be more particular to individuals with BPD, for example, the meaning of self-acceptance, developing self-confidence, re-claiming identity, struggling with shame and guilt, not because of having a diagnosis of mental illness, but simply finding it very difficult to come to terms with who they are (Katsakou et al., 2012). Katsakou and Pistrang (2018) comment that this might be reflective of enduring challenges in developing a sense of identity and self-compassion, 'which often reflects a lack of secure attachment relationships and a history of abuse or neglect among people with BPD' (citing Gilbert, 2010).

Katsakou and Pistrang (2018) state that their findings suggest that therapy with people with BPD might facilitate change by focusing on two main areas – firstly, creating a safe, caring, and respectful environment, where clients feel valued and actively participate in coming to a better understanding of their difficulties; and secondly, promoting practical change, for example, confronting stressful situations, engaging more in community activities, managing finances, and getting involved in voluntary or paid employment. A characteristic of GLOW11 which was given much attention was the importance of creating a safe, caring, and respectful and structured coaching environment, within which both support and challenge could be experienced. In this regard, Katsakou and Pistrang (2018) write that 'when the therapeutic environment and relationships within therapy were experienced as a safe haven, people could internalise this feeling of safety and feel contained' and 'feeling contained in the therapeutic relationship also led clients to develop a sense of trust in other people' (p. 951). The central importance of a therapeutic relationship in BPD-specific therapies is a particularly important point.

The creating of a working relationship was also a pivotal aspect of the GLOW11 experience. Stelter (2019) states that research in the fields of coaching and psychotherapy 'underscores the importance and meaning of the relationship and the dialogue guide's abilities and virtues as the foundation of a successful dialogue' (p. 111). We will expand on the importance of this topic in GLOW11 further in the book and implications arising for coaching psychology engaging with people with BPD.

Katsakou and Pistrang (2018) citing Shepherd, Boardman, and Burns (2010) also draw attention to the finding in their review that 'full recovery' may be an inappropriate way of framing improvement in BPD because of enduring challenges to defining individuals' sense of self throughout their lives.

Ng, Bourke, and Grenyer (2016) carried out a systematic review of literature regarding both symptom remission (clinical recovery) and personal recovery which included views of individuals with BPD, clinicians, family and carers. The authors observed that most of the current literature has been focused on the clinical recovery of people with BPD, the observations of clinicians and consumers predominating, but with limited attention to the lived experience of individuals with BPD and their support networks. They state that the focus on clinical recovery is not surprising 'given the severity of the disorder and the significant impact BPD can have on quality of life' (p. 15). The personalised nature of recovery for individuals with BPD is indicated in a strong desire for both work-related activities and being able to carry out day-to-day activities to completion (Ng et al., 2016). This study also highlighted that the word 'recovery' and clinical recovery in particular may not fully capture the experiences of people with BPD (Ng et al., 2016). However, the authors also posit a view that while there are clear differences in the definitions of personal recovery and clinical recovery, there may also be complementary elements, citing Slade (2009). Ng et al. (2016) conclude that gaining an understanding of individual goals for therapy and recovery and incorporating this into clinical research and psychotherapy research may help to make interventions more personal and relevant.

Barnicot et al. (2012) carried out a systematic review of psychotherapy for BPD given that there is significant variation between individuals with BPD in terms of benefits from psychotherapy. This study identified three clinical implications consistent across studies – there is no evidence that older persons with BPD are more difficult to engage and work with in psychotherapy, as may be assumed (citing Lievesley, Hayes, Jones, Clark, and Crosby, 2009) and the successful adaptation and effectiveness of DBT for older people with DBT is referenced (citing Lynch et al., 2007); there is no evidence to date that people with very severe symptoms of BPD benefit less from therapy, again as may often be assumed – in fact, it is such individuals who may have most potential for change; and the findings also strongly reinforce the importance of the therapeutic alliance in the provision of therapy for BPD and recommend that therapists make developing and maintaining the alliance a priority (Barnicot et al., 2012).

Donald et al. (2017) set out to explore the meaning of the word 'recovery' and identify processes of recovery that are important to people with BPD. A key finding regarding the challenges implicit around self-acceptance for people with BPD is the importance of self-inquiry, whereby 'curiosity about the self, particularly if guided by a supportive other, may lend itself to a more balanced appraisal of the self (which is often problematic for individuals with BPD), and accordingly lead to greater self-awareness and self-acceptance' (p. 367). While all of the participants in this study supported the idea of positive change in life, recovery was also described as 'risky' or 'scary' to consider in the context of an already-established sense of self – a fear about change resulting in 'not knowing who I am at all' with debilitating consequences for the individual (Donald et al., 2017, p. 357). The authors caution that professionals need to be sensitive to this perceived risk in working with people with BPD, especially in the early stages of change, where anxieties might be particularly heightened (Donald et al., 2017). Conditions identified in this study as central to a process of change for people with BPD were support from others; acceptance of the need for change; work on past trauma without blaming oneself; curiosity about oneself; and reflection on one's behaviour (Donald et al., 2017). The authors conclude that for professionals working with individuals with BPD, 'operating from a conventional recovery-oriented viewpoint may not be sufficient or even desirable; rather it may be necessary to find ways to explicitly incorporate each of the conditions of change identified by consumers in this study' (Donald et al., 2017, p. 358).

Donald et al. (2017), in a follow-on study interviewed 16 clinicians who had specialist training and experience in working with people with BPD regarding their perspectives on the meaning and relevance of the recovery concept in the context of BPD. The study found that clinicians' understanding of recovery was broadly consistent with frameworks of recovery such as CHIME (Leamy et al., 2011), though there was also a point of divergence towards a clinical understanding of recovery as remission of symptoms and improved psychosocial functioning (Donald et al., 2017). Most clinicians in this study expressed some caution, even ambivalence regarding the concept of recovery for people with BPD. This appeared to be related to a divergence between clinicians' theoretical understanding of recovery as a powerful paradigm for change and actual 'recovery-oriented practices' as carried out in mental health services (Donald et al., 2017). For example, actual practice included the use of pro-forma worksheets or identical protocols for every person, that do not necessarily accord with official policy or the recovery principles found in the recovery literature (Donald et al., 2017). While there were points of agreement between individuals with BPD and clinicians across the two studies (Donald et al., 2017; Donald et al. 2017) for example, the importance of change to self-representation and the need to nurture and maintain personal relationships, consumers were more specific about the range of conditions needed for recovery to occur. Other examples of divergence included accepting the need for change and taking responsibility for one's behaviour being emphasised by consumers but not by clinicians; and while clinicians used more abstract language that emphasised agency and creative resourcefulness, consumers were insightful about the everyday features of recovery in lived experiences (Donald et al., 2017). Clinicians also referred to a need for individuals to have space and support in order to have capacity to act in the world – in this context the authors stated that 'the importance of understanding recovery from the perspective of lived experience is clear in our data, but clinicians also have an important contribution to make to understandings of the specific features, practices and dynamics of recovery' (p. 207).

Finally, in a study whose results have resonance with GLOW11, Mohi, Deane, Bailey, Mooney-Reh, and Ciaglia (2018) carried out a study to explore the ways in which people seeking treatment for BPD identify with values across a range of key life domains, for example, relationships, health and wellbeing, education and personal development, work and career, spirituality, recreation and leisure, and community involvement. The authors make a number of important points regarding the concept of recovery, BPD and the importance of clarification of values as essential towards values-based goals and actions:

- that the improvements monitored and measured in the clinical literature, such as symptom reduction, don't necessarily correspond with people's own evaluation of meaningful progress and life improvement on the road to recovery.
- that while specialist therapies for BPD do address important treatment targets, for example, reductions in self-harm, more personally important goals being sought by people with BPD require greater attention (citing Katsakou et al., 2012).
- that there is a need to increase clarification of individuals values and connect these to personally meaningful goals in the treatment of BPD (citing Ng et al., 2016).
- that values are a universal source of motivation and a fundamental driver of behaviour for human beings across cultures (citing Schwartz, 1992).
- that values can be generally understood as guiding life principles that provide a basis from which people draw their personally meaningful goals and consequently influence daily decision-making (citing Hayes et al., 1999).

While all life domains were identified as highly important to people with BPD in the study, interpersonal relationships (family, friends, romantic partners) and health and wellbeing were given highest priority (Mohi et al., 2018). Levels of personal commitment to values were rated highest for interpersonal relationships compared to all other life domains (Mohi et al., 2018). Challenges in interpersonal relationships and functioning is consistently identified as inherent to BPD (Mohi et al., 2018; citing American Psychiatric Association, 2013; World Health Organisation, 1993).

Mohi et al. (2018) conclude that therapeutic approaches such as ACT can help people to identify, connect and operationalise values in important life domains and that 'broadening BPD treatments to include a focus on people's values may be one way to help close the gap between treatment targets and the more personally meaningful goals people are wishing to pursue in treatment' (p. 8).

Livesley (2017) provides a useful integrating overview of the current situation regarding specialist approaches to supporting individuals with BPD. He argues that the emphasis on specialist therapy approaches for BPD needs to be replaced by a more integrated and evidence-based approach combining effective methods from all therapies. He also argues that current specialist therapies are limited because 'they do not recognise or accommodate the extensive heterogeneity of borderline personality disorder and its complex etiology' (Livesley, 2017, p. 47). Livesley (2017) recommends that an integrated therapeutic framework be organised around principles of therapeutic change common to all effective therapies (citing Castonguay & Beutler, 2006) supplemented by more specific therapeutic techniques as needed. Breakthroughs in research have now shown that most people with BPD can be successfully helped towards recovery, whether clinical (symptom recovery) or personal recovery and critical commentary is identifying a much broader range of possible therapy approaches to correspond with the heterogeneity associated with the diagnosis of BPD. Livesley (2017) concludes that it is important to recognise that any particular individual 'shows features shared with *all* other individuals with BPD, features shared with *some* but not with all individuals, and features *unique* to the individual' (p. 70). We mention this broadening out of therapeutic approaches to BPD here to highlight that this is an opportune time to critically reflect on possible contributions coaching psychology might offer to people with BPD. As previously noted, this book is not offering definitive recommendations, but hopefully a more nuanced beginning exploration of the topic and the opening out of a conversation.

Personal recovery and clinical recovery: Incompatible?

Slade (2009) asks whether clinical recovery and personal recovery are incompatible, noting that mental health professionals gravitate towards a definition of recovery as clinical, while consumers find greater value in recovery as a personal phenomenon. Slade (2009) argues that clinical recovery and personal recovery are clearly different and 'in some respects incompatible as primary goals for a mental health system' (p. 43). However, the values, goals, and work practices associated with clinical recovery make clinical recovery a sub-set of personal recovery and 'prioritising clinical recovery is helpful for many people in supporting their personal recovery, but inadequate for others, and toxic for some' (Slade, 2009, p. 43). Slade (2009) states that for clinical recovery, symptom remission is necessary, while personal recovery does not involve any mandatory position about symptoms, and identifies five justifications for giving primacy to personal recovery over clinical recovery in mental health services:

(i) **Epistemological:** personal recovery places more value than clinical recovery on the knowledge of the individual.
(ii) **Ethical:** acting in the professionally defined best interests of the individual should not be a primary value of services.
(iii) **Effectiveness:** the most common treatment (medication) does not cure, so the central promise of a clinical recovery approach is not fulfilled.
(iv) **Empowerment:** 'their' life has not been safe in professional hands.
(v) **Policy-based:** national policy requires a focus on personal recovery.

Regarding the tension and interplay involving personal recovery and clinical recovery, Andresen et al. (2011) state that 'we now know that people can recover in the clinical sense from serious mental illness – that is, in terms of objective measures of symptoms and functioning' and 'we also know that people can recover psychologically from the impact of mental illness, while still experiencing recurring symptoms' (Andresen et al., p. 153). These author/researchers further state that while one way of conceptualising recovery is living a fulfilling life 'within the limits of disability,' it is important that professionals don't implicitly impose these limits, 'inadvertently returning consumers to square one in their battle for hope' (Andresen et al., pp. 153/4). Citing Tenney (2000), Andresen et al. (2011) conclude that while it might be too early to claim unequivocally that everyone *can* recover from serious mental illness, there is no means of determining that any person can *not* recover – 'the hope and the opportunity to live *beyond* mental illness must be there for everyone. Recovery should be the expectation' (p. 1540).

Ultimately, in mental health services with a focus on personal recovery, disagreement with a clinical model will not matter, what matters is that the person discovers their own meaning, to make some sense of their experience and give some hope for the future (Slade, 2009). Slade (2009) asks why this is important and states … 'because suffering with meaning is bearable – meaningless suffering is what drives you mad. Finding meaning *is* moving on' (p. 42).

In the kindly light of post-GLOW11 retrospection, it became evident that across all of the coaching journeys, the relationship of participants to their symptoms of BPD was important in terms of how particular symptoms were experienced, perceived and interpreted. The concept of 'choice-point' was particularly helpful as an orientation for coaching in this regard. One of the functions of the choice-point concept is to help a person to become more aware of the sources of their emotional suffering, with particular reference to difficult thoughts and feelings, difficult life situations being faced, behaviours that move the person away from values and towards values, depending on context and from the person's perspective (Harris, 2019).

Luoma, Hayes, and Walser (2017) refer to 'choice' as the experience of values being freely selected and not swayed by avoidance, rigid rules, social manipulation, shoulds, musts, acknowledging that 'clients often feel coerced by others or by their own history, feelings, thoughts, and even by their values' (p. 208).

In GLOW11, it seems in retrospect that one of the reasons why participants actually enjoyed the challenges implicit in working with personal values was a growing realisation of how over-identification or fusion with particular symptoms of BPD resulted in individuals thinking they were unable to choose their values freely. Coaching in this context appeared to help particular participants to somewhat defuse from this story. Luoma et al. (2017) characterise this as follows … 'if you can disrupt fusion with this story and help clients connect with the possibility of being able to choose their own path, they often have a sense of innocence re-found despite the harshness with which they may have learned to treat themselves in order to cope … they may come into contact with parts of themselves (e.g. their values) that feel untouched, unjaded, and pure' (p. 208).

GLOW11 participants retrospective reflections from final group meeting following conclusion of coaching sessions and a final review group session

- 'I have a problem with the word recovery, my word is moving forward.'
- 'Maybe the word for recovery should be uncovered or discovered.'
- 'Stepping back and laying out the pieces resonates with me instead of recovery.'
- 'To recover is not a word that is useful! To recover something that is gone and beyond use now.'
- 'My mother used to recover our school books to make them perfect. I am not perfect!'
- 'This was my opportunity to unplug, reset and begin again.'
- 'My family may not value me, but I am still of value to myself.'
- 'I was always looking to fix what I thought was broken in myself. The dichotomy between fantasy/illusion and the perfect me. The "perfect me" exists in-between and that's good-enough, not perfect, but not bad either.'
- 'Its so good not having guilt about taking time for myself. Where I can read, go into nature and just be.'
- 'Understanding my need for self-control was huge for me, in my thinking, my reactions, my impulses and behaviours. And what happens when I lose it? The impact on me. On others. I learned that for me self-control means I want to choose to act and behave in any situation with kindness, fairness and compassion for myself.'

- 'All I wanted was better time management. I felt like a prisoner of time. Always trying to reach the future, preoccupied with looking too far ahead. Time management is a waste of time, trying to steal time by not really living in the moment. What's important to me even more now are my friends, home and health and making time for each.'
- 'I always felt that depression had me, rather than me feeling depressed. That shift in my thinking is important.'
- 'My true values are not a destination I will reach. But now I have a North Star in view that stays constant by me trying to stay true to my values.'
- 'Life throws things at you and will continue to throw things at me, I know. It's important that I stay with values and keep peace in my heart.'
- 'This journey has taught me to focus on my strengths, my values, my purpose in life and find my place in the world. It has taught me to let things go, be more flexible and free.'
- 'Coaching allowed me to look at my relationships where it seemed I took ten steps forward and twenty steps back. Why? It has helped me learn so much about myself, my feelings, thoughts, my physical being, knowing what my body is doing as part of me.'
- 'I realised during GLOW my ability to help others by giving a listening support to them, using what I have learned here. One of my core values is helping others, it's an inner strength. And it has brought to the front the importance of having a support network around me.'
- 'At the start I didn't really want to be involved in GLOW even though I signed up. But I did show up. And here I am. It has helped to know I am not alone and there are others who understand and resonate with me, and my feelings and thoughts. I didn't trust the relationship with my coach first, and now, well there is no one I would trust more with my life.'
- 'I have learned that even when I feel afraid, I am still able to keep going, that I am a resilient person.'
- 'I questioned the idea of coaching. What is it? Support? Thinking openly? Telling me what to do? I expected someone to come with a list of things I had to do, but that wasn't the case. I was expected to do it myself, with support! This is different. It has shown me there is no right or wrong way for me to think.'
- 'I thought I had some values, but wasn't really aware of the things that are important to me, I discovered through GLOW that saying no is okay for me, that being true to my values is a lifeline and that using my values to plan my life day by day really helps me.'
- 'My biggest aha moment was the Ballymaloe mindful walking day. I was amazed at how I was that day. Breathe. Eat. Walk. Be there and comfortable with silence. An awareness kicked in. Being mindful helps me now tune into times when mood is low.'

- 'GLOW has helped me discover that as well as being a wife, a mother, a sister, an aunt, a carer, I am also me! The me I had forgotten about. The me who is often overlooked by this mental illness. There was no me at all. I thought first my coach would get me to where I needed to be, maybe even find me and fix me. But I learned that my coach was a companion, sometimes giving me a gentle nudge but that ultimately it was me controlling my journey. It was actually that sense I got of myself that showed me a real sense of me, me doing the thinking, me talking about my thoughts and feelings to another person. I felt that I mattered in the relationship. That was amazing. Because if I mattered to my coach, did I matter to myself? Believing in myself and that that is good enough is huge for me.'

- 'Knowing my values has helped me stay more focused on what I enjoy and am good at. I love art and painting and I am good at it. I want to be able to show people that side of me. I don't want people only seeing behaviours and saying it's because of BPD. Now I don't over-react so much at home. The tension is gone which is great.'

- 'I have started to take time for myself now. It might only be ten minutes away from the noise of a busy house with small kids who always want something from me. I no longer feel guilty about taking time out, to read a book or just look out the window watching and listening to the birds. And I can handle it now if one of the kids comes looking for me during my time out.'

- 'GLOW for me is about someone who could support me in the right direction. I already had a hold on my life, I knew my purpose and where I want to go. What I was missing was the steps on how to get there. I want to move country, I need my finances to improve and get back to work. I am doing that now and have overcome the fear.'

From the overview of different concepts of recovery described in the book, it will be evident that the retrospective reflections of GLOW11 participants were located primarily in the realm of personal or psychological recovery. As previously stated, it may be the case that participants experienced reduction of BPD symptoms during the DBT programme and that the coaching psychology interaction in GLOW11 built upon this in moving towards working with values as a vehicle for considering personal recovery or perhaps more to the point, consideration of a life worth living.

Key challenges

It is beyond the remit of this book to explore a wide range of important issues arising from the implications of personal recovery policy and practice, for example, the measurement of personal recovery; how to build recovery-oriented mental health service provision; the coaching of mental health professionals in a recovery context; how to ensure personal recovery is not 'colonised' by the mental health system; the ongoing research and practice applications of CRM and CHIME frameworks; and the empirical evidence for personal recovery.

Vignette

Evelyn is a woman in her mid-40s who has a diagnosis of Borderline Personality Disorder (BPD). At the start of coaching, Evelyn speaks about having completed a DBT programme, finding it very helpful at the time, but is also struggling emotionally now and feeling 'a bit in limbo.' She is finding it a struggle to keep motivated every day and feels she is keeping busy doing things for everyone else in her life, particularly in her family, but is also feeling isolated in herself.

Evelyn identifies the life domain of health and wellbeing as the area of her life that she wants to focus on in the coaching sessions. Evelyn struggles simply to express that it is her own wellbeing that she wants to address. It is as if she is needing to come up with words whose emotional meaning are previously unknown to her. Evelyn visibly struggles and is emotional in the process of acknowledging and expressing a wish 'to do coaching just for me, just for me.' The coaching psychologist suggests to Evelyn that it seems to go against the grain for her to focus on her own needs in life and to bring these to coaching. Evelyn replies, 'yes, that's the word, I'm going against the grain here' and smiles, shaking her head. The coaching psychologist comments that as she is smiling Evelyn is also shaking her head. Evelyn says 'you don't know how hard it is for me to say to you, to anyone, that I want something just for me.'

The coaching psychologist explores with Evelyn how she is feeling in the session about saying that she wants something just for herself, about going against the grain. Evelyn refers to feelings of 'guilt' and 'embarrassment.' The coaching psychologist explores with Evelyn the particular personal history of these emotions in her life. A personal history of submissiveness emerges. The coaching psychologist explores this aspect of Evelyn's personal history because both her learned roles in life and her emerging desire to change are evident as they converse together in the session.

In the literature on BPD, Livesley (2017) writes about the nature of submissiveness and its behavioural manifestations as 'indiscriminately acceding to others' demands, always deferring to others, placating and appeasing others, consistently seeking to please others, accepting other peoples' opinions readily, difficulty expressing personal needs, problems voicing one's own opinions, discounting one's own opinions, allowing others to be excessively critical and abusive, being exploited and taken for granted, having difficulty in being assertive, putting others' needs first, putting one's self down, and needing constant advice and reassurance' (p. 204). Evelyn's description of her personal history in her family highlights a history of submissive behaviour. The coaching psychologist slowly reads the above information on submissiveness to Evelyn and then hands her a copy. Evelyn is asked to identify any particular behaviours named that she recognises and that she wants to change. Evelyn is encouraged to take her time and is given a yellow highlighter. Eventually she says – 'the ones I recognise as my be-haviours are always trying to please others, not saying what I need, partly because I've really never thought about what I need for me, and putting myself down. I've always seen myself as a problem.' As she speaks, Evelyn becomes tearful and apologises. She is asked what her tears are about. 'I feel upset just now at how much of my life has been about making sure everyone else is okay, as if that was my job in life.' She is asked why she apologised. 'I don't really know now,' she replies.

The coaching psychologist says 'Evelyn, it sounds to me like there are particular behaviours that you want to change?' Evelyn looks at the coaching psychologist directly and replies 'yes, I do.' 'I wonder whether there is a particular behaviour you would like to focus on, a behaviour that if it changes will make a positive difference to how you see yourself and give you a sense of wellbeing that perhaps you don't feel at the moment?' Evelyn identifies the behaviour she wants to change as not saying what she needs. In discussion, she realises that a first step is her actually becoming aware that she has needs of her own that have been compartmentalised away.

The coaching psychologist says to Evelyn, 'I'm imagining that as you have been going about each day looking after everybody at home, there must be times when a thought crosses your mind about something you would like to do for yourself and you have pushed that thought away?' Evelyn becomes tearful. She starts talking about a wish she has often felt to sit on her own in a particular room in her home which overlooks a garden. She has never acted on this wish. The coaching psychologist asks Evelyn to picture herself being in that room on her own. Evelyn smiles and laughs. 'It sounds daft, I just had a thought there about drawing! I used to love drawing as a child. It went by the wayside when my life started to go pear-shaped.' The coaching psychologist says, 'It sounds like you surprised yourself just now?' Evelyn replies, 'Yes, I did.'

The coaching psychologist asks Evelyn to read through her values list to see if there is a particular value that she recognises that might fit with her wish to draw. Initially, Evelyn selects the value of freedom – meaning to live freely and to choose how she lives and behaves. Evelyn speaks about wanting to be free enough in herself and with others to be able to say that she is going to sign up for 'drawing classes.' Evelyn's new sense of self-awareness becomes evident when she says 'My feeling is that going to drawing classes and doing drawing at home in the room over the garden will give me a feeling of freedom. But I know I will need to be brave in myself to say this at home. I don't think at this stage anyone will mind. It's just they are so used to me being me.' Evelyn is asked to look at the word 'courage' in her values list and to read it aloud. 'Courage: to be courageous or brave; to persist in the face of fear, threat, or difficulty.' She is asked to say what this means to her now and to take time to think about it. When Evelyn looks up again she says 'the big thing there for me is my own courage in facing up to my own fear … of making changes in my life.'

Discussion points

To what extent are your assumptions about coaching individuals with BPD and other forms of diagnosed mental distress based on knowledge about clinical recovery only?

How does learning about personal/psychological recovery change your assumptions about the possibilities of coaching in mental health?

Suggested reading

1 Andresen, R., Oades, L. G., & Caputi, P. (2011). *Psychological recovery: Beyond mental illness*. Chichester, UK: Wiley-Blackwell. (Provides a comprehensive overview of psychological recovery).

2 Deegan, P. (1996). Spirit breaking: When the helping professions hurt. *Humanistic Psychologist, 18*(3), 301–313. (Written by a person with personal experience of mental health services).

3 Livesley, W. J. (2017). *Integrated modular treatment for borderline personality disorder: A practical guide to combining effective treatment methods*. Cambridge, UK: Cambridge University Press. (Chapter 21 has an interesting perspective on building a more coherent self in a context of BPD, and which may also be of interest to coaching practitioners regarding issues around identity).

4 Mohi, S. R., Deane, F. P., Bailey, A., Mooney-Reh, D., & Ciaglia, D. (2018). An exploration of values among consumers seeking treatment for borderline personality disorder. *Borderline Personality Disorder and Emotion Dysregulation, 5*(8), 1–10. (A research article that examines the importance of values in different life domains for individuals with BPD).

5 Oades, L. G., Deane, F. P., & Crowe, T. P. (2017). Collaborative recovery model: From mental health recovery to wellbeing. In M. Slade, L. G. Oades, & A. Jarden (Eds.), *Wellbeing, Recovery and Mental Health* (pp. 99–110). Cambridge, UK: Cambridge University Press. (Provides a clear overview of the Collaborative Recovery Model (CRM)).

6 Slade, M. (2009). *Personal recovery and mental illness: A guide for mental health professionals*. Cambridge, UK: Cambridge University Press. (Provides a comprehensive overview of personal recovery).

7 Slade, M., & Wallace, G. (2017). Recovery and mental health. In M. Slade, L. Oades, & A. Jarden (Eds.), *Wellbeing, recovery and mental health* (pp. 24–34). Cambridge, UK: Cambridge University Press. (This chapter provides a concise overview of CHIME recovery framework).

References

American Psychiatric Association. (2013). *Diagnostic and statistical manual of mental disorders: DSM-5*. Washington, DC: American Psychiatric Publications.

Amering, M., & Schmolke, M. (2009). *Recovery in mental health: Reshaping scientific and clinical responsibilities*. London, UK: Wiley.

Andresen, R., Oades, L. G., & Caputi, P. (2011). *Psychological recovery: Beyond mental illness*. Chichester, UK: Wiley-Blackwell.

Anthony, W. A. (1993). Recovery from mental illness: The guiding vision of the mental health system in the 1990s. *Psychosocial Rehabilitation Journal, 16*, 11–23.

Anthony, W. A. (2000). A recovery-oriented service system: Setting some system level standards. *Psychiatric Rehabilitation Journal, 24*(2), 159–168.

Barnicot, K., Katsakou, C., Bhatti, N., Savill, M., Fearns, N., & Priebe, S. (2012). Factors predicting the outcome of psychotherapy for borderline personality disorder: A systematic review. *Clinical Psychology Review, 32*, 400–412.

Bateman, A., & Fonagy, P. (2004). *Psychotherapy for borderline personality disorder: Mentalization-based treatment*. Oxford, UK: Oxford University Press.

Bracken, P., & Thomas, P. (2005). *Postpsychiatry: Mental health in a postmodern world*. Oxford, UK: Oxford University Press.

Bracken, P., & Thomas, P. (2015). Challenges to the modernist identity of psychiatry: User empowerment and recovery. In K. W. M. Fulford, M. Davies, R. G. T. Gipps, G. Graham, J. Z. Sadler, G. Stanghellini, & T. Thornton (Eds.), *The Oxford handbook of philosophy and psychiatry* (pp. 123–138). Oxford, UK: Oxford University Press.

Brookfield, S. D. (2012). *Teaching for critical thinking: Tools and techniques to help students question their assumptions*. San Francisco, CA: Jossey-Bass.

Cameron, K., Dutton, J. E., & Quinn, R. E. (Eds.). (2003). *Positive organisational scholarship: Foundations of a new discipline*. San Francisco, CA: Berrett-Koehler Publishers.

Campone, F. (2014). At the border: Coaching a client with dissociative identity disorder. *International Journal of Evidence Based Coaching and Mentoring, 12*(1), 1–13.

Castonguay, L. G., & Beutler, L. E. (2006). *Principles of therapeutic change that work*. New York: Oxford University Press.

Deegan, P. (1996). Spirit breaking: When the helping professions hurt. *Humanistic Psychologist, 18*(3), 301–313.

Donald, F., Duff, C., Broadbear, J., Rao, S., & Lawrence, K. (2017). Consumer perspectives on personal recovery and borderline personality disorder. *The Journal of Mental Health* Training, Education and Practice, *12*(6), 350–359.

Donald, F., Duff, C., Lawrence, K., Broadbear, J., & Rao, S. (2017). Clinician perspectives on recovery and borderline personality disorder. *The Journal of Mental Health Training, Education and Practice, 12*(3), 199–209.

Farkas, M., Gagne, C., Anthony, W., & Chamberlain, J. (2005). Implementing recovery oriented evidence based programs: Identifying the critical dimensions. *Community Mental Health Journal, 41*(2), 141–158.

Fortune, B., Bird V., Chandler, R., Fox J., Hennem R., Larsen J.,..., Slade, M. (2015). *Recovery for real. A summary of findings from the REFOCUS programme*. London: Rethink Mental Illness.

Galvin, K., & Todres, L. (2013). *Caring and well-being: A lifeworld approach.* London, UK: Routledge.

Gilbert, P. (2010). *Compassion-focused therapy: Distinctive features (CBT distinctive features).* Hove, UK: Routledge.

Glover, H. (2005). Recovery-based service delivery: Are we ready to transform the words into a paradigm shift? *Australian E-Journal for the Advancement of Mental Health, 4*(3), 1–3.

Gray, J. (2011). The chasm within: My battle with personality disorder. *Philosophy, Psychiatry & Psychology, 18*(3), 185–190.

Hanlon, P., & Carlisle, S. (2008). What can the science of well-being tell the discipline of psychiatry – and why might psychiatry listen? *Advances in Psychiatric Treatment, 14*, 312–319.

Harris, R. (2019). *ACT made simple* (2nd ed.). Oakland, CA: New Harbinger Publications.

Hayes, S. C., Strosahl, K., & Wilson, K. G. (1999). *Acceptance and commitment therapy: An experiential approach to behaviour change.* London, UK: Guilford Press.

Katsakou, C., Marougka, S., Barnicot, K., Savill, M., White, H., Lockwood, K., & Priebe, S. (2012). Recovery in borderline personality disorder (BPD): A qualitative study of service users' perspectives. *PLoS ONE, 7*, e36517.

Katsakou, C., & Pistrang, N. (2018). Clients' experiences of treatment and recovery in borderline personality disorder: A meta-synthesis of qualitative studies. *Psychotherapy Research, 28*(6), 940–957.

Kramer, P. J., & Gagne, C. (1997). Barriers to recovery and empowerment for people with psychiatric disabilities. In L. Spaniol, C. Gagne, & M. Koehler (Eds.), *Psychological and social aspects of psychiatric disability* (pp. 467–476). Boston, MA: Center for Psychiatric Rehabilitation.

Leamy, M., Bird, V., Le Boutillier, C., Williams, J., & Slade, M. (2011). Conceptual framework for personal recovery in mental health: Systematic review and narrative synthesis. *The British Journal of Psychiatry, 199*, 445–452.

Libermann, R. P., & Kopelowicz, A. (2002). Recovery from schizophrenia: A challenge for the 21st century. *International Review of Psychiatry, 14*, 242–255.

Lievesley, N., Hayes, R., Jones, K., Clark, A., & Crosby, G. (2009). *Ageism and age discrimination in mental health care in the United Kingdom. A review from the literature.* Department of Health, Centre for Policy on Ageing.

Linehan, M. (1993). *Cognitive-behavioural treatment of borderline personality disorder.* New York: Guilford Press.

Livesley, W. J. (2017). *Integrated modular treatment for borderline personality disorder: A practical guide to combining effective treatment methods.* Cambridge, UK: Cambridge University Press.

Luoma, J. B., Hayes, S. C., & Walser, R. D. (2017). *Learning ACT: An acceptance & commitment therapy skills training manual for therapists* (2nd ed.). Oakland, CA: Context Press.

Lynch, T. R., Cheavens, J. S., Cukroqicz, K. C., Thorp, S. R., Bronner, L., & Beyer, J. (2007). Treatment of older adults with co-morbid personality disorder and depression: A dialectical behaviour therapy approach. *International Journal of Geriatric Psychiatry, 22*, 131–143.

McGregor, J., Repper, J., & Brown, H. (2014). The college is so different from anything I have done: A study of the characteristics of Nottingham recovery college. *The Journal of Mental Health Training, Education and Practice, 9*(1), 3–15.

Mohi, S. R., Deane, F. P., Bailey, A., Mooney-Reh, D., & Ciaglia, D. (2018). An exploration of values among consumers seeking treatment for borderline personality disorder. *Borderline Personality Disorder and Emotion Dysregulation, 5*(8), 1–10.

Ng, F. Y. I., Bourke, M. E., & Grenyer, B. F. S. (2015). *Recovery from borderline personality disorder*. Wollongong: 9th Annual Conference for the Treatment of Personality Disorder.

Ng, F. Y. I., Bourke., M. E., & Grenyer, B. F. S. (2016). Recovery from Borderline Personality Disorder: A systematic review of the perspectives of consumers, clinicians, family and carers. *PLoS ONE, 11*, 8.

Oades, L. G. (2012). Responding to the challenge of mental health recovery policy. In L. L'Abate (Ed.), *Mental illnesses – Evaluation, treatments and implications* (pp. 391–406). Vienna, Austria: InTech.

Oades, L. G., & Crowe, T. P. (2008). *Life journey enhancement tools (LifeJET)*. Wollongong, Australia: Illawarra Institute for Mental Health, University of Wollongong.

Oades, L. G., Crowe, T. P., & Nguyen, M. (2009). Leadership coaching transforming mental health systems from the inside out: The collaborative recovery model a person-centered strengths based coaching psychology. *International Coaching Psychology Review, 4*, 25–36.

Oades, L. G., Deane, F. P., & Crowe, T. P. (2017). Collaborative recovery model: From mental health recovery to wellbeing. In M. Slade, L. G. Oades, & A. Jarden (Eds.), *Wellbeing, recovery and mental health* (pp. 99–110). Cambridge, UK: Cambridge University Press.

Oades, L., Deane, F., Crowe, T., Lambert., G., Kavanagh, D., & Lloyd, C. (2005). Collaborative recovery: An integrative model for working with individuals who experience chronic and recurring mental illness. *Australasian Psychiatry, 13*, 279–284.

Oh, H., Noorsdy, D., & Robert, G. (2013). Eight steps toward recovery-oriented psychiatry education. *The Journal of Mental Health Training, Education and Practice, 6*(1), 38–46.

Paris, J. (2020). *Treatment of borderline personality disorder: A guide to evidence-based practice* (2nd ed.). London, UK: The Guilford Press.

Petrova, M., Dale, J., & Fulford, B. (2006). Values-based practice in primary care: Easing the tensions between individual values, ethical principles and best evidence. *British Journal of General Practice, 56*, 703–709.

Prior, C. (2000). Recovering a meaningful life is possible. *Psychiatric Bulletin, 24*(1), 30.

Ralph, R. O. (2000). Recovery. *Psychiatric Rehabilitation Skills, 4*(3), 480–517.

Repper, J., & Perkins, R. (2003) *Social Inclusion and Recovery*. London, UK: Bailliere Tindall.

Schwartz, S. H. (1992). Universals in the content and structure of values: Theoretical advances and empirical tests in 20 countries. *Advances in Experimental Social Psychology, 25*, 1–65.

Shepherd, G., Boardman, J., & Burns, M. (2010). *Implementing recovery. A methodology for organisation change.* Sainsbury Centre for Mental Health.

Slade, M. (2009). *Personal recovery and mental illness: A guide for mental health professionals.* Cambridge, UK: Cambridge University Press.

Slade, M. (2010). Mental illness and well-being: The central importance of positive psychology and recovery approaches. *BMC Health Services Research, 10,* 26.

Slade, M. (2012). The epistemological basis of personal recovery. In A. Rudnick (Ed.), *Recovery of people with mental illness: Philosophical and related perspectives* (pp. 78–94). Oxford, UK: Oxford University Press.

Slade, M., Amering, M., Farkas, M., Hamilton, B., O' Hagan, M., Panther, G., ..., Whitley, R. (2014). Uses and abuses of recovery: Implementing recovery-oriented practices in mental health systems. *World Psychiatry, 13,* 12–20.

Slade, M., Amering, M., & Oades, L. (2008). Recovery: An international perspective. *Epidemiologia e Psichiatria Sociale, 17*(2), 128–137.

Slade, M., & Wallace, G. (2017). *Recovery and mental health.* In M. Slade, L. Oades, & A. Jarden (Eds.), (pp. 24–34). Cambridge, UK: Cambridge University Press.

Slade, M., Williams, J., Bird, V., Leamy, M., & Le Boutillier, C. (2012). Recovery grows up. *Journal of Mental Health, 21*(2), 99–104.

Slade, M., Leamy, M., Bacon, F., Janosik, M., Le Boutillier, C., Williams, J., & Bird, V. (2012). International differences in understanding recovery: Systematic review. *Epidemiology and Psychiatric Sciences, 21*(4), 353–364.

Soloff, P., Lynch, K., & Kelly, T. M. (2002). Childhood abuse as a risk factor for suicidal behavior in borderline personality disorder. *Journal of Personality Disorders, 16,* 201–214.

Stelter, R. (2019). *The art of dialogue in coaching: Towards transformative exchange.* London, UK: Routledge.

Sterling, E. W., von Esenwein, S. A., Tucker, S., Fricks, L., & Druss, B. G. (2010). Integrating wellness, recovery, and self- management for mental health consumers. *Community Mental Health Journal, 46,* 130–138.

Tenney, L. J. (2000). It has to be about choice. *Journal of Clinical Psychology, In Session, 56*(11), 1433–1445.

Tooth, B. A., Kalyanasundaram, V., Glover, H., & Momenzadah, S. (2003). Factors consumers identify as important to recovery from schizophrenia. *Australasian Psychiatry, 11* (Supplement), S70–S77.

Trivedi, P. (2010). A recovery approach in mental health services: Transformation, tokenism or tyranny? In T. Bassett, & T. Stickley (Eds.), *Voices of experience: Narratives of mental health survivors* (pp. 152–164). London, UK: Wiley.

Uppal, S., Oades, L. G., Crowe, T., & Deane, F. (2010). Barriers to the transfer of collaborative recovery training into Australian mental health services: Implications for the development of evidence-based services. *Journal of Evaluation in Clinical Practice, 16,* 451–455.

Watts, M., & Higgins, A. (2017). *Narratives of recovery from mental illness: The role of peer support.* London, UK: Routledge.

World Health Organisation (1993). *The ICD-10 classification of mental and behavioural disorders: diagnostic criteria for research* (vol. 2). Geneva: World Health Organization.

Young, J. E. (1999). *Cognitive therapy for personality disorders: A schema-focused approach* (3rd ed.). Sarasota, FL: Professional Resource Press.

Zanarini, M. C., Frankenburg, F. R., Reich, D. B., & Fitzmaurice, G. (2010). Time to attainment of recovery from borderline personality disorder and stability of recovery: A 10-year prospective follow-up study. *American Journal of Psychiatry, 167*(6), 663–667.

Zanarini, M. C., Frankenburg, F. R., Reich, D. B., & Fitzmaurice, G. (2012). Attainment and stability of sustained symptomatic remission and recovery among patients with borderline personality disorder and axis 11 comparison subjects: A 16-year prospective follow-up study. *American Journal of Psychiatry, 169*(5), 476–483.

Chapter 5

A life worth living

This chapter will describe what was a unique aspect of the GLOW11 coaching interaction with individuals with BPD, a day spent in a rural ecological habitat by all concerned (GLOW11 participants and coaching psychologists). The day introduced participants to elements of the natural MEDSS framework (described below) that could be incorporated into their thinking about what constitutes a personal life worth living, with hope, meaning, and purpose. The chapter opens with an overview regarding the tendency to pathologize what is called mental illness, the importance of validation in the GLOW11 coaching experience and how GLOW11 built upon the DBT programme previously completed by participants.

Overview

In highlighting the developmental nature of human experience Csikszentmihalyi (2006), states that a final stage of personal psychological integration is — 'a point at which a person comes to accept his or her past, no longer seeks to change or achieve the impossible, yet is vitally connected to the immediate environment' (p. 4). However, consciously or unconsciously, we often distance ourselves from the possibility of greater psychological integration as we grapple in the present with different life experiences that bring stress or emotional pain. Also, we may have experienced significant trauma in our lives, where a learned and now habitual fear response in the body can trigger us to take fright, avoid, run away, or angrily lash out at a sometimes real or perhaps more often a perceived danger. If we lean too strongly towards such reactions and experiences, we may at the same time not give sufficient attention to our psychological needs for recognition, validation, affection, and feeling connected to a secure sense of self, to others, and to the wider world. Such experiences positively contribute to our sense of a life worth living, with meaning and a purpose in living. While all of what has just been described can be considered as occurring within a continuum of 'normal' human experience, such experiences also resonate strongly for individuals with BPD, frequently triggering dysregulation on the one hand and a yearning for

DOI: 10.4324/9781003048978-5

psychological safety on the other Linehan (2020). writes that one of the toughest challenges faced by people with BPD is regulating their emotions, being quick to become very emotional in response to a trigger in the environment and slow to come back down. She adds that 'people who have a tendency toward emotion dysregulation will have problems in an invalidating environment but will fare quite well in a validating environment' (p. 301), what she calls the biosocial theory of borderline personality disorder. The importance of GLOW11 as a validating experience for each participant cannot be stated too often and was central to each person's motivation in showing up, participating in and contributing to coaching sessions.

Traditionally, the experience of mental illness has been pathologized. If we pathologize mental illness or significant mental distress we are also pathologizing the human condition per se. In the speed of time it takes to make an assumption, people with BPD can be categorized into some 'separate' grouping of human beings, making it very difficult to imagine and conceptualise how such individuals might be able to connect or reconnect with their sense of what makes for a life worth living. We believe that the pathologizing of what is called mental illness is a significant ethical and professional challenge for counsellors, psychotherapists and coaches/coaching psychologists and consequently can be a major stumbling block to engaging with individuals with BPD, for example, with the belief that a life worth living, even with symptoms, is possible. This is an important challenge for coaching practitioners to consider since it includes thinking about whether coaching/coaching psychology can be an option for individuals with BPD, for example.

Building on the DBT programme that GLOW11 participants had previously completed (described by Linehan, 2020, as 'a very pragmatic, down-to-earth therapy ... literally, a programme of self-improvement' p. 172), GLOW11 as a five-session one-to-one coaching interaction assisted individuals to open out a space where important personal values could be clarified, explored for meaning and capable of being translated into decision-making and actions in domains of daily life identified as where change was desired. During five group sessions, personal learning was shared and further explored. Participants had previously expressed the wish for such group sessions.

This book so far has considered in some detail the considerable challenges faced by individuals with a diagnosis of BPD and the rationale above that underpinned a coaching psychology approach to diagnosed mental illness in general and BPD in particular. The book has explored the concept of recovery and its implications for mental health policy and practice. The book has also drawn attention to the conceptual and practice tensions between personal/psychological and clinical recovery, with an emphasis in this book on personal/psychological recovery in particular and it's relevance to the search for a life worth living by persons with BPD.

Our previously stated stance of engaging with GLOW11 from a 'not knowing' perspective as coaching psychologists is not to ignore the personal and professional experience, education, training and ongoing development and learning that we each brought to it. Implicit in our stance was to fully embrace and explore particular innate needs, that we all share – to be emotionally and socially connected with others, to feel valued by significant others, to feel psychologically safe in the company of others, and to hope that we can make a positive difference to the lives of others in the world. As with the concept of recovery and its personal meanings, these needs are not unique, though clearly important, to people with a diagnosis of BPD. We too, as individuals who work as coaching psychologists, also seek for a life worth living. In the coaching sessions each of us in different ways shared such thoughts about needs with GLOW11 participants where each discerned it to be appropriate and helpful. On receipt of such information, participants invariably were initially surprised, but always warmly welcomed what they heard. Our sense now is that such moments were critical to the process of coaching in GLOW11, conveying both mutual respect, that mattering to one another was a shared need and that the emerging relationship was inter-dependent and reciprocal.

Visioning for a life worth living

During the process of sharing and discussion among coaching psychologists during GLOW11, particular elements, arising from learning in coaching interactions with participants, emerged as important in contributing to re-flection on a life worth living. These elements are by definition incomplete, as yet, not robustly tested, but were echoed consistently by GLOW11 par-ticipants as important. We hope that this adds to the discourse as we accept our professional responsibility for whatever healing and personal recovery is possible in our own lives and in the lives of others. We also hope that it inspires others to continue the work of measuring but with a softer heart.

Cox (2013) refers to the importance of visioning and self-efficacy, through remembered previous successes, 'as pertinent to potential future events that may then be transferred into new situations via the new knowledge created in the coaching analysis' (p. 153). A pivotal challenge in GLOW11 was how to constructively build on the prior necessary DBT intervention and to create a validating environment for each participant that would facilitate and help further develop respective levels of self-understanding that would translate into visions of lives worth living that were possible and hopefully achievable. In this context, there was also the need to consider our own vision of how we might develop the capability to help participants 'develop their capacity to pay attention to their own actions, thoughts, feelings, emotions and moods and the interplay with the events in their (own) en-vironment.' (Bachkirova, 2020). This involved us in a process of focusing on and deeply listening to the lived experiences of participants to help each co-create 'potentially new ways of being and doing in the world' (Hawkins & Turner, 2020). In that sense we set out to identify, be with, validate and experiment with the self-knowledge of participants to create their own life worth living and in the process to open up 'the possibility of adaptation, reorientation, integration, and the other responses to the experience by the individual.' (Slade, 2012). Such words may seem somewhat incongruous at times. However, the 'down-to-earth' existential issues frequently faced by individuals with BPD is captured succinctly by Linehan (2020) where she refers to working with individuals who are highly suicidal. She writes 'I totally believe that you can build a life that you will view as worth living. Even in your tears, you have to believe whether you believe or not, letting go of disbelief, holding on to hope' (p. 230). Hopefully, this puts into context what is at issue when we refer to the concept of a life worth living, the inherent challenges for individuals with BPD and one's own assumptions, beliefs, and values in coaching interactions with those concerned.

Elements of a life worth living that emerged in GLOW11 coaching interactions

BPD affects the way a person feels about self in relation to trusting others (fears of abandonment, separation or rejection), how that person then might relate to others (unstable relationships) and how she/he might behave (inappropriate comments, bouts of intense anger). In such a context, then, specific needs take on a heightened degree of importance when considering elements that might contribute to a life worth living. For example, a healthy connection to a relatively stable sense of self and relationally to significant others, access to meaningful work or occupation, and involvement in personally meaningful recreational and/or artistic activities. Implicit in these types of experiences being meaningful and having a purpose for the individual, will be the importance of good-enough recurring experiences of recognition, acceptance and validation that communicates a felt sense that one matters in this world. Underpinning this are personally chosen values that are capable of being accessed and chosen for values consistent rather than values inconsistent behaviour. As stated elsewhere in this book, the coaching psychologists' own capabilities in conveying respect and mattering to participants was critical towards their openness and capacity for trust and engaging in working with values. Our consideration of these elements also prompted reflection on our own assumptions and unconscious biases about the nature of what is called mental illness – what if the symptoms of mental illness are 'voices' of grief for lost connections to what makes one's life worth living? If recovery is 'a journey of the heart' (Deegan, 1996) recovery then begins to make sense also in terms of an emotional journey of reconnection to what it means to be human, to what we truly value and care about and why. This is a journey of hope, action and love. In the process it is about 'recovering a new sense of self and of purpose within and beyond the limits of mental illness' (Deegan, 1988, p. 11).

Natural MEDSS framework and a day in an ecological setting

The natural MEDSS framework (see Table 5.1) as proposed by the authors (O'Connor & O'Donovan, 2020) refers to an overarching mind / body/ emotion capacity-building approach that can be adapted for use in coaching practice. The framework was used to inform and guide an experiential day spent by the whole group (GLOW11 participants and coaching psychologists) in a rural ecology centre that comprised 250 sprawling acres of natural habitat and animal life. The framework was introduced as an educational input at the start of the day, with a view to offering particular information to

Table 5.1 (O'Connor and O'Donovan (2020))

Physical Fitness	Mental Fitness	Emotional Fitness	Fitness & Conditioning
• **Exercise** / Movement.	• Thinking styles.	• Emotions.	
• **Diet** / Nutrition.	• Values.	• Moods.	
• **Sleep**.	• Goals.	• Feelings.	
• Hydration.	• Mental attitude /	• Awareness.	
• Full spectrum light.	toughness.	• Meta-cognition.	
• Fresh air.	•	• **S**ocial	
• Nature.	Cognitive distortions/bias.	(connection and belonging).	
	• Judgements.		
	• Resilience.		
INTENTION.	**ATTENTION.**	**ATTITUDE.**	**Mindful Living Life Skills.**
• Values (goals & actions).	• Focus (being more present to experience and the challenges faced, both favourable and unfavourable)	• Choice.	
• Mindfulness / mindful living		• **M**indfulness (adopting an attitude of wonder, curiosity, compassion, kindness and acceptance).	
TRIGGERS &CUES.	**ROUTINES & HABITS.**	**REWARDS**	**Goals, Habits & Routines.**
• Tension / stress / low energy & mood.	• Good / Bad Habits	• I am excited....	
	• Instead of	• Energy / resilience / confidence / coping / self-worth / self-efficacy.	
	• Remembering & forgetting.		
	• New habits	• I will.........	

participants that could be helpful in their thinking about a personally chosen and valued life.

The natural MEDSS framework asks questions about a range of mental, emotional, and physical aspects of human life, along with mindful living skills involving attention, attitude and intention that can be incorporated by coaching practitioners in their practice. The areas of the framework are viewed as being interdependent, flexible, and adaptive in practice. On the day in question, the questions identified focused in particular on participant's habits around diet and nutrition, sleep and exercise and movement. We viewed these questions as of particular importance for GLOW11 participants, given their self-acknowledged propensity to spend inordinate amounts of daily time engaging in unproductive introspection and rumination. The natural MEDSS framework was not offered as a teaching tool to GLOW11 participants but as an input consistent with adult development in inviting each person to formulate a personal agenda with a view to incorporating considerations around diet and nutrition, sleep, exercise, and movement into a vision of a life worth living. Among questions asked at the beginning of the day and in consideration of the time available were:

- Have you considered gentle exercise and movement as possibly contributing to a life worth living?
- Have you considered diet and nutrition as possibly contributing to a life worth living?
- Have you considered sleep and sleep hygiene habits as possibly contributing to a life worth living?
- Have you considered how gentle walking in the fresh air of nature might increase your wellbeing and contribute to a life worth living?
- Who do you socially connect with that gives you a sense of acceptance and belonging?

The possible benefits of developing more positive habits and daily routines regarding diet and nutrition, sleep, exercise, and movement were discussed by participants. We also highlighted how improved adaptation of such habits might contribute to an increased sense of personal wellbeing, with complementary positive influence on mood and emotion. Participants were also facilitated to participate in exercises regarding mindful breathing, mindful eating, mindful walking, and balance.

Natural MEDSS – building capability towards a life worth living

Arising from the experience of the day spent in the ecological centre, we believe that the natural MEDSS framework provides important elements towards helping individuals with BPD in particular to factor in considerations around physical exercise, diet and nutrition, sleep habits, and so on within the broader context of the GLOW11 coaching interaction focus of clarifying and engaging in values-based decisions and actions in identified life domains. Of particular interest on the day was sharing by a number of participants about an increased awareness of tendencies to notice and engage more often than not with negative aspects of what the mind produces and how this can result in increased emotional pain and suffering, and ongoing feelings of helplessness that give voice to 'this is as good as it gets.' We suspect that this was not an entirely new insight for the individuals concerned, but that mindful walking in natural habitats provided opportunities to experience and observe a 'slowed down' sense of self supported by and somewhat contained by communities of trees, fauna, flora, and exotic animals.

What we pay attention to is important. How we pay attention is also important McGilchrist (2019). writes that attention is not just another 'cognitive function' – 'it is actually nothing less than the way in which we relate to the world. And it doesn't just dictate the *kind of relationship* we have with whatever it is: it dictates *what it is that we come to have a relationship with*' (p. 13).

In a coaching context the natural MEDSS framework echoes what Heinzig (2017) references as the need to go beyond the normal 'uni-focus on performance' or goal related approaches and also consider exploring other and relevant areas of uniqueness to the coachee's lived experience, such as sleep and diet. With such a particular focus on performance and goals in many genres of coaching, Heinzig (2017), importantly, in our view, highlights the need to understand where our own values as coaches/coaching psychologists fit and the need to be increasingly conscious of who such frameworks are serving. In that sense MEDSS is not a framework to improve performance or rehabilitate a coachee and send them back to the frontline, as it were. Its purpose in GLOW11 during the day in question was to raise awareness with a view to finding out from GLOW11 participants what they found interesting and helpful in the framework in their search for a life worth living. In highlighting this, the framework is also presented here to invite discussion amongst coaches/coaching psychologists about what needs to be considered in the wider context of the training and formation of coaches.

Particular applications of MEDSS framework during a day in an ecology centre

'My goal that day was intimacy – the tactile, olfactory, visual, and sonic details of what, to most people in my culture, would appear to be a wasteland. This simple technique of awareness had long been my way to open a conversation with any unfamiliar landscape. Who are you? I would ask. How do I say your name? May I sit down?' (Lopez, 2020).

Nature: Do I see the trees?

The judging mind is potentially an instrument of sometimes painful disconnection from ourselves, others, the environment and ultimately, for increasing numbers, disconnection from hope. The body is a powerful instrument of connection Linehan (2020). refers to the power of the body over one's feelings – 'not just in the way that intense exercise and paced breathing change feelings by changing the body's chemistry, but merely through effects of posture and facial expression' (p. 203). She writes that the reverse is also true – 'that if you adopt the posture of anger or happiness, you have the tendency to experience the same feeling. The power of body over mind' (Linehan, 2020, p. 204). Somewhere during the day one of the participants shared that the experience of being with nature 'helped me to get out of my head for one day.' Another shared, 'My biggest aha moment was the mindful walking. I was amazed at how I was during that time. Breathe. Eat. Walk. Be there and comfortable with silence. An awareness kicked in. Being mindful helps me now tune into times when mood is low' And a further sharing was 'as I walked about and stopped to look at where I was, I became immersed in nature and for awhile at least stopped thinking about who or what I am … it was lovely just to be.'

Bratman, Anderson, Berman, and Cochran (2019) while noting the limitations of the current evidence base, report that a growing body of evidence is revealing the value of nature experiences for mental health and positive mood states. These authors point to the impacts of rapid urbanization and decline in human contact with nature globally and the need for critical decision-making at government and community levels about how to preserve and enhance opportunities for nature experience (Bratman et al., 2019). Citing a range of studies, the authors report that nature experience is associated with increased positive affect; happiness and subjective wellbeing; positive social interactions, cohesion, and engagement; a sense of meaning and purpose in life; improved manageability of life tasks; and decreases in mental distress (Bratman et al., 2019). The day spent at the rural ecological centre was a first such nature-based experience for all of the GLOW11 coachees. It was perhaps as Elgin (2010) cited in Koger (2015) suggests, an opportunity 'to live a simpler, less stressful, spiritually grounded and healthier life' (p. 246). The benefits of such experiences can be significant as new possibilities are practiced and taken away.

We underestimate the value of time spent in nature (Nisbet & Zelenski, 2011). Spending time in nature can improve eudaimonic well-being and higher levels of self-reported personal growth (Pritchard, Richardson, Sheffield, & McEwan, 2020) Schertz and Berman (2019). Point to improvements in cognitive flexibility and attentional control Capaldi, Dopko Raelyne, and Zelenski (2014). Found that people who are more connected to nature tend to experience more positive affect, vitality, and life satisfaction than people who are less connected to nature O' Riordan and Palmer (2019). Draw attention to ecopsychology informed coaching practice, beyond the coaching room into green and blue space. Researchers (Crust, Henderson, & Middleton, 2013) and practitioners are also recognizing and creatively integrating exercise and movement in nature settings into coaching practice to enhance well-being, e.g. walking (Palmer & Di Blasi, 2019); mindful walking (O'Donovan, 2015); walk and talk (O'Donovan, 2009 Di Blasi, McCall, Twomey, & Palmer, 2014;). The natural world can provide a powerful context for coaching and we the authors would suggest a powerful context for those who have experienced significant physical, mental, and emotional distress and disconnection in their lives.

Mindfulness and mindful living: What needs my attention now?

The opening focus on the natural MEDSS framework during the day spent in the ecological habitat included mindfulness-based exercises as stated earlier Panchal, Palmer, and Green (2019). describe mindfulness as 'the foundation of flourishing with the recognition that mindfulness contributes directly to well-being' (p. 54) along with its 'evidence-based interpersonal, affective, and intrapersonal benefits' (Davis & Hayes, 2011, p. 199). This also built on GLOW11 participants prior exposure to mindfulness and its practice in the DBT programme.

This focus was on facilitating participants to intentionally show up to the day and engage with the experience of greater present moment awareness. A guided five-minute mindful sitting meditation was offered with the intention to notice the breath/feet in contact with the ground, thoughts, moods etc. In consideration of the fact that much of the time, most human beings are on unconscious auto-pilot (Kahneman, 2012) and absent from present moment experience, this exercise provided a simple and accessible experiential starting point.

Intentionality is an element of the natural MEDSS framework and also central to mindfulness and developing the skills of focusing on what needs one's attention most Kabatt-Zinn and Kabatt-Zinn (2008). note that 'Intentions remind us of what is important … intention informs our choices and our actions … our intentions serve as blueprints, allowing us to give shape and direction to our efforts … and our lives.'

The opportunity for GLOW11 participants to be with and mindful of their experiences in the present moment during the day seemed to matter to coachees. In the words of one participant; 'This was my opportunity to unplug, reset and begin again.' A participant said, 'All I wanted was better time management. I felt like a prisoner of time. Always trying to reach the future, preoccupied with looking too far ahead. Time management is a waste of time, trying to steal time by not really living in the moment.' Another participant shared, 'It is comfortable and comforting just to sit here.'

Exercise and movement: How well am I looking after my body?

Prior to an opportunity to walk about the ecological habitat, participants were facilitated to engage with gentle movement exercises that highlighted the centrality of the body to our experience and learning and also the centrality of exercise and movement to promoting positive mood states and wellbeing.

To the knowledge of the authors, exercise and movement as part of practice is neither mentioned in the academic psychology (Weir, 2011) nor current coaching psychology literature. This appears to be an omission in that Anderson and Shivakumar (2013) point to the indisputable benefits of regular physical activity on health and that exercise is often the first step in modifying current lifestyles in the prevention of chronic diseases. In a series of randomized controlled studies, Blumenthal et al. (2007) provide evidence for the exercise-mood connection. They point to exercise as being 'generally comparable to antidepressants for individuals with major depressive disorders. Ströhle (2008) suggests that in order to optimize exercise programmes 'a multidisciplinary approach involving scientists and practitioners in psychiatry, psychology, sport medicine and health care providers as well as public funding,' (p. 781) is needed. This has yet to be realised but it raises interesting possibilities for the use of exercise as part of the coaching psychologists' overall approach to practice and also for consideration and inclusion in the training and formation of coaching psychologists. It also raises interesting research possibilities for further exploration of exercise and mindfulness activities (i.e. mindful walking) in nature.

An exercise which captured the essence of the day spent in the ecology centre was one which incorporated a full mind/body experiential activity that invited coachees to explore the estate with a particular intention to be present to whatever attracted their attention at whatever sensory level i.e. sound, sight, taste, touch, kinesthetic. Coachees were invited individually to choose their own direction, and to proceed in silence, alone for 60 minutes' duration. They were also asked to create the intention to be curious, to 'stand and stare,' and notice beyond the initial judgement, something that resonated with them at a deeper personal level. This could have been an image, a memory, a sound, a smell, an item they saw along the way, or something they picked up. The invitation was to take time to reflect on the meaning and to return to the group to share, as much as they wished, what they had noticed. This was a powerful exercise of aloneness and belonging which resonated deeply in the reflective sharing. A participant later remarked; 'I no longer feel guilty for taking ten minutes for myself. Sometimes, I just look out the window, watching and listening to the birds but because I no longer feel guilty, I no longer feel angry and annoyed.'

Diet and nutrition: How well am I eating?

As part of a day of mindful living and in preparation for a mindful eating exercise on the day, coachees and coaching psychologists were invited to prepare their own favorite food for lunch. The food was eaten in silence. Even the simple act of slowing down to eat more mindfully can help a person become more grounded and connected in the moments of chewing and swallowing food or water. A slowing down during the eating of food can enhance the taste of food and savor the different flavours, the sweetness, the saltiness and smell and appreciate the aromas. This was also an opportunity to identify and share the important link between diet and mental health (Adan et al., 2019), diet and mood (Zepf, Hood, Guillemin, & International Society for Tryptophan Research, 2015), and diet and wellbeing (Anderson, Cryan, & Dinan, 2019).

Anderson et al. (2019) while highlighting that while the exact mechanism is unclear, note that the bacteria that is secreted in the gut (microbiota), 'respond to neurotransmitters including dopamine, serotonin and GABA all of which can have antidepressant properties in the brain. It's likely that this is one of the ways gut bacteria influence your mood' (p. 120).

The natural MEDSS framework as used during the day in the ecological centre allowed us as coaching psychologists to move beyond 'sit and coach' formats, to be creative and intuitive in our practice and interactions and importantly to understand more about the interactions between mental health and well-being, positive mood states both high and low and exposure to natural habitats which can nourish the human body, soul, and spirit.

Sleep: How well am I sleeping?

Along with diet, sleep is important to effective human functioning and positive mood states also. Lack of sleep presents very real dangers to physical and psychological health and wellbeing Walker (2017). Points out that while the association between sleep disturbance and mental illnesses has long been known by psychiatry, the effects of sleep loss on emotional stability are now being more fully explored and understood and suggests that sleep is perhaps of greater importance for health than diet or exercise.

Baglioni et al. (2016) in a meta-analysis of research on sleep and mental disorders and in particular BPD, suggest that, sleep continuity, depth and sleep disturbances may be associated with borderline personality disorder but that more research is needed based on the low number of studies considered. Bernert, Kim, Iwata, and Perlis (2015) identify sleep disturbances as an evidenced based suicide risk factor. While the science of sleep and its effects may not be of immediate interest to every coaching psychologist, for those of us who choose to work with people with a diagnosed mental illness in general and those with a diagnosis of BPD in particular, possible suicidal ideation and propensity to self-harm was a factor we were acutely aware of throughout the GLOW11 coaching interaction. The link between sleep disturbance and suicide should flag another area for consideration in the training of coaching psychologists and particularly for work in this area.

Furthermore, while we as coaching psychologists are not professionally qualified in any of the domains mentioned above i.e. exercise, diet, or sleep, they were areas of general interest and consideration in our ongoing coaching work with our coachees. Bad eating habits and sleep deprivation are life stressors in their own right and any consideration of mental health and wellbeing by coaches and coaching psychologists should include them.

Finally, as part of the natural MEDSS coaching framework and during the day in the ecological centre, basic sleep hygiene principles were shared with coachees, i.e. reducing caffeine intake, regular bedtime routines for waking, and sleeping, etc.

Social connection: When I am alone, where do I belong?

Clifton, Pilkonis, and McCarty (2007) note that BPD in particular is associated with chronic interpersonal problems including ambivalent attachment, impaired social cognition, and poor interpersonal boundaries. The hypervigilance and tendency to readily take offence associated with BPD can lead to disconnection from the powerful benefits of group membership and a resulting sense of belonging. The original coaching psychology intervention with a BPD cohort (GLOW 1) did not have a group element as all coaching was delivered one-to-one. Arising from feedback and also the group work associated with DBT, it was considered essential to incorporate this aspect into GLOW11.

Seppala, Rossomondo, and Doty (2012) define social connection as a person's subjective sense of having close and positively experienced relationships with others in the social world. While different domains within psychological research i.e. developmental, clinical, social, personality psychology may use different terms to describe social connection, for example, attachment, social support, belongingness, social connectedness; the research is consistent in pointing to the importance of interpersonal connection to mental health and wellbeing. In reviewing the literature around social connection and wellbeing, Seppala et al. (2012) further state that it is closeness, intimacy, and affection that constitute social connection and that it is the affective quality of relationship that matters.

Throughout the GLOW11 coaching interaction and in particular on the day in the ecological centre, it was important for us as coaching psychologists to create a sense of sharing within the group and a sense of intimacy to that sharing, that had meaning and value and mattered to each individual member of the group. The connections we endeavoured to create and coach that day were face to face, inviting the vulnerability that can accompany sharing one's thoughts and feelings in a group. The approach taken was consistent with being wide-angled, empathic and compassionate (Hawkins & Turner, 2020). Implicit in the approach was to locate problems, difficulties or conflict, not in the individuals who were present, but in the connections between everyone present and to speak to those connections with self, with peers and by extension to their wider world of family, friends, partners and in some instances, lost loves along the way. In so doing mindfully, the choice to reconnect with and appreciate the full range of one's experience, the 'positives' and the 'negatives' being accepted with greater kindness and compassion also was noted for some individuals.

Whether goal-setting in GLOW11? – a note

In the context of what is described in this chapter and perhaps more generally in the context of the book itself, some readers or perhaps many readers, may be asking whether or to what extent the GLOW11 coaching interaction was concerned with assisting participants with goal-setting. The question is important to discuss briefly in the context of coaching interaction with individuals with BPD.

GLOW11 coaching interaction helped participants to focus primarily on the present and future Paris (2020). Writes that while not every individual with BPD 'gets better' 'but those who do find a way to commit themselves to a purpose in life' (p. 189), adding that this is why therapy must be oriented towards present and future Paris (2020). Writes that getting better requires 'getting a life' (p. 190). GLOW11 focused on this primary and higher-order goal of assisting each individual to move towards realizing important elements of their vision of a life worth living.

The use of goals in coaching is a topic that has drawn a number of different perspectives into play Clutterbuck (2013). Makes the point that in exploring the experiences of coaches in the context of working with coachee goals, 'the more, it seemed that the approaches espoused in so much of the coaching literature were rooted in simplistic assumptions about both goals and the complexity of clients' lives' (p. 332) David (2013). Cautions that goals can imply linearity and predictability, where none exists, that goals can narrow focus and hinder successful change, and that the goal is not always the goal David (2013). Adds that in her own practice she has found that 'the simple remembering of the universal needs for autonomy, competence, and relatedness is a powerful anchor … regardless of the client's presenting issues, can we sense that one or more of these needs is yet to be fulfilled? And in this regard, what support can we offer?' (p. 337) Grant (2013). Makes the case for 'a goals hierarchy that calls for attention to values in order to ensure subordinate goals and action plans do not become dominant' (p. 328) Berkman, Donde, and Rock (2013). Argue that in setting goals, motivation (approach or avoidance), planning, social context, and self-control all need to be taken into account. These are factors that many individuals with BPD struggle with in developing habits of being, thinking, and acting out a life worth living. Ultimately, the primary focus in GLOW11 coaching interaction echoed what has been strongly identified in the literature on BPD as the fundamental importance of living a life that is viewed as worth living (Linehan, 2020), getting a life (Paris, 2020) or 'achieving and maintaining recovery indicates an ability to take care of oneself and possibly experience a certain satisfaction with one's life' (Zanarini, 2019, p. 120).

Conclusion

Recovery in the context of mental illness is not some holy land where a person returns to a 'normal' state of health or mind, where she/he is clinically symptom free. Recovery is not some destination of enduring high mood where wellbeing and happiness are in some way attainable or guaranteed. Recovery as we understand it is an invitation and a commitment to a difficult, uneasy, at times uncomfortable and unpredictable journey, step by sometimes very painful step, where the destination may be fuzzy and changing, but one is sustained by personal hope and validating support. The recovery journey of a life worth living is sustained by the search for connectedness, hope, identity, meaning to life and empowerment (Leamy, Bird, Le Boutillier, Williams, & Slade, 2011).

Livesley (2017) writes that if there is a single rule in working with individuals with BPD it is 'keep it simple and keep it consistent' (p. 271). Our primary and consistent coaching focus in GLOW11 was assisting individuals to clarify, explore and work with their personal values both in continuing to apply DBT life skills, develop behavioural habits (Duhigg, 2012) towards creating a realistic vision of a life worth living and the potential rewards associated. Clarifying, exploring, and working with values was enhanced by supporting individuals to view values from a perspective of what each person cared about, what mattered most when considering their view of the life desired. In varying degrees, this approach brought into light a sense of each person as knower, what Livesley (2017) refers to as strengthening the self as knower – 'the self as knower is crucial in constructing a more coherent self and a life worth living' (p. 231) and that unless individuals with BPD 'trust their basic feelings and wants, there is no basis for elaborating a sense of who they are and what they want from life' (p. 231).

In this context, the natural MEDSS framework helped in validating each person's motivation and stated reasons for participating in GLOW11 and provided additional practical and experiential food for consideration in their quest Livesley (2017). Refers to the idea of a personal niche, writing that while the environment is an important aspect of a person's life, it is frequently neglected in therapeutic work on the basis of being assumed to be independent of the person. In the context of seeing the value of the natural MEDSS framework for GLOW11 participants, we are in agreement with Livesley (2017) arguing that healthy individuals do not react passively to the environment, 'they actively shape their world to create a personal niche that is congenial to them ... they seek out situations and individuals to establish a niche that organizes their lives, offers outlets for needs, abilities, talents, and aspirations, supports their interests, and provides opportunities for personal satisfaction and a contented way of living' (p. 255).

Discussion points

1. What might be some of the benefits of incorporating nature and natural settings into coaching practice?
2. Are the concepts of exercise and movement, diet and nutrition and sleep hygiene practices irrelevant to coaching and coaching psychology?
3. Should mindfulness training be included in coach education programmes?
4. What are the main challenges you might see for coaches working beyond the coaching room and into blue and green spaces?
5. As a coach what physical, mental and emotional habits have you developed to keep you safe and well in the world. What are the cues and primes that trigger those habits?

Recommended reading

Anderson, S. C., Cryan, J. F., & Dinan, T. (2019). *The psychobiotic revolution: Mood, food and the new science of the gut-brain connection.* National Geographic Society.

Duhigg, C. (2012). *The power of habit: Why we do what we do in life and business.* New York: Random House.

Walker, M. (2017). *What we sleep: The new science of sleep and dreams.* London, UK: Penguin Books.

References

Adan, R., van der Beek, E. M., Buitelaar, J. K., Cryan, J. F., Hebebrand, J., Higgs, ...Dickson, S. L. (2019). Nutritional psychiatry: Towards improving mental health by what you eat. *European Neuropsychopharmacology: The Journal of the European College of Neuropsychopharmacology, 29*(12), 1321–1332.

Anderson, E., & Shivakumar, G. (2013). Effects of exercise and physical activity on anxiety. *Frontiers in Psychiatry, 4*, 27.

Anderson, S. C., Cryan, J. F., & Dinan, T. (2019) *The psychobiotic revolution: Mood, food and the new science of the gut-brain connection.* National Geographic Society.

Bachkirova, T. (2020, in press). Understanding yourself as a coach (Chap 4). In J. Passmore (Ed.), *The coaches handbook: The complete practitioner's guide for professional coaches* (1st ed.). London, UK: Routledge.

Baglioni, C., Nanovska, S., Regen, W., Spiegelhalder, K., Feige, B., Nissen, ...Riemann, D. (2016). Sleep and mental disorders: A meta-analysis of polysomnographic research. *Psychological Bulletin, 142*(9), 969–990.

Berkman, E., Donde, R., & Rock, D. (2013). A social neuroscience approach to goal setting for coaches. In S. David, D. Clutterbuck, & D. Megginson (Eds.), *Beyond goals: Effective strategies for coaching and mentoring* (pp. 109–123). Farnham, UK: Gower.

Bernert, R. A., Kim, J. S., Iwata, N. G., & Perlis, M. L. (2015). Sleep disturbances as an evidence-based suicide risk factor. *Current Psychiatry Reports, 17*(3), 554.

Blumenthal, J. A., Babyak, M. A., Doraiswamy, P. M., Watkins, L., Hoffman, B. M., Barbour, K. A., ...Sherwood, A. (2007). Exercise and pharmacotherapy in the treatment of major depressive disorder. *Psychosomatic Medicine, 69*(7), 587–596.

Bratman, G. N., Anderson, C. B., Berman, M. G., Cochran, B. (2019). Nature and mental health: An ecosystem service perspective. *Science Advances, 5*(7), 1–14.

Capaldi, C. A., Dopko Raelyne, L., & Zelenski, J. M. (2014). The relationship between nature connectedness and happiness: A meta-analysis. *Frontiers in Psychology, 5*, 1–15.

Clifton, A., Pilkonis, P. A., & McCarty, C. (2007). Social networks in borderline personality disorder. *Journal of Personality Disorders, 21*(4), 434–441.

Clutterbuck, D. (2013). The way forward. In S. David, D. Clutterbuck, & D. Megginson (Eds.), *Beyond goals: Effective strategies for coaching and mentoring* (pp. 327–338). Farnham, UK: Gower.

Cox, E. (2013). *Coaching understood: A pragmatic inquiry into the coaching process.* London, UK: Sage.

Crust, L., Henderson, H., & Middleton, G. (2013). The acute effects of urban green and countryside walking on psychological health: A field-based study of green exercise. *International Journal of Sports Psychology, 44*, 1–19.

Csikszentmihalyi, M. (2006). *A life worth living: Contributions to positive psychology.* Oxford, UK: Oxford University Press.

David, S. (2013). The way forward. In S. David, D. Clutterbuck, & D. Megginson (Eds.), *Beyond goals: Effective strategies for coaching and mentoring* (pp. 327–338). Farnham, UK: Gower

Davis, D. M., & Hayes, J. A. (2011). What are the benefits of mindfulness? A practice review of psychotherapy-related research. *Psychotherapy, 48*(2), 198–208

Deegan, P. E. (1988). Recovery: The lived experience of rehabilitation. *Psychosocial Rehabilitation Journal, 11*(4), 11–19.

Deegan, P. (1996). Recovery as a journey of the heart. *Psychiatric Rehabilitation Journal, 19*, 91–97.

Di Blasi, Z., McCall, J. Twomey, M., & Palmer, S. (2014). A pilot study examining the influence of 'Walk and Talk' v 'Sit and Talk' coaching sessions. Conference paper given at the ISCP International Congress of coaching Psychology, London, 12 October, 2014.

Elgin, D. (2010). *Voluntary simplicity* (2nd ed.). New York: Harper Collins.

Grant, A. M. (2013). New perspectives on goal setting in coaching practice: An integrated model of goal-focused coaching. In David, D. Clutterbuck, & D. Megginson (Eds.), *Beyond goals: Effective strategies for coaching and mentoring* (pp. 55–85). Farnham, UK: Gower.

Hawkins, P., & Turner, E. (2020). *Systemic coaching: Delivering value beyond the individual.* London, UK: Routledge.

Heinzig, E. (2017). *The future of coaching: Vision, leadership and responsibility in a transforming world.* London, UK: Routledge.

Kabatt-Zinn, J., & Kabatt-Zinn, M. (2008). *Everyday blessings.* New York: Hyperion.

Kahneman, D. (2012). *Thinking fast and slow.* London: Penguin.

Koger, S. M. (2015). A burgeoning ecopsychological recovery movement. *Ecopsychology. 7*(4), 245–250.

Leamy, M., Bird, V., Le Boutillier, C., Williams, J., & Slade, M. (2011). Conceptual framework for personal recovery in mental health: Systematic review and narrative synthesis. *The British Journal of Psychiatry, 199*, 445–452.

Linehan, M. M. (2020). *Building a life worth living: A memoir.* New York, NY: Random House Books.

Livesley, W. J. (2017). *Integrated modular treatment for borderline personality disorder: A practical guide to combining effective treatment methods.* Cambridge, UK: Cambridge University Press.

Lopez, B. (2020). Love in a time of terror: On natural landscapes, metaphorical living and Warlpiri Identity. Retrieved from https://lithub.com/barry-lopez-love-in-a-time-of-terror/

McGilchrist, I. (2019). *Ways of attending: How our divided brain constructs the world.* London, UK: Routledge.

Nisbet, E. K., & Zelenski, J. M. (2011). Underestimating nearby nature: Affective forecasting errors obscure the happy path to sustainability. *Association of Psychological Science, 22*(9), 1101–1106.

O' Connor, M. & O' Donovan, H. (2020). Coaching Psychology for Mental Health: Borderline Personality Disorder and Personal Psychological Recovery. London, UK: Routledge.

O'Donovan, H. (2009, December). CRAIC: A model suitable for Irish coaching psychology. *The Coaching Psychologist, 5*(2), 35–40.

O'Donovan, H. (2015). *Mindful walking: Walk your way to mental and physical well-being.* Ireland: Hachette Books.

O'Riordan, S., & Palmer, S. (2019). Beyond the coaching room into blue space: Ecopsychology informed coaching psychology practice. *Coaching Psychology International, 12*(2), 8–18.

Palmer, S., & Di Blasi, Z. (2019). Reflections on walking for enhancing creativity and well-being: A way forward for coaching and coaching psychology practice. *Coaching Psychology International, 12*(1), 19–24.

Panchal, S., Palmer, S., & Green, S. (2019). From positive psychology to the development of positive psychology coaching. In S. Palmer and Whybrow, A. (Eds.), *Handbook of coaching psychology: A guide for practitioners*. London: Routledge.

Paris, J. (2020). *Treatment of borderline personality disorder: A guide to evidence-based practice* (2nd ed.). London, UK: Guilford Press.

Pritchard, A., Richardson, M., Sheffield, D., & McEwan, K. (2020). The relationship between nature connectedness and eudaimonic well-being: A meta-analysis. *Journal of Happiness Studies 21*, 1145–1167.

Seppala, E., Rossomondo, T., & Doty, J. R. (2012). Social connection and compassion: Important predictors of health and well-being, *Social Research, 80*(2), 411–430.

Schertz, K. E., & Berman, M. G. (2019). Understanding nature and its benefits. *Current Directions in Psychological Science, 28*(5), 496–502.

Slade, M. (2009). *Personal recovery and mental illness: A guide for mental health professionals*. Cambridge, UK: Cambridge University Press.

Slade, M. (2012). The epistemological basis of personal recovery. In A. Rudnick (Ed.), *Recovery of people with mental illness: Philosophical and related perspectives* (pp. 78–94). Oxford, UK: Oxford University Press.

Ströhle, A. (2008). Physical activity, exercise, depression and anxiety disorders. *Journal of Neural Transmission, 116*, 777–784.

Walker, M. (2017). *What we sleep: The new science of sleep and dreams*. London, UK: Penguin Books.

Weir, K. (2011). The exercise effect. Retrieved from https://www.apa.org/monitor/2011/12/exercise

Zanarini, M. C. (2019). *In the fullness of time: Recovery from borderline personality disorder*. Oxford, UK: Oxford University Press.

Zepf, F. D., Hood, S., Guillemin, G. J., & International Society for Tryptophan Research (2015). Food and your mood: Nutritional psychiatry. *The Lancet. Psychiatry, 2*(7), e19.

Chapter 6

Coaching psychology and mental distress

In this chapter we will discuss some of the core issues pertaining to BPD identified in the literature, which we encountered to varying degrees in GLOW11. We also outline the process involved in working with values in GLOW11. Core issues identified for consideration in coaching individuals with BPD include one's way of being, containing anxiety, suffering, trauma, working with emotions, personal narratives of individuals with BPD, the coaching relationship, power as influence or imposition, positive psychology and recovery, and 'getting a life!' These topics are recommended as important for coaching psychologists interested in this work in terms of relevant information, critical reflection on one's assumptions about mental distress/mental illness and coaching readiness and practice considerations.

At the same time, we want to reiterate our view that coaching psychology has much to offer individuals with BPD in a context where symptom reduction has occurred and is being sustained (clinical recovery) with a view to exploring the meaning and purpose of a life worth living and practical daily implications for decision-making and actions (personal/psychological recovery).

Previously in the book we mentioned what has traditionally been the normative position in coaching psychology regarding engaging only with the non-clinical population, the 'worried well.' We also highlighted that coaching psychology has begun of necessity to acknowledge that simple distinctions between non-clinical and clinical groupings no longer make sense, as 'the boundary between clinical and non-clinical is imprecise and fluid' (Cavanagh & Buckley, 2018, p. 451). GLOW11 was a coaching psychology engagement with members of a 'clinical population' with BPD that started approximately 12 months after the individuals concerned had completed a DBT therapy programme. Corrie (2016) has proposed that because of the seeming acceleration of emotional and psychological distress in society, a science of wellbeing and self-care is needed, developed by 'specialists by practice' rather than specialists by profession and that coaching practitioners are well placed to play a central role given the diversity of the coaching community and the trans-disciplinary nature of its knowledge.

DOI: 10.4324/9781003048978-6

Consequently, we do not advocate that coaching psychology should be a first port of call for supporting people with a diagnosis of mental illness, in particular Borderline Personality Disorder (BPD). However, we do advocate that coaching psychology can be of potentially significant assistance to individuals with BPD who have completed a specialist programme such as DBT, or indeed a more generalist programme, where there is consensus that as a result the person concerned has experienced symptom reduction and has not self-harmed for a period of 6–12 months. From the perspective of GLOW11 as a coaching psychology intervention, we agree with Breggin (1997) writing in a therapy context that 'as helping persons, if we *think* we are adequate to any task, situation, or person, then we are misleading ourselves and may possibly cause harm to others. As a therapist, if we're frightened by a situation or client – and don't admit it to ourselves – we're likely to behave with the sensitivity of a steamroller' (p. 25). Consequently, the context we advocate for coaching psychology interventions for individuals with BPD is that there would be close collaboration with existing therapy programme clinical personnel, similar to how GLOW11 was planned, managed and sustained, and completed.

Recovery revisited

In the context of moving into a COVID-19 world and what is worth giving attention to, as authors and practicing coaching psychologists we have a renewed appreciation of the relevance of the psychological processes that underpin the recovery journey (for example, connectedness; hope and optimism; identity; meaning in life; and empowerment) (Leamy, Bird, Le Boutillier, Williams, & Slade, 2011). These psychological processes and others are in fact applicable to every human being, not only people with a diagnosis of mental illness. As a coaching psychologist, one's own mental health is always a matter to keep in awareness, without degenerating into circular introspection and rumination. In this regard, Mussey (2016) writes about the recovery process 'revealing a human journey that is not unique to those who have been diagnosed with a 'mental-illness.' Who among us has not struggled to recover from some form of distress – like the loss of a loved one, a debilitating illness or accident, abandonment, betrayal, war, trauma, violence, abuse or addiction? During dark times, haven't we too needed someone to listen with compassion to our story, inspire hopefulness and remind us of our resilience?' The ubiquitous nature of mental distress is captured by Myers (2015) who writes in an ethnographic study from the perspective of her own recovery journey with BPD, that when she asked people in recovery about their lives 'they had meaningful lives, jobs and children. I met authors, artists, psychologists, psychiatrists, and lawyers, all in recovery from serious mental illness' (p. 4).

Our bottom-line commitment in preparing for and during GLOW11 was that whatever value might accrue for participants, we would at least do no harm. Egan (2014) cautions that doing no harm is the first rule of the skilled helper, yet some do harm by being unprincipled or are incompetent, adding that helping is not a neutral process – it is for better or for worse.

Grenyer et al. (2015) recommend the following key principles for application in working with people with BPD:

- Be compassionate
- Demonstrate empathy
- Listen to the person's current experience
- Validate the person's current emotional state
- Take the person's experience seriously, noting verbal and non-verbal communications
- Maintain a non-judgmental approach
- Stay calm
- Remain respectful
- Remain caring
- Engage in open communication
- Be human and be prepared to acknowledge both the serious and funny side of life where appropriate
- Foster trust to allow strong emotions to be freely expressed
- Be clear, consistent, and reliable
- Respect aspects of challenging behaviours that have survival value given past experiences
- Convey encouragement and hope about capacity for change, while validating current emotional experience.

Many of these principles were confirmed and affirmed by GLOW11 participants at our final group meeting, as referenced in the previous chapter.

Questions for participants in GLOW11

As described earlier, at the heart of GLOW11 was a focus on co-exploring with participants their personal, freely chosen values as chosen life directions, exploring questions such as:

- What was fundamentally important to each person in life?
- What gave each person a unique sense of purpose?
- What kind of person did each aspire to be in their relational world?
- What kind of things did each want to stand for? (Hill & Oliver, 2019)
- What did each person really care about?

Our motivation with such questions was to facilitate and enable each participant to identify and take ownership of their own agenda in the one-to-one sessions. Coaching from an ethical emancipatory perspective of adult-to-adult communication, relationship and co-creation was central. Something of this has been captured by Bachkirova, Cox, and Clutterbuck (2018) in the context of adult learning theory, stating that adults need to know that they have ownership of the agenda, know the course of the learning and want to be treated as equals and shown respect both for what they know and how they prefer to learn. This 'agenda' was certainly put to the test on occasions in both one-to-one coaching sessions and in group coaching sessions in the context of participants personal struggles around self-functioning. For example, Gold and Kyratsous (2017) write that identity disturbance is one of the core features of BPD manifesting in 'the self is … poorly developed, or there is an unstable self-image, which is often associated with excessive self-criticism; chronic feelings of emptiness; and dissociative states under stress' (p. 1020). While in GLOW11 we met with individuals of tremendous courage and resilience, these same individuals also revealed the fragility and vulnerability of their experience of themselves at a personal level.

Questions for GLOW11 coaching psychologists

When working with people who have experienced significant destabilising psychological trauma and dislocation in periods of their lives, there can be a particular challenge in trying to locate oneself as a coaching psychologist, in order to help rather than do harm. Engaging with GLOW11 did involve a sense of dislocation, there being no existing theory for coaching psychology practice that would provide reliable guidance. In the context of our participation in GLOW11 and in authoring this book, particular questions seemed to recur, for example:

- What have been the life experiences and narratives arising that have contributed to shaping my practice as a coaching psychologist?
- How am I being drawn to particular life narratives and perspectives and perhaps avoiding others?
- How do I understand my motivation in being drawn to a process such as GLOW11?
- What do I really desire in my leaning into GLOW11 and how do I maintain awareness of how my ego may answer this question?
- Is what I do in one-to-one sessions motivated to helping the person to live their freely chosen values?
- What do I really care about here?
- What is the worst thing that could happen here?
- What are the questions we will realise we should have asked in six months?

Related to some of these questions, Western (2012) writes that 'we are all authored by our experiences, as individuals and collectively, through the cultures and contexts that shape us. Coaches are shaped by their personal and collective experiences in coaching and beyond, and through the coaching narratives and discourses that inform their thinking and practice' (p. 19). Related to questions about care, values and meaning, Stanghellini and Rosfort (2013) ask 'what do I care about and how am I supposed to make sense of and cope with my concerns? I have to understand myself by making sense of the values that are revealed by my feelings and emotions. The question of meaning is therefore inescapably connected to the affective origins of values' (p. 64). Even now, some considerable time after completion of GLOW11, the individuals we met still figure in clear outline in our respective memories. We still wonder how each is getting on in life. During the time of COVID-19 we made e-mail enquiries as to their wellbeing.

Given that GLOW11 was a first for coaching psychology in the context of diagnosed mental illness, we could travel light! We were also cognisant of what Western (2012) calls the reality principle, that the external environment may not enable a person to achieve their desires and goals, given the reality of social and structural power and economic inequality, in addition to factors such as mental, physical, and emotional health, in contrast to 'the positivist coaching ideology that says we can achieve anything we want …' (p. 19).

Mental distress as a way of being can quite easily become a 'calling card' for a person with BPD. At the same time as distress is manifest there is a parallel searching for a safe shore on which to land. The demeanour of the helping professional sitting with or walking with the person with BPD is important. An over-emphasis on positivity or a collusive attitude to distress will derail the coaching process and more importantly, the coaching relationship. Balance and perspective-taking are important elements in carrying off support and challenge as inherently respectful and empathic attitudes and behaviours. The coaching psychologist is not immune either to the pleasure principle or to the reality principle. Being true to oneself can frequently sound trite. In this work it demands frequent reflection and consideration with a view to one's way of being as one sits with the other person (with BPD). Even the slightest, unintentional gesture, sound or word of invalidation can be amplified in the moment. Vaughan-Smith (2019) writes that individuals who are traumatised have had their boundaries and autonomy breached and therefore it is so important that coaches do not contribute to that being repeated. We can strongly identify with how Vaughan-Smith (2019) describes a coaching interaction that helps rather than harms when being with a person who has known trauma – 'our contribution to the healing of trauma starts with our ability to create a safe space and to be fully present in our healthy self, listening attentively to all that is said or not said. Never underestimate the value of an individual being listened to attentively, without being judged. Even when questions addressed to the healthy self, seem to be answered by the survival self, the question is not wasted, as it triggers some possibility for the healthy self to become active' (p. 112). Vaughan-Smith (2019) concludes with a reference to how interacting with individuals who have known trauma can make the coach feel vulnerable to bringing one's own survival responses into play – becoming directive, avoidant, insecure, trying rescue, and becoming entangled. Stelter (2018) states that without attention to oneself, one cannot pay attention to the other person and asks a series of very helpful questions, for example – what happens to me when I listen to the person?; how am I drawn into the story of the person?; what kind of pain, sorrow, compassion, joy, enthusiasm so I experience as I listen?; am I becoming too engaged?; am I trying to realise my own agenda through the other person? Suffice to say, in all forms of coaching work but in this type of work in particular, different forms of quality supervision is non-negotiable.

Values as helping to live a life worth living

We have discussed the topic of values previously in the context of our preparation for GLOW11. Here we refer to how working with values was carried out in the coaching process of GLOW11. We also consider whether working with values is a 'good fit' in a coaching context, in trying to assist people with BPD towards a life worth living to consider values post – GLOW11. Stelter (2018) describes values as a key anchor for one's identity and refers to the importance of digging deeper 'in order to understand how certain values, beliefs, aspirations, dreams and hopes can form the basis of actions...' (p. 64). This perspective on values is important since it refers to questions of self-identity, capacity for reflection and motivation for taking action, all issues identified as being problematic for many people with BPD. Cameron, Reed, and Gaudiano (2014) state that dropout rates from DBT programmes by people with BPD are high with concomitant low motivation for homework completion and use of skills. Citing ACT, Cameron et al. (2014) suggest that values work towards increasing values-consistent behaviour or valued or committed action, may be one way to improve motivation concerning DBT, both in-session and out of session. Cameron et al. (2014) view working with values as more motivating as it 'deemphasises reaching a specific goal, and instead emphasises choosing behaviours that are consistent with a personal value from moment to moment' (p. 110).

This perspective resonates with the experience of working with values in GLOW11. While GLOW11 participants did strongly connect with a process of clarifying their personal values across different life domains and did engage with exploring how behaviours associated with their values might become more of a behaviour pattern, in general they were less motivated to link their values to setting concrete and specific goals and step-by-step actions. Cameron et al. (2014) capture something of what might be important here where they refer to the linking of valued directions and associated behaviours giving individuals opportunity 'to move about in their lives in ways that are not simply attempts to escape from uncomfortable thoughts or emotions, but instead are chosen as a way to move toward something that is important to them as a *person living a life'* (p. 112), which they refer to as an 'appetitive process' that loosens the focus on escape and strengthens commitment to living with chosen purpose. The 'appetitive process' referenced here is perhaps quite apt in the sense of pointing to a more embodied emotional experience by GLOW11 participants rather than a singularly cognitive exercise. It's also worth mentioning here that the initial commitment and engagement by each individual involved in GLOW11 was sustained throughout, with no person dropping out.

A study by Mohi, Deane, Bailey, Mooney-Reh, and Ciaglia (2018) regarding the role of values for people with BPD is also relevant to a post-GLOW11 reflection. These author researchers echo again what is now a common refrain that the progress monitored and measured in the clinical literature, for example, symptom reduction, though very important (e.g. reductions in self-harm) 'does not necessarily correspond with people's actual evaluations of meaningful progress and life improvement on the road to recovery' (p. 1), citing Schrank and Slade (2007) and Slade, Amering, and Oades (2008). Mohi et al. (2018) suggest that value focused interventions may have therapeutic benefit towards targeting some of the core features of BPD, for example, identity disturbance and chronic feelings of emptiness (citing American Psychiatric Association, 2013; World Health Organisation, 1993), as connection to one's values can provide purposeful direction and meaning in life (citing Huguelet et al. (2016). Using the Personal Values Questionnaire (Blackledge, Ciarrochi, & Bailey, 2006), Mohi et al. (2018) set out to describe the ways in which individuals with BPD who are seeking treatment identify with values across a range of key life domains. Of interest in terms of GLOW11 is that interpersonal relationships were rated as most important in the sample (as well as health and wellbeing) (Mohi et al., 2018) given that problematic interpersonal relationships and functioning is common in BPD (citing American Psychiatric Association, 2013; World Health Organisation, 1993). Mohi et al. (2018) suggest that that in addition to established approaches such as DBT and MBT 'a more structured values clarification process may help identify the importance of personal relationships as a treatment goal' (p. 7). The findings also showed discrepancies between the importance of valued life domains and lower levels of value commitment, desire to improve and success, bringing internal/external value motivations into consideration (Mohi et al., 2018). The authors/researchers conclude that understanding what motivates people with BPD to pursue values in key life domains will assist professionals to work with the motivational needs of individuals in pursuing what is important to them (Mohi et al., 2018).

In GLOW11, we provided each participant with a brief overview of values using Hill and Oliver (2019) reference to values as 'what is important to us and gives us a sense of purpose; the person we want to be and the things we want to stand for' (p. 37). We used a brief adaptation of the Valued Living Questionnaire (Wilson, Sandoz, Kitchens, & Roberts, 2010) to capture a broad range of life domains. The life domains included were personal growth and learning; health and wellbeing; money and finance; partner and love; fun and recreation; work and career; family and friends; community and environment. Each life domain had a brief number of clarifying questions to help with reflection. We also used a comprehensive list of values-based words with brief explanatory add-ons for participants to identify associated values in each life domain identified as personally important. As it turned out, each participant warmed strongly to the process of identifying and exploring their personal values in different life domains. It was interesting and informative to help coachee's make a distinction between the values they felt they 'should' have or socially desirable and the actual values that resonated with them in their heart. The affective aspect of values was highlighted as a way to help each coachee become more aware of their leaning towards particular values. The valued life domains prioritised by GLOW11 participants in the main were family and intimate relationships; health and wellbeing; personal growth and development; money and finance; work and career; and recreation and fun (in order of priority). Particular values associated with different life domains included self-compassion; self-forgiveness; self-control; courage; honesty; personal expression; beauty; humour; happiness; creativity; fairness; and happiness, in particular. Participants spoke about wanting to be 'honest, truthful and sincere' in their relationship with their partner and with self; about 'depression having me, rather than me having depression'; 'just wanting this voice in my head to stop the criticism and the judging of everything I do'; 'self-control means I want to choose to act in any situation with kindness, fairness and compassion to myself'; 'I want to be calmer, warmer and more forgiving to myself'; 'I wish my brain didn't go so fast with thought after thought, it's so stressful'; 'my whole life I have been looking to others to affirm me, now I want to do it for myself'; 'I really need to look after my health and wellbeing now, before it's too late; 'trying to be perfect in every way has sucked the life out of me'; 'I want to stop seeing myself as a problem to be fixed'; 'I know who I am for everyone else, but I don't know who I am for me.'

A noted feature of working with values in GLOW11 was how the process became significantly more an affective rather than a predominantly cognitive exploration. Zanarini (2008) states that Linehan (1993) has suggested that BPD is best understood as a disorder of emotional dysregulation and that Gunderson (1984) has suggested that BPD is best understood as a disorder of attachment, where fear of aloneness and abandonment are the core conflicts experienced Stanghellini and Mancini (2019) state that the values-related needs of the person with BPD make high demands – requiring the other person to be present and loyal, a source of validation, spontaneous – so much so that the 'need for recognition and fear of abandonment force the borderline person to insatiably aspire to a sort of emotional osmosis with the other…' …'the other is needed as a source of recognition' …'the other's absence, or incomplete presence, is often the reason for feelings of un-recognition and desperate loss of selfhood' (p. 679).

Working with emotions

Cox (2017) writes that the part played by emotions in coaching is an area that is mainly under-theorised, with very little research devoted to working with emotions in coaching. She mentions that researchers in other fields have identified how emotions have an important part to play in formulating ethical judgments (citing Nussbaum, 2004) and as creating meaning (Dirkx, 2008; Greenberg, 2004), for example. Cox (2017) provides an emotional climate inventory for coaching which could be adapted to working with emotions with individuals with BPD. The inventory has a coach and a coachee focus along with helpful reflection points for each and a similar framework within which to consider coachee needs and coach needs.

Emotions motivate us to turn our attention to or away from a given object; to move towards or away from a given direction; contribute to our feeling of being involved in the world (engagement); to grasping the meaning of things and situations (enactment); and to our pre-reflective understanding of other people (attunement) (Stanghellini & Rosfort, 2013). Stanghellini and Rosfort (2013) write that the source of our basic sense of being a self is affective in nature and that 'emotions bind the self to, make it feel attuned to and engaged with, the world, other people, and itself' and that 'to be a *self* is to feel rooted in one's emotional life' (p. 306). They state that both BPD and schizophrenia 'illustrate one fundamental aspect of human emotional ex-perience, of the relationship between emotions and selfhood, and of the entanglement of emotions and rationality' (p. 11). These authors further state that the core of primary emotional complex demonstrated by people with BPD is dysphoric mood as a permanent and enduring characteristic (usually accompanied by irritability, internal agitation, hyper-emotionality, and sometimes boredom) and anger (may be accompanied by shame and may trigger acute crises of rage) (Stanghellini & Rosfort, 2013).

Related to the difficulties experienced by individuals with BPD in managing emotions, Linehan (2020) provides an interesting perspective, which she describes as 'reasonable mind' and 'emotion mind.' When a person is in reasonable mind, reason is in control – 'ruled by facts, reason, logic and pragmatism' and 'emotions such as love, guilt, and grief are irrelevant' (Linehan, 2020, p. 281). When a person is in emotion mind 'you are ruled by your moods, feelings, and urges' and 'facts, reason and logic are not important' (p. 281), which some people might term being unreasonable. Linehan (2020) states that mindfulness skills can help to balance emotion mind and reasonable mind, with the intention of making wise decisions. She concludes with a reference to what she calls 'wise mind' – the synthesis of emotion mind and reasonable mind and which 'adds intuitive knowing to emotional experience and logical analysis' (p. 282).

Inevitably, as coachees were supported in working with personal values towards their picture of a life worth living, emotions related to historical experiences of acceptance, belonging and sense of self also emerged. Cox (2013) refers to the distinction between emotions and feelings identified by Damasio (2000). Cox (2013) refers to emotions as pre-set – 'bioregulatory devices which are instinctive and automatic' (citing Damasio, 2000, p.15) and that 'consciousness allows feelings to be known and thus promotes the impact of emotion internally, allows emotion to permeate the thought process through the agency of feeling' (citing Damasio, 2000, p. 56). Consequently, feelings are sensory signals that in interacting with human consciousness, bring emotions and experience to our attention (Cox, 2013). Cox (2013) writes that traditionally coaches have been reluctant to work with feelings (citing Bachkirova & Cox, 2007) 'but this aversion should be seen as misplaced since feelings are the initial mechanism through which understanding is ultimately achieved' (p. 17). As referenced by Stanghellini and Rosfort (2013) (the source of our basic sense of being a self is affective in nature) and Linehan (2020) (the importance of balancing reasonable and emotion mind with the intention of making wise decisions), in interacting with individuals with BPD coaching psychologists need to be open to addressing feelings that will emerge in sessions.

Based on our experience in GLOW11 we believe that working with values as referenced earlier helped to provide participants with a safe physical and psychological space in which a reliable coaching relationship could be created and provided a clear focus for coaching (working with values towards a life worth living). Within this coaching context, understandably on occasions feelings were expressed that connected to some strong emotions related to a coachee's sense of acceptance, belonging and self, both historically and currently. This is an important issue for consideration in terms of coaching psychologists interacting with individuals with BPD. Whittington (2020) writes that we are all born into relationship systems, beginning with the family system, extending to other relationship systems – educational, professional, organisational, and that our sense of belonging in each system informs our identity and sense of our place in the world, as 'each offers us powerful experiences and we soon learn how it is to feel included or excluded' (p. i). Whittington (2020) goes on to say that our sense of belonging and our need to belong begins in the family and that 'all of our experiences of belonging in different systems are held within us for life' (p. 52). Paris (2020), citing Linehan (1993), writes that each future client with BPD is born with a temperamental risk factor that may lead to emotional dysregulation, being a child that gets upset more easily and coming down from upsets more slowly, and that while of itself such a trait need not result in BPD, difficulties can arise if parents react with invalidating advice as a pattern. Paris (2020) describes a scenario as an example – when children are told 'Don't get so upset' or 'Be strong' 'this well-meant advice is *invalidating*. It leaves these children with the same emotions, and adds a feeling of shame about ex-periencing them' (p. 119). Consequently, and of critical importance here, interactions where strong emotions are invalidated can be a risk factor for BPD and individuals with BPD will need support to recognise and validate their emotions (Paris, 2020; citing Linehan, 1993). Paris (2020) also makes the point that while affective instability can be problematic, it is not always a negative thing to be emotional and that 'in some ways, people who respond to life events with strong feelings are more interesting and appealing' (p. 119). In any event, strong emotions and BPD invariably go hand-in-hand and for coaching psychologists interested in this work, it is an important matter for one's own consideration and indeed one's own temperamental profile and history of invalidation-validation.

Containing anxiety

Our frequent references to the critical importance of 'mattering' in the context of bringing coaching psychology to people with BPD does of course have implications for the coaching psychologist – their own wellbeing and mental health, and capability to bring containment to what emerges in the coaching process. Day, de Haan, Blass, Sills, and Bertie (2008) refer to particular types of anxiety and doubt that can be manifest for coaches in the context of critical moments in coaching sessions, for example, anxieties about the boundaries of coaching, anxiety about role, anxiety about sa-tisfying outcomes, anxiety about trusting one's intuition and feelings, an-xiety about one's own contribution to a critical moment, anxiety due to specific behaviour by the coachee, and anxiety stemming mainly from oneself. These different forms of anxiety will surface in working with in-dividuals with BPD, for any number of reasons, for example, the challenge of entering a previously unknown coaching psychology terrain, and the difficulties many individuals experience in processing and communicating their inner pain.

Implicit also in the coaching sessions in GLOW11 was the importance of the containment of coachee anxiety, in particular in the first session. If coaching is to be effective, there needs to be a containment process at work. Cavicchia and Gilbert (2019) refer to Western (2012) setting out a model of containment that has relevance here. Western (2012) identifies two types of containment, paternal containment from a Lacan (2007) view representing the external world, incorporating structure, action, activity, and relationships that have to be negotiated. The paternal containment also includes the reality principle, the fact of there being an external reality which needs to be faced and negotiated (as distinct from a closed personal inner world of feelings and thoughts; Cavicchia & Gilbert, 2019). Paternal containment is described as important at both the beginning and ending of the coaching engagement, as well as in individual sessions, for example, through clear contracting, exploring expectations, number, duration, location and frequency of sessions, confidentiality, and fees where applicable (Cavicchia & Gilbert, 2019). Maternal containment represents the inner world, emotional containment, close relations, intimacy, play, creativity, thinking, and emergence, and is the capacity to hold and manage difficult emotions and responses, plus returning them in the form of meaning (Cavicchia & Gilbert, 2019). Cavicchia and Gilbert (2019) conclude that 'coaches under pressure to achieve quick results, busily rushing to technique, goals and solutions, risk missing the generative potential and opportunities for new associations and learning afforded by maternal containment' (pp. 125/6) and similarly, 'without paternal containment towards the end of a coaching process, the coaching relationship risks remaining primarily a safe and supportive space, but one where changes in the external world are not made' (pp. 125/6). The importance of containment is also reflected in observations by Paris (2020) in the context of therapy for people with BPD, where he states 'if any one principle can be drawn from empirical studies, it is that all proven therapies for BPD are well structured' and that people with BPD 'lack these structures – both in their inner worlds and in their outer lives' (p. 223).

How do we want to be with one another?

GLOW11 as a coaching psychology project was complex, in its undertaking and in the process of engagement with individuals with BPD, individually and collectively. We explored and experienced ongoing a pivotal question – how did we want to *be* with GLOW11 participants? This question is now of no little importance existentially. COVID-19 has surfaced existential questions regarding life and death, in particular, how do we as human beings now want to *be* with one another in a post-Covid-19 world, as it emerges? Does physical distancing as a necessary step back also provide opportunity for reflection on how to move toward rapport and relationship with renewed respect and care? There are continuous references in the media to something called a 'new normal.' The labelling of a person's life or a society as 'normal' is in fact simply an imposition without any meaning. It captures a particular type of attention and similar to so many other 'media' words it takes up permanent residence in human discourse.

The post-COVID transition raises particular questions about how coaching psychology can become relevant to individuals with diagnosed mental illness, including BPD, who frequently inhabit a fragmented sense of self and presence in the world. In the post-COVID world, every human being is facing into ongoing and probably increasing societal and global volatility, uncertainty, complexity, and ambiguity (VUCA). This experience is likely to be more intense and disorientating for people with BPD. This is not to discount the undoubted resilience and adaptive skills of individuals with BPD, in particular those who have participated in and gained critical life skills from DBT programmes (Linehan, 1993).

Linehan (2020) writes that DBT skills fall into four categories, each designed to address a different set of problems:

Mindfulness skills: which help to reduce pain and increase happiness.

Distress tolerance skills: which teach how to tolerate crisis situations so that the person can effectively find a solution to whatever is causing the stress.

Emotion regulation skills: which teach how to control one's emotions so that the person doesn't react to what is happening without reflection and doesn't say or do things that make a situation worse.

Interpersonal effectiveness skill: which help the person to be effective in relationship with others.

According to Linehan (2020) mindfulness skills and distress tolerance skills open the path to *acceptance* of reality as it is, while emotion regulation skills and interpersonal effectiveness skills, taken together, are *change* skills, that help individuals address the changes they need to make in their lives. Linehan (2020) writes that 'the goal of DBT is to help people find the path to getting out of hell' (p. 170). In explaining this to people with BPD, Linehan (2020) tells them 'if you want to get out of hell, you have to get through the fire to the other side … you have to go through your anger, open up to your therapist, keep going through the pain. It isn't overnight that you are going to feel better. But you will' (p. 171).

Coaching psychology can play an important role in helping individuals with BPD to further internalise individual processes of acceptance and change. For example, from the perspective of Acceptance and Commitment coaching, Hill and Oliver (2019) emphasise the active nature of the process of acceptance in the sense that uncomfortable thoughts and feelings are elements of a fully lived life, whereby individuals are encouraged 'to willingly come into contact with this stuff in service of their values' (p. 27). From an ACT perspective, the opposite of acceptance is experiential avoidance, the habitual or pervasive avoidance that leads to behavioural harm. Hill and Oliver (2019) state that the key context is valued action and the extent to which experiential avoidance impedes steps towards values. In the context of change, Hill and Oliver (2019) speak about committed action as 'the behavioural component of valued living, where we turn our values from intentions and ideals into action' (p. 40).

The question of how to be as a person and a coaching psychologist with individuals with BPD is helpful when considered in a context of acceptance and change. How am I in responding to my own particular anxiety in daily life, the anxieties of family members, of friends, of colleagues? Do I recognise my limitations and possibilities in how I negotiate issues and situations where acceptance is necessary and where change is necessary, for my mental health and wellbeing as I interact with others in my connected world?

Suffering and Borderline Personality Disorder

While the research to date regarding recovery and people with BPD is encouraging, BPD presents significant life and identity challenges for those affected. Zanarini (2019) writes that achieving and maintaining recovery suggests 'an ability to take care of oneself and possibly experience a certain satisfaction with one's life' (p. 120). She adds that the reverse is probably also true – the failure to recover, both symptomatically and psychosocially will likely be associated with ongoing dependency on family of origin 'and a continuing high level of inner pain, particularly feelings of shame that they have not achieved the life they planned for when younger, and worry that they might end up all alone with no one to help them or care for them' (p. 120). It is also true that a certain number of people with BPD experience significant ruptures with their family of origin and can find themselves quite alone in life.

Experience of trauma and suffering is standard for people with BPD. Rosfort (2019) writes that a person's identity is at stake in suffering, in the sense that 'our experience of being a self is troubled, and in severe cases it is so dramatically disturbed that we lose our sense of agency and ownership of our experiences and actions' (pp. 340/341).

Slade (2014) writes that a focus on personal recovery does not mean ignoring or avoiding the all-too-real experience of human suffering and 'also does not involve being relentlessly up-beat in the face of this suffering' (p. 219). Slade (2014) adds that in acknowledging when life is difficult is a helpful and authentic response for both the person with a mental illness and the other people in their life. Slade (2014) concludes that 'the development and consolidation of identity, the finding of hope, the creation of meaning and the grasping of personal responsibility all create ways forward from this suffering' (p. 219). Watts and Higgins (2017) cite Frank (1995) identifying that bearing witness to suffering is key to healing and that unless suffering is witnessed by a sympathetic other, it remains as 'an embodied memory ... a memory of experience now written into tissues' (p. 185) and that a recurring theme in many narratives is the absence of someone to tell. This is echoed in Orange (2011) who writes that there may be many reasons that we don't really want to allow the other person to affect us so much and that suffering breaks down meaning – at least until we respond. Orange (2011) cites Levinas' (1981) statement that a compassionate response to the suffering of others adds meaning to human life.

A consideration of emotional pain and suffering is likely to be unfamiliar and perhaps unnerving for many coaches and coaching psychologists. Coaching with individuals with BPD brought us face to face with people who have suffered much in life. Being receptive to suffering with non-judgment and acceptance is being receptive to the person with non-judgement and acceptance. The person has chosen to be present in the coaching space and she/he has shown up. In some ways suffering as experienced in the other person is abstract and therefore it is more difficult to know how one might be able to help. However, the abstraction of suffering becomes more tangible and concrete as one is attentive to words, tone of voice, facial expression, bodily posture, pace of speech, in both the coachee and in oneself, as coaching psychologist. Breggin (1997) writes that we should not focus exclusively on relief of distress rather than on trying to understand the underlying sources of pain, but neither should we focus on the suppression of pain. Suppression of pain gives a particular message to the other person, that her/his suffering is the problem, rather than a signal of their problems (Breggin, 1997).

In the context of BPD, Linehan (2020) advocates for a radical acceptance – surrendering and radically accepting life as it is, with willingness, without resentment, without anger – 'then you are in a place from which you can move on' (p. 252). To radically accept something is to stop fighting it and needs to be done and practiced over and over and over, until gradually acceptance becomes acceptance and 'if you do that, what happens? Suffering gets less intense. Suffering goes down to being ordinary pain' (p. 253).

Lenihan (2020) offers a verse of poetry that she says is germane to the lives of DBT therapists working with people with BPD, which also resonates with us as coaching psychologists. The verse reads:

'Do not believe that he who seeks to comfort you lives untroubled among the simple and quiet words that sometimes do you good. His life has much difficulty and sadness... Were it otherwise he would never have been able to find those words' (Rilke, 2002).

Trauma and Borderline Personality Disorder

Stanghellini and Rosfort (2013) write that it is customary that therapeutic conversations with persons with BPD will be about some stressful event that has very recently happened and that it is also common that if the therapist asks the person about that particular event during a subsequent session, she/

he will have great difficulty recalling the event and the circumstances. In a similar vein, Paris (2020) writes that whether in individual or group therapy sessions, individuals with BPD will frequently bring up examples of dysregulated emotions brought on by recent events. People with BPD are mainly focused on the present moment in such a way that they 'are not able to liberate themselves from what they are thinking, experiencing, or suffering right now' (p. 289), the capacity to distance oneself from an event, take a perspective on it, integrate it into a narrative sequence and so give a personal meaning, being defining characteristics of trauma (Stanghellini & Rosfort, 2013). This tendency to be immersed in the here-and-now, what is called an intra-festum mentality, can serve to exacerbate the person's sense of isolation, causing further irritation, frustration and, consequently, anger (Pazzagli & Monti, 2000). These authors state that dysphoria, anger, and aloneness, as three main characteristics of BPD can provide a theoretical reference model for therapists, with dysphoria resulting from a revolving door of emotional oscillation between a hope for stability and disappointment due to it being experienced as unattainable (Pazzagli & Monti, 2000).

Stanghellini and Rosfort (2013) helpfully advise that an individual's current traumatic experiences should not be assumed to be a re-enactment of earlier traumatic experiences and cite the advice of Correale (2007) that the focus of attention in therapy sessions should be on the daily traumas suffered by individuals with BPD rather than a search of earlier psychological experiences. Correale (2007) is referenced further to the effect that a focus on daily traumas is a way to meet the person's need to recount the experience and share it's burden with another person, thus enhancing their capacity to describe their experience and reflect on them by situating them in time and history (Stanghellini & Rosfort, 2013). This would also enhance the helping professional's understanding of what is actually occurring in the person's life-world through a type of slow-motion recollection of one of the daily traumatic events that make up the person's existence (Stanghellini & Rosfort, 2013).

Paris (2020) writes that while not all individuals with BPD 'get better,' those that do 'find a way to commit themselves to a purpose in life' (p. 189) and that therapeutic work with people with BPD must be focused on finding goals in the present and in the future, towards 'getting a life.' GLOW11 participants generally were able to work from this basis, while also needing to bring the coaching psychologist up to date with any recent painful event or experience. One participant needed to withdraw from GLOW11 due to a deterioration in mental health, suicidal ideation, and subsequent hospitalisation. We did recognise in working with each individual the varying degree to which each had and continued to experience trauma.

From a coaching perspective, Vaughan-Smith (2019) writes that both the word and the idea of trauma can raise worries and anxieties in coaches and cites the type of questions she has been asked, for example 'What's trauma got to do with coaching?' 'Surely it's the field of therapy?' 'Surely, better to focus on positive thoughts?' She writes that the word trauma comes from the Greek word for wound and that consequently it is the 'wounds' we are left with (Vaughan-Smith, 2019). In a more generic context of coaching, Vaughan-Smith (2019) refers to the signs of trauma that are ever-present in our daily lives and that many people who come to coaching, both clients and coaches, including those who seem to be successful, are traumatised. An accurate understanding of trauma provides a way to think about what is happening in the 'here and now' for clients and coaches and how it might be connected to the 'there and then' of the past (Vaughan-Smith, 2019). As we have seen, while many individuals with BPD have experienced trauma in early life and ongoing, it is the 'here and now' present moment manifestation of trauma that is perhaps more relevant for coaching psychology. Vaughan-Smith (2019) states that coaching does share an overlap with therapy when considering trauma and that coaching has a contribution to make to healing trauma, in the sense that while coaching is not therapy, it can be therapeutic 'if we consider it to be the achievement of healthy and favourable outcomes for the client through supporting the mobilisation of inner resources to bring about desired personal change' (p. 4). Vaughan-Smith (2019), while not addressing BPD specifically in her text, offers a helpful lens through which to think about possible perspectives regarding coaching psychology and BPD. She writes that with psyche-trauma, while we cannot see the wound directly, we are aware of the impact, and what we encounter 'is the externalised result of the trauma on behaviour (Vaughan-Smith, 2019). This includes how we relate to others, how safe we feel, our thoughts, emotional responses, levels of stress, and our bodily experience' (p. 5).

In the coaching sessions, we endeavoured not to engage in coaching as a linear, cause-and-effect approach. We coached on the basis that there was not a problem to be solved at all. As a priority, we endeavoured to bring an attitude of respect, care, compassion, and validation to each person, particularly in one-to-one coaching sessions. This emphasis on care may at first glance strike the reader as an odd primary focus for a coaching psychologist. There are a number of reasons that underpin this emphasis. Firstly, there is a stigma associated with a diagnosis of Borderline Personality Disorder. Zanarini (2019) writes that reluctance to give a diagnosis of BPD is frequently due to stigma, with many mental health professionals believing that the borderline diagnosis is pejorative, indicating a person who is difficult to handle and has a poor prognosis. Both Zanarini (2019) and Paris (2020) state that stigmatic views of BPD are based on mistaken ideas about outcome and treatability and a lack of awareness that Borderline Personality Disorder has the best symptomatic prognosis of any of the major psychiatric illnesses. Hence the critical importance of a demonstrated attitude of respect, care, compassion, and validation. Secondly, our emphasis on respect, care, compassion, and validation may strike the reader as odd, simply because so much of coaching and coaching psychology research and literature has been concerned with the world of corporate organisations, executive coaching, leadership, and the necessary importance of systemic approaches to coaching in these contexts (Hawkins & Turner, 2020). GLOW11 was a coaching intervention carried out with a relatively marginalised group of people associated with the psychiatric mental health service system in Ireland. However, GLOW11 was also carried out in a systemic context. Hawkins and Turner (2020) define systemic coaching as 'individual systemic coaching is a collaborative and dialogical inquiry between two people (coach and coachee), exploring how the coachee can learn and develop in relation to the worlds they are embedded within, in a way that creates positive benefit for them and all the nested systems of which they are part' (p. 28). GLOW11 as a coaching psychology intervention was fully cognisant of the systemic nature of the worlds that participants are embedded in, or struggling to experience a sense of acceptance and belonging. These are the worlds of family of origin, mental health services and associated mental health professionals, work environments, frequently part-time, searching for further educational and personal growth opportunities that are available and affordable, taking the risk of stretching oneself into creative and artistic endeavours, either as a solitary activity or with others, and the ever-present challenges and opportunities for intimacy in interpersonal relationships frequently fraught with fears of abandonment.

Narratives of persons in recovery and BPD

In the context of the impacts on mental health of a globalised, always-changing VUCA world (volatility, uncertainty, complexity, ambiguity) with the current and ongoing impacts of COVID-19, Stanghellini and Rosfort (2013), citing Fuchs (2007) make an interesting observation about BPD. Fuchs (2007) suggests that the increasing prevalence of BPD may in part be attributed 'to the development of a mainly externally driven, fragmented character of post-modern society, whose main features, such as the acceleration of momentary events, the mobility of work life, the futility of communication, the fragility of relationships, the receding loyalty and commitment, overlap with the borderline type of existence' (p. 277). Consequently, the narratives of individuals with BPD in this time may offer interesting and important insights about the interaction between sense of self with an almost out-of-control sense of society.

The narratives of persons in recovery were an important consideration in GLOW11. Narrative is endemic to human living. Watts and Higgins (2017) cite Barthes (1982) as follows: '...myth, legend, fable, tale, novella, epic, history, tragedy, drama, comedy, mime, painting... stained glass windows, cinema, comics, news items, conversation. Moreover, under this almost infinite diversity of forms, narrative is present in every age, in every place, in every society; it begins with the very history of mankind and there nowhere is nor has been a people without narrative ... it is simply there like life itself' (p. 251). Andresen, Oades, and Caputi (2011) citing McAdams (2001) state that the stories of people in recovery can be understood in terms of 'narrative identity,' in that the person builds a story 'that links their past, present and future in a way that brings them to an understanding of how they fit in with the world, thus imbuing their lives with a sense of unity and purpose' (p. 109).

However, in the field of mental health systems and wider society, the narratives of individuals in recovery has traditionally been relegated to a status of secondary importance compared to the narratives of mental health and psychiatry. Morgan, Felton, Fulford, Kalathil, and Stacey (2016) write that what is termed the 'universally true' knowledge of psychiatry and mental health is often considered to be based on the expertise of professionals and practitioners, and not on the experiential expertise of the people who have lived with mental distress' (p. 83). Rhodes and De Jager (2014) citing Madigan (2011) differentiate between two different types of knowledge in the therapeutic process – 'outsider' or 'global knowledge' used by professionals and 'insider' or 'local knowledge' based on the experience of individuals living with and having overcome difficulties. They go on to state that the recovery movement in mental health relies mainly on insider knowledge, 'in the form of stories circulated between consumers to build solidarity and inspire hope' (p. 99).

In relation to people with BPD and narrative, Fuchs (2007) makes the important point that narrative implies a continuity of the personal past, present and future, based around the capacity of a person to integrate often contradictory aspects and tendencies into a coherent, overarching sense and view of self. As mentioned in the section above on BPD and trauma, individuals with BPD tend to bring to sessions the most recent traumatic event experienced. In this context, Fuchs (2007) comments that individuals with BPD seem to struggle with the capacity to establish a coherent self-concept and instead 'adopt what could be called a 'post-modernist' stance towards their life, switching from one present to the next and being totally identified with their present state of affect' (p. 379), in effect showing what he describes as a fragmentation of the narrative self. According to Fuchs (2007) this fragmentation of the narrative self in individuals with BPD manifests in they having significant difficulties recalling specific autobiographical experiences. The difficulties experienced by individuals with BPD regarding narrative identity are mirrored in difficulties sustaining long-term relationships, with life becoming a series of disconnected episodes with people entering and leaving their lives in ongoing succession (Fuchs, 2007). Ultimately Fuchs (2007) describes BPD as 'a disorder of intersubjectivity' (p. 383), making the point that studies of attachment in people with BPD have found that a majority (75–90%) show overinvolved-preoccupied or avoidant attachment patterns, primarily due to negative or traumatic early experiences, in particular with abusive caregivers (citing Levy, Meehan, Weber, & Reynoso Clarkin, 2005; Fonagy et al., 1996). He concludes that when experiences of trusting relationships are missing in early childhood, inner representations of others necessary to form coherent narratives of oneself will not be established. In the context of coaching and narrative, Drake's (2018) observation regarding narrative and life seem apt here – that the stories people tell about their lives are of considerable significance in coaching because there is a very close connection between the ways in which individuals narrate their experiences and how they live their lives.

Fuchs (2007) analysis of the challenges experienced by people with BPD regarding narrative identity are interesting in the context of situating GLOW11 as a coaching psychology intervention, following on from a DBT intervention with the same individuals with BPD. Working with values within particular important life domains appeared to provide individuals with an accessible and reliable framework for reflecting on chosen current life domains, associated values and desired actions or behaviours consistent with their values. This provided a functioning anchor point in sessions and from session to session for constructive relationship-building and change-nudging conversation. Given the focus of DBT on mindfulness skills, distress tolerance skills, and emotion regulation skills, it seems reasonable to hypothesise that GLOW11 participants entered the coaching space having made use of these skills, resulting in less dysregulated emotions and therefore more open to and available for creating and sustaining interpersonal effectiveness skills with each coaching psychologist. In this context, it may also be the case that a post-DBT coaching psychology intervention of GLOW11 nature may well provide the listening presence of another person who can understand intentions and actions of the individual with BPD and thereby assist in the expression of a more coherent narrative identity. Certainly, from the anecdotal comments of GLOW11 participants this perspective warrants consideration.

The coaching relationship in GLOW11

Fuchs (2007) refers to BPD as a disorder of intersubjectivity, largely related to particular invalidating and/or abusive experiences in early childhood family life. The coaching process implicit in GLOW11 was essentially predicated on the possibilities implicit in creating a coaching relationship with each participant in one-to-one sessions. A key orientation point for each coaching psychologist was to be experienced as a trustworthy person by each coachee. The observations and feedback from participants suggest that this was their experience and was important. In the context of psychotherapy approaches to BPD, Paris (2020) states that several therapies based on different theories, using different techniques, can produce similar results and asks might they have something in common? Paris (2020) refers to what are called 'common factors' being the best predictors of effectiveness in all forms of psychotherapy, citing Lambert (2013). Paris (2020) goes on to state that the most important common factor in psychotherapy is the quality of the alliance or relationship between therapist and client.

In a coaching context, Stelter (2018) also refers to 'common factors.' Stelter (2018) states that research has documented that the following common factors 'promote the conversation's positive impact on the dialogue partner who is seeking help and on the outcome of the process also outside the field of therapy' (p. 114).

i.   **Social network factors:** factors within the social context of the person seeking support that have a key impact on the long-term outcome of the conversation. Important social network factors are core values, social support, supportive knowledge, procedures and guidelines, and the dialogue partner's recognition of the value of the conversation.

ii. **Dialogue guide factors:** the dialogue guide's *way of being* in the conversation makes an important contribution to the outcome. This includes the dialogue guide's own wellbeing, authenticity, empathy, and acceptance of the dialogue partner's situation.

iii. **Client factors:** the dialogue partner's engagement and involvement frame the third group of factors – a sense of concern and need and an active search for help play an important role in framing the conversation. Hope and an expectation of change form an important perspective. The person who is seeking support has to perceive the dialogue guide as credible for the conversation to develop in a fruitful and transformative manner.

iv. **Relational factors:** the aim of the relationship itself is foundational for a positive dialogue process. Productive and fruitful direct and indirect communication and good cooperation between the parties are important for building a successful relationship. A common understanding of the problem, tasks, and purpose/goal and of the distribution of roles promotes a good relationship and thus increases the likelihood of a positive outcome.

v.   **Practice strategies:** any transformative and fruitful dialogue is based on a change rationale, where the dialogue guide has faith in the positive effect of the dialogue. Specific dialogue strategies also play a key role – includes approaches to reflection, feedback, wondering, attention, insight, emotional learning, knowledge, information sharing, the development and testing of new ways of acting, success and mastery experiences, appreciation and suggestions, and the dialogue guide's way of offering support (Stelter, 2018).

As coaching practitioners involved in GLOW11 we strongly resonate with each of the common factors detailed by Stelter (2018), as key orientation points for considering and reflecting on practice. A term used by Stelter (2018) – heteroenticity (citing Kirkeby, 2009) – relating to oneself through the other – also resonates in terms of the coaching process that emerged in GLOW11 – 'the dialogue guide generously makes him/herself available to the other with a basic stance of never knowing more than the other' (p. 90). This is inclusive of developing practice, interaction, collaboration and dialogue approaches that 'do away with the limitations of considering development and responsibility as exclusively individual endeavours, rather than something that unfolds in a shared space' (p. 36).

Stelter (2018) emphasises the critical importance of the availability of social support for the dialogue partner, either their organisation or general life context, for a successful outcome, as an individual is rarely able to move forward alone. GLOW11 participants at all times had support available to them from the local mental health services/clinical psychology team who had delivered the DBT programme. Social support of a more informal nature, for example through family, friends, or intimate partners frequently surfaced as problematic for a number of participants.

Further, Stelter (2018) also states that 'the dialogue partner has to be able to link the chosen dialogue approach with an ability to include and attend to the common factors outlined above, with their emphasis on the relational dimension of the interaction' (pp. 115–116) and that a key factor in the dialogue guide's own development is the ability to reflect on their own practice. Stelter (2018) cites Schon (1983) referring to the capacity to *see-as* and act-as that enables one to have a feel for problems that do not fit existing rules, and further cites Schon's (1983) important concept of *reflection-in-action* – 'our knowing is ordinarily implicit in our patterns of action and in our feel for the stuff with which we are dealing' (p. 140). In a related coaching context, Cavicchia and Gilbert (2019) refer to as the implicit and explicit dimensions of interaction and building relationship. They suggest 'the crucial importance for change practitioners to understand the interface between what is termed the explicit verbal level of relating, the domain of the 'narrative.' and the implicit, non-verbal, somatic embodied level of relating – how it feels to be with another person moment by moment' (p. 93). Crucial also in this process is not only the words spoken, but how these words are spoken in tone of voice, 'the rhythm and textures of our language, how we sit and move in the process of communicating, the melody of our voice (prosody)...' (p. 95). Again, these references have both implicit and explicit relevance and importance when coaching with individuals with BPD given the need to both recognise the phenomenon of invalidation and to provide a validating coaching experience.

Power in the immediacy of the coaching interaction

In this book, as stated previously, we are not advocating that coaching psychology be the first port of call for people experiencing significant mental distress, such as BPD. GLOW11 was planned and launched from a very strong cooperative, indeed systemic baseline involving clinical psychologists working in local mental health services in Cork (Ireland), with necessary protocols and procedures in place. Each of the participants in GLOW11 had previously completed a DBT programme. At the same time, the individuals who chose to participate in GLOW11 did so from a stated hope that their experiences of self and life could be enhanced. During the coaching sessions, individuals experienced varying degrees of mental distress and vary degrees of insight, emotional release and commitment to values-based actions or behaviours. Trust needed to be established. Safety needed to be established. Containment of anxiety needed to be evident. In-session checking in with coachees regarding their experience of the coaching relationship and process occurred. Coachees were regularly invited to identify which elements of coaching were working for them or otherwise. Coachees were asked to think about the interpersonal communication and interaction process within each session and more widely in group sessions. As coachees experienced the risk of honest feedback being worth taking in this regard, an element of coaching that emerged frequently was the critical importance to each participant that she/he mattered as a whole person to each coaching psychologist and the implication that coaching interactions were based around invitation to collaborate rather than acceptance of expertise. In this context, Chefetz (2003) lists some questions that connect to the importance of mattering in a professional-client relationship – how does the other person matter to you?; how does the other person affect you?; what is it like for you when you matter too much, or too little to the other person?; how does mattering influence how you work with the person?.

There are a number of issues here that are relevant to a consideration of coaching psychology and whether it can bring value to the lives of individuals with BPD. One critical issue is that of power. Bruning (2014) states that our social system is constructed on the assumed pairing of power with vulnerability and that 'individually and collectively, power can be used as a defence against a sense of vulnerability; power without vulnerability can lead to abuses; and vulnerability without any power can result in an ineffectual positioning and failure both at an individual and organisational level' (pp. xviii–xix). GLOW11 participants were emerging from varying degrees of involvement with mental health services. Their applications for participation in GLOW11 were facilitated for processing within mental health services. Their individual interviews were attended by the DBT therapists who had supported and built relationship with them. This information is shared simply to put in context power and vulnerability is implicit in every professional-client engagement and interaction. To our knowledge, this issue has received very little attention in the coaching psychology literature. We are open to correction here! An exception is Welman and Bachkirova (2010) who make a helpful distinction between power as imposition and power as influence, in the sense that while people influence one another all the time to get needs met, there is a point where influence can become imposition in *all* relationships, including coaching and counselling. They highlight a number of factors that may influence the predisposition of coaches towards use of power, such as professional factors like fear of the unpredictability of the coaching process, attachment to particular outcomes, status as specialists in a position to deliver a needed service, perceived professional expertise, and more personal factors such as personality traits, with self-deception added for good measure (Welman & Bachkirova, 2010). The aspect of power as discussed by Welman and Bachkirova (2010) that resonates most strongly with us is their reflection on dealing with power in the immediacy of the coaching interaction and that in the 'here and now' of the coaching interaction 'it is the awareness (of the coach) and consent (of the coachee) that makes the crucial difference between 'forceful influence' and 'imposition of will' (p. 151). These authors conclude that if coaches want to avoid temptation towards power, 'we believe that they need to be aware of its possibility moment by moment' (p. 153). Stelter's (2019) invitation to consider oneself to be *a fellow human being and a co-creative partner* in the coaching dialogue contains within it multiple potential perspectives for an ethical reflection of how one *is* as a coaching psychologist, *with* oneself and *with* the other person, and a yardstick for a consideration of power as imposition or as influence.

Validation

In GLOW11 we endeavoured to relate to participants individually and collectively cognisant of a key issue for BPD identified by Linehan (1993; 2020) and others, that of emotional validation. The history of traumatic emotional invalidation shared by many people with BPD presents very particular challenges for professional helpers of all professions and disciplines, especially in the context of building a positive working alliance or relationship. Paris (2020) in acknowledging Linehan's (1993) introduction of the term *validation*, states that validating need not mean agreeing with a person's feelings or behaviours, but does mean understanding them in an interpersonal context and that doing so avoids dismissing the person's reactions, leaving opportunity for reframing and reappraisal. Paris (2020) adds that failures of empathy can trigger strong emotional reactions in individuals with BPD 'who are unusually sensitive to being misunderstood ... the trick is to avoid being in any way insistent about one's own position and to shift gears rapidly when necessary' (p. 213), a flexibility that most individuals will appreciate.

Stanghellini and Rosfort (2013) writing about people with BPD state that the integrity of the self can be damaged by trauma, not the kind of trauma arising from sexual abuse or violent acts, but trauma that takes the form of an invalidating environment. These authors add that 'an invalidating environment is one in which communication of private experiences is not met by appropriate responses. Instead of being validated, private experiences are trivialised, their expression is discouraged, and emotions (especially painful emotions) are disregarded. The kind of trauma that may jeopardise the development of a warm and intimate sense of self is the absence of *recognition*' (Stanghellini & Rosfort, 2013, p. 275). As a result, the person is left with the experience of an internal emptiness, of being no one, feeling the loss of one's *own* value, and consequently 'feelings of discontinuity over time, of inner emptiness, and a fragile sense of being 'myself' are indeed the principal symptoms of borderline personality disorder' (pp. 275/276).

Linehan (1993) describes the invalidating environment as one where communication of private experiences is invariably met by erratic, inappropriate, and extreme responses and where the expression of private experiences is not validated, instead is often punished and/or trivialized. There is a disregard for experience of painful emotions in addition to the factors that to the person seem causally related to the emotional distress. The person's interpretations of their own behaviour, including intention and motivation, are dismissed. Invalidation has two primary characteristics. Firstly, it tells the person that she is wrong in her description and her assessment of her own experiences, especially in her views of what is causing her own emotions, beliefs, and actions. Secondly, her experiences are attributed to socially unacceptable characteristics of personality traits. The environment insists that the person feels what she says she does not feel ('You are angry, but you just won't admit it'), likes or prefers what she says she does not (the proverbial 'When she says no, she means yes'), or has done what she said she did not do. Negative emotional expressions tend to be attributed to traits like over-reactivity, oversensitivity, paranoia, a distorted view of events, or failure to adopt a positive attitude. Behaviours that have unintended negative consequences for other people are likely to be attributed to hostile or manipulative motives. Failure, or any deviation from socially defined success, is identified as resulting from lack of motivation, lack of discipline, not trying hard enough, and so on. Positive emotional expressions, beliefs, and action plans can be invalidated similarly by being attributed to lack of discrimination, naivete, over-idealization, or immaturity. Overall, the person's private experiences and emotional expressions are not viewed as valid responses to events (Linehan, 1993). In her memoir, Linehan (2020) writes about invalidating environments where there is constant disapproval, constant pressure to be someone else, sometimes resulting in traumatic invalidation – 'it can be an accumulation of pervasive misreading of emotions by others, such as when someone insists incorrectly that a person is angry, jealous, afraid, or lying or insists that the person has internal motives he or she doesn't have. Trauma is most likely when these actions make the individual feel like an outsider' (p. 55). Linehan (2020) concludes that in the extreme, traumatic invalidation can lead to thoughts of self-harm and suicide as a source of relief from the toxic emotional environment they are in. Again in the context of BPD, Paris (2020) writes that while validation is an essential element of any therapy, it is especially important for individuals with BPD – they 'may not listen to anything else their therapists have to say unless their feelings are accepted and validated' (p. 170). Galen (2016) suggests that validation can support emotion regulation, frequently a major area of challenge for people with BPD, helping the person to understand their own experience as an experience that is real and makes sense, thereby improving communication and relationship. In a similar vein, Livesley (2012) comments that a collaborative approach is facilitated by a validating approach that serves multiple functions – validation is empathic and supportive; helps to counter earlier invalidating experiences (citing Linehan, 1993), which can promote self-validation. Livesley (2012) adds that the challenge is 'to validate experience without validating causes and consequences of experiences and responses that are invalid' which involves helping the individual 'to distinguish the experience from the reasons given for the experience and responses to it' (p. 61).

Hopefully, this detailed outline helps with the importance of understanding the nature and impacts of invalidating environments on people with BPD. We highlight its core importance, not just as a concept for understanding, but as a reminder of how any professional helper can unintentionally engage in invalidating words, gestures, facial expressions. Hence the importance, of moment by moment 'observation' of oneself as coaching psychologist – one's idiosyncratic turns of phrase, one's smile or facial expression in conjunction with speaking particular words, one's implicit assumptions about good intentions and how communication will be received. All added to a particularly heightened sense of being involved in the co-creating of a coaching relationship genre in GLOW11 we had not previously experienced as coaching psychologists. In the context of coaching, Cavicchia and Gilbert (2019) refer to the importance of listening deeply to the richness of data that is entering the space shared by coach and coachee, where we cannot but notice and select certain aspects that capture one's attention related to the filtering of one's experience, emotional responses and attention. However, this is also when one needs to be paying attention to what might be missing, avoided or not being said, 'minding the gap' (citing Western, 2012).

In GLOW11, peer-supervision sessions were invaluable in the context of sharing and reflecting on our individual coaching processes. In these sessions, we learned to communicate and relate to one another, not from trying to pretend all was in hand, but from what became our far more habitual home of not-knowing, being curious, putting learning to good effect, awareness of both vulnerability and resilience, exploring our own values and recognising the critical importance of 'letting go of our own system of values and to communicate within the other person's value system' (De Haan & Sills, 2012, p. 6).

Positive psychology and recovery

Slade (2010) writes that generating a science of illness within mental health services has been far more successful to date in comparison to creating a science of wellbeing. Slade (2010) argues that in the context of personal recovery, assessment and treatment of the person needs to change if the goal is to promote wellbeing rather than treating illness, on the basis that wellbeing is possible for people experiencing mental illness. He also suggests that mental health professionals need to acquire additional skills on the basis that the typical mental health worker will know far more about treating illness and far less about promoting wellbeing (Slade, 2010).

Slade (2010) also highlights relevant new areas of knowledge, for example, recovery which emphasises the centrality of hope, identity, meaning, and personal responsibility (citing Andresen et al., 2003; Spaniol, Wewiorski, Gagne, & Anthony, 2002; Ralph, 2000). Regarding recovery, Slade (2010) highlights that recovery is a multifaceted concept, there being no right way for an individual to recover, with eliciting idiographic knowledge and understanding subjective phenomena an important clinical skill. Slade (2010) also highlights positive psychology as a relatively new area of knowledge relevant to wellbeing, emphasising it being about valued subjective experiences – wellbeing, contentment, satisfaction (in the past), hope and optimism (for the future), and flow and happiness (in the present), as well at a group level being about civic virtues such as better citizenship – responsibility, nurturance, altruism, civility, moderation, tolerance, and work ethic (citing Seligman & Csikszentmihalyi, 2000).

Slade (2010) refers to one important advance regarding empirical investigation of mental health, a conceptual framework – the Complete State Model of Mental Health (citing Keyes & Lopez, 2002). In the context of the Complete State Model of Mental Health, Keyes and Martin (2017) propose that constructs of mental health and mental illness are distinct, with mental health/wellbeing on a spectrum from low to high and mental illness on a spectrum from absent to present. Slade (2010) states that the conceptual framework maps easily onto the themes emerging from the recovery narratives. He cites a frequent question asked – 'how can you be recovered if you still have a mental illness?' and that any answers given 'can be only partial answers since the term recovery is an illness term. By contrast, access to mental health is open to all' and this provides an alternative frame of understanding for recovery (citing Slade, 2014).

Andresen et al. (2011) state that the stage model of psychological recovery highlights the need of a positive psychological approach in recovery. These authors/researchers write that while qualitative research methods are very important in understanding and communicating the richness of individual experience and narrative, developing and linking with relevant quantitative approaches will strengthen the impact and reach of the recovery movement (Andresen et al., 2011). They make connections between psychological recovery concepts, positive psychology research and relevant constructs and relevant measures mainly used in non-clinical populations, for example – hope, meaning, and purpose (psychological recovery concept), hope theory/ purpose in life (positive psychology research), and State and Trait Hope (Snyder, 2000); Purpose in Life Scale (Marsh, Smith, Piek, & Saunders, 2003).

Slade (2014) in referring to interventions to promote wellbeing, also mentions cognitive behavioural therapy, mindfulness, narrative psychology, and positive psychotherapy.

Resnick and Rosenheck (2006) propose that the recovery concept and positive psychology have followed separate but parallel paths, adding that positive psychology provides a potentially useful framework for services seeking to support the recovery orientation, and that the recovery orientation can help to broaden the hitherto overly narrow scope of positive psychology' (p. 120). They add that while the underlying philosophies and goals of positive psychology and the recovery movement have similarities, two differences have functioned to keep them from constructively engaging (Resnick & Rosenheck, 2006). The differences identified are that positive psychology focuses on improving the lives of people who do not have a mental illness, while advocates of recovery argue that the existence of 'pathology' should not exclude a focus on what is healthy; and that positive psychology focuses on empirical research, while the recovery movement focuses on action, advocacy, and self-determination (Resnick & Rosenheck, 2006). Resnick and Rosenheck (2006) also state that leaders of positive psychology have developed an overarching theoretical framework that functions as the basis of an intellectual movement 'led by prominent academic psychologists, that challenges the dominance of 'negative psychology' (p. 121), while the recovery movement by and large is 'a grassroots movement of the disenfranchised that has placed itself distinctly apart from the human service professions, the academy, and the empirical research tradition' (p. 121). Schrank et al. (2014) also state that the goals of positive psychology and recovery appear to be congruent, however, recovery has been historically built on personal narratives, theories and opinions, with empirical research lagging behind, while positive psychology 'offers a quantitative research focus in need of defensible theories and contextual knowledge on which to base its application' (p. 98).

Slade (2010) argues that advocates of the recovery approach (via developing position statements (Mental Health Commission, 2005), consensus statements (Substance Abuse and Mental Health Services Administration, 2005), frameworks (National Institute for Mental Health in England, 2004), guidelines (Tondora & Davidson, 2006) and other action and change-oriented approaches has been more successful than positive psychology (via empirical research, scientific methods, nomothetic approaches, and convergence on overarching theories (Seligman, 2002) in influencing policy on mental health.

Green and Palmer (2019) state that positive psychology interventions have been used for both clinical and non-clinical populations, 'however, in the main, the majority of research have been conducted on the 'normal' or 'non-clinical' population; whereas, despite some debate, EBC (Evidence Based Coaching) is primarily for those in the 'normal' population' (p. 13). They add that this is based on a concern that coaching a person, involving actively pushing towards a stretch goal, 'may be detrimental to someone experiencing clinical depression or anxiety for example' (p. 13) (Green & Palmer, 2019). Green and Palmer (2019) also state that 'second wave of positive psychology (citing Lomas & Ivtzan; Sims, 2017) attempts to embrace both the positive and the negative (or dark) sides of the human condition and experience' (p. 14). Citing Grant (2007) and his Model of Goal Striving and Mental Health, Green and Palmer (2019) refer to individuals in the 'languishing' quadrant of the model who may be experiencing clinical or subclinical issues which may present a challenge to coaches without clinical training (citing Grant & Spence, 2010). Slade (2010) also queries why there has not been greater rapprochement between the recovery movement and positive psychology. He suggests that the 'positioning of positive psychology as a branch of psychology invokes unhelpful tribal loyalties – it suggests a relevance to psychologists but not other types of researchers or professionals' (p. 6) and that wellbeing is a focus for many disciplines (Slade, 2010). Slade (2010) suggests that the divergence of recovery and positive psychology has impoverished both groups given the complementary aims of both. Slade (2010) recommends that for recovery, the development of a clinically credible evidence base has the potential to be significant to transforming mental health services and for positive psychology, 'the incorporation of the central recovery focus on the individual and their differing ways of seeing the world (including giving primacy to familial or cultural affiliation over personal identity) will address criticisms that it is ethnocentric (being based mainly on US research)...' (p. 7). He adds that if people with mental illness are outliers, for example, in terms of having a relatively low ratio of protective to risk factors, 'then excluding them from consideration makes the development of generalisable theories more difficult' (p. 7).

It may well be that a 'third wave' of positive psychology as posited by Lomas, Waters, Williams, Oades, and Kern (2020) will contribute to addressing the identified divergence between recovery and positive psychology. Among the core characteristics of this posited 'third wave' are a broadening 'beyond the individual' towards recognition and appreciation of greater complexity, in terms of enquiry (interest in super-individual processes and phenomena); disciplines (becoming more interdisciplinary); culture (becoming more multicultural and global); and methodologies (embracing other ways of knowing) (Lomas et al., 2020). These authors propose that going beyond the individual person as the primary focus of enquiry implies looking deeply and critically at groups, organisations and broader systems that impact on people's wellbeing.

Getting a life!

We include a reference to positive psychology in the context of recovery to highlight some of the tensions evident between what are called 'non -clinical' or 'normal' groupings of people and people consigned to the 'clinical' grouping. The term 'abnormal' is rarely enough used currently, however the implication is ever-present in language used. We urge that coaching psychology creates and sustains a wide intercultural landscape of focus and application in the contemporary world, in which all perspectives and possibilities are carefully examined and where our existing assumptions about the limits and possibilities of coaching psychology are always a topic for critical reflection. This aspiration is already reflected in the coaching psychology literature. Examples include Cox, Bachkirova, and Clutterbuck (2014) who highlight the multifaceted nature of coaching, with many practical and theoretical traditions influencing the field leading to a wide variety of coaching genres and theory-base traditions and view this as an opportunity rather than a problem; and Western (2012) who advocates in his theoretical approach an emancipatory approach as an ethical position, 'ethics, liberation, autonomy and justice: coaching to help create the 'good society' (p. 28).

In some respects, people with BPD have been outliers in the world of mental illness and mental health services. As already mentioned in this book, the majority of the narratives, commentary and research on personal recovery has been concerned with other forms of significant mental distress, for example, schizophrenia, clinical depression, and psychosis. In GLOW11 as coaching psychologists, we engaged with particular individuals with BPD, extending and stretching the good work already carried out by clinical psychology colleagues working in local mental health services. More than anything, as we reflected on how we would welcome these particular individuals with BPD, we also had a unique experience of being individually and collectively welcomed by each of them. We did experience the importance of the coach being 'a fellow human being and a co-creative partner in the dialogue' (Stelter, 2018, p. 3).

As regards the possibility of a coherent engagement between coaching psychology and BPD we particularly highlight the following comments by Livesley (2017) – that the final phase of therapeutic work with people with BPD seeks to construct a more adaptive self and a life worth living, however, systematic work on these issues probably only occurs with relatively few individuals. He writes that even following seemingly successful therapy many individuals with BPD continue to experience difficulties and 'hence this phase is important if treatment is to achieve something more than symptomatic improvement' and individuals are to be helped to live more satisfying lives (Livesley, 2017). This resonates strongly with the stated hopes and aspirations of the individuals who participated in GLOW11, the ongoing search for more satisfying lives. Livesley (2017) adds that the search for a more satisfying life can build on the work of specialist (e.g. DBT) or generic therapy approaches by helping individuals with BPD build a sense of a more integrated self, formulate a more coherent self-narrative, and 'develop a life worth living by building a personal niche that provides opportunities for a contented and rewarding life' (p. 229). These sentiments are echoed by Linehan (2020) stating that she wants the individuals she works with to understand that they are much more than the disorders they present with… 'too often, this is how people view those who are diagnosed with certain behavioural conditions … it's a label that sticks and seems to define … my message to clients is, no, you are more than that … you have made bad decisions in the past … but you still have the capacity for wisdom, you have the capacity to know what is right for you' (p. 282).

Finally, in observations that echo something fundamentally important in all forms and approaches to skilled helping, including coaching psychology, Livesley (2017) writes that 'what matters is not just what therapists do but how they do it. This is more nebulous and difficult to describe. It is captured in part by the emphasis on an empathic, supportive, and validating therapeutic stance. But this is only part of what matters. Other features of the therapeutic interaction that therapists need to create are the following: respect, compassion, acceptance, attentiveness, involvement, and empathic attunement' (pp. 11/12), adding that these elements characterise a process that offers new experiences to challenge old ways of interacting with the interpersonal world and this aspect needs to be got right, because while technical competence may be necessary, it is not at all sufficient.

Based on the experience of GLOW11, we strongly endorse the observations above (Livesley, 2017). Our considered view is that there is an opportunity for coaching psychology to assist people with BPD in the quest for more satisfying lives and that the planning and operational elements of GLOW11 offer potentially a coherent and workable framework.

Discussion points

1. In a COVID-19 world does the recovery framework/s have a more universal application to human resilience and wellbeing?
2. In the context of the sense of dislocation triggered by COVID-19,

what are the questions you are asking in terms of trying to locate/ relocate yourself as a coaching psychologist, and have you colleagues with whom to share?

3. To what extent is working with emotions an integral aspect of your coaching psychology practice? If you tend to shy away from working with emotions have you reflected on your reasons?

4. What do you know about the relevance of the 'common factors' to the practice of coaching psychology?

5. When reflecting on your coaching practice, do you consider the issue of power in the coaching relationship?

Suggested reading

Cameron, A. Y., Reed, K. P., & Gaudiano, B. A. (2014). Addressing treatment motivation in borderline personality disorder: Rationale for incorporating values-based exercises into dialectical behaviour therapy. *Journal of Contemporary Psychotherapy*, *44*, 109–116. (While the article addresses working with values in the context of DBT, it provides food for thought for coaching psychologists considering how to incorporate values work in their practice).

Cox, E. (2017). Working with emotions in coaching. In T. Bachkirova, G. Spence, & D. Drake (Eds.), *The Sage Handbook of Coaching* (pp. 272–290). (An excellent article on the importance of working with emotions in coaching practice).

Stelter, R. (2019). *The art of dialogue in coaching: Towards transformative exchange*. London, UK: Routledge. (In addition to important considerations for the coach to be a fellow human being and a co-creative partner, pp. 61–69 discusses working with values and pp. 111–121 looks at the relevance of "common factors" to coaching psychology practice).

Vaughan-Smith, J. (2019). *Coaching and trauma: From surviving to thriving*. London, UK: Open University Press. (An excellent foray into the possibilities of coaching and trauma. Chapter 7 as a final chapter is particularly helpful in discussing issues around boundaries, challenges and healing).

Welman, P., & Bachkirova, T. Power in the coaching relationship. In S. Palmer, & A. McDowall (Eds.), *The coaching relationship: Putting people first* (pp. 139–158). London, UK: Routledge. (This chapter provides an excellent overview of the issue of power in the coaching relationship).

Western, S. (2012). *Coaching and mentoring: A critical text*. London, UK: Sage. (in chapter 6, the author provides a very interesting reflective exercise on "locating ourselves" which we suggest also asks questions that are relevant to a Covid-19 world (p. 145).

References

American Psychiatric Association (2013). *Diagnostic and statistical manual of mental disorders: DSM-5*. Washington, DC: American Psychiatric Publications.

Andresen, R., Oades, L., & Caputi, P. (2003). The experience of recovery from schizophrenia: Towards an empirically-validated stage model. *Australian and New Zealand Journal of Psychiatry, 37*, 586–594.

Andresen, R., Oades, L. G., & Caputi, P. (2011). *Psychological recovery: Beyond mental illness.* London, UK: Wiley-Blackwell.

Bachkirova, T., & Cox, E. (2007). Coaching with emotion in organisations: Investigation of personal theories. *Leadership and Organization Development, 28*(7), 600–612

Bachkirova, T., Cox, E., & Clutterbuck, D. (2018). Introduction. In E. Cox, T. Bachkirova, & D. Clutterbuck (Eds.), *The complete handbook of coaching* (3rd ed., pp. xxix–xiviii). London, UK: Sage Publications Ltd.

Barthes, R. (1982). *La Litterature et realite.* Paris: Editions Du Seuil.

Baumeister, R. F., Bratslavsky, E., Finkenhauer, C., & Vohs, H. D. (2001). Bad is stronger than good. *Review of General Psychology, 5*(4), 323–370.

Blackledge, J. T., Ciarrochi, J., & Bailey, A. (2006). *Personal values questionnaire* [Internet]. http://www.contextualscience.org/resources.

Breggin, P. (1997). *The heart of being helpful: Empathy and the creation of a healing presence.* New York: Springer.

Bruning, H. (Ed.). (2014). *Power and vulnerability.* London, UK: Karnac.

Cameron, A. Y., Reed, K. P., & Gaudiano, B. A. (2014). Addressing treatment motivation in borderline personality disorder: Rationale for incorporating values-based exercises into dialectical behaviour therapy, *Journal of Contemporary Psychotherapy, 44*, 109–116.

Cavanagh, M. J., & Buckley, A. (2018). Coaching and mental health. In E. Cox, T. Bachkirova, & D. Clutterbuck (Eds.), *The complete handbook of coaching* (pp. 451–464). London, UK: Sage.

Cavicchia, S., & Gilbert, M. (2019). *The theory and practice of relational coaching: Complexity, paradox and integration.* London, UK: Routledge.

Chefetz, R. A. (2003). On matters of mattering. *Journal of Trauma and Dissociation, 4*(1), 1–4.

Correale, A. (2007). *Area traumatica e campo istituzionale, seconda edizione.* Roma: Borla Edizioni.

Corrie, S. (2016). *Promoting self-care in a complex world: What every coach should know.* Keynote presentation at the SGCP Coaching Psychology Workshops & Conference 2016.

Cox, E. (2013). *Coaching understood: A pragmatic inquiry into the coaching process.* London, UK: Sage.

Cox, E. (2017). Working with emotions in coaching. In T. Bachkirova, G. Spence, & D. Drake (Eds.), *The Sage handbook of coaching* (pp. 272–290). London, UK: Sage Publications Ltd.

Cox, E., Bachkirova, T., & Clutterbuck. D. (2014). Theoretical traditions and coaching genres: Mapping the territory. *Advances in Developing Human Resources, 16*(2), 139–160.

Cristea, I. A., Gentilla, C., Cotet, C. D., Palomba, D., Barbui, C., & Cuijpers, P. (2017). Efficacy of psychotherapies for borderline personality disorder: A systematic review and meta-analysis. *JAMA Psychiatry, 74*, 319–328.

Damasio, A. (2000). *The feeling of what happens: Body, emotion and the making of Consciousness*. London, UK: Vintage.

Day, A., de Haan, E., Blass, E., Sills, C., & Bertie, C. (2008). Coaches' experience of critical moments in the coaching. *International Coaching Psychology Review, 3*(3), 207–218.

De Haan, E. & Sills, C. (Eds.). (2012). *Coaching relationships: The relational coaching field book*. Faringdon, UK: Libri Publishing.

Dirkx, J. M. (2008). The meaning and role of emotions in adult learning. *New Directions for Adult and Continuing Education, 120*, 7–18.

Drake, D. (2018). Narrative coaching. In E. Cox, T. Bachkirova, & D. Clutterbuck (Eds.), *The complete handbook of coaching* (3rd ed., pp. 109–123). London, UK: Sage Publications Ltd.

Egan, G. (2014). *The skilled helper: A client-centred approach*. Andover, UK: Cengage Learning Inc.

Fonagy, P., Leigh, T., Steele, M., Kennedy, R., Mattoon, G., Target, M., & Gerber, A. (1996). The relation of attachment status, psychiatric classification, and response to psychotherapy. *Journal of Consulting and Clinical Psychology, 64*, 22–31.

Frank, A. (1995). *The wounded storyteller: Body, illness and ethics*. Chicago: University of Chicago Press.

Fuchs, T. (2007). Fragmented selves: Temporality and identity in borderline personality. *Psychopathology, 40*(6), 379–387.

Galen, G. (2016). *Validation: Making sense of the emotional turmoil in borderline personality disorder*. www.mcleanhospital.org. Retrieved: 24/06/2020.

Gold, N., & Kyratsous, M. (2017). Self and identity in borderline personality disorder: Agency and mental time travel. *Journal of Evaluation in Clinical Practice, 23*, 1020–1028.

Grant, A. M. (2007). A model of goal-striving and mental health for coaching populations. *International Coaching Psychology Review, 2*(3), 248–262.

Grant, A. M., & Spence, G. B. (2010). Using coaching and positive psychology to promote a flourishing workforce: A model of goal-striving and mental health. In P. A. Linley, S. Harrington, & N. Page (Eds.), *Oxford handbook of positive psychology and work* (pp. 175–188). Oxford, UK: Oxford University Press.

Green, S., & Palmer, S. (Eds.). (2019). *Positive psychology coaching practice*. London, UK; Routledge.

Greenberg, L. S. (2004). Emotion-focused therapy. *Clinical Psychology & Psychotherapy, 11*(1), 3–16.

Grenyer, B. F. S., Jenner, B., Jarman, H., Carter, P., Bailey, R., & Lewis, K. (2015). Treatment guidelines for personality disorders (2nd ed.), University of Wollongong, Illawarra Health and Medical Research Institute. www.projectairstrategy.org

Gunderson, J. G. (1984). *Borderline personality disorder*. Washington, DC: American Psychiatric Press.

Hawkins, P., & Turner, E. (2020). *Systemic coaching: Delivering value beyond the individual*. London, UK: Routledge.

Hill, J., & Oliver, J. (2019). *Acceptance and commitment coaching: Distinctive features*. London, UK: Routledge.

Huguelet, P., Guillaume, S., Vidal, S., Mohr, S., Courtet, P., Villain, P., ...Perroud, N. (2016). Values as determinant of meaning among patients with psychiatric disorders in the perspective of recovery. *Scientific, 6.* http://www.nature.com/articles/1srep27617.pdf

Kane, S. (2001). "4.48 Psychosis." In S. Kane (Ed.), *Complete plays* (pp. 203–246). London, UK: Methuen.

Keyes, C. L. M., & Lopez, S. J. (2002). Toward a science of mental health. In C. Keyes, & S. J. Lopez (Eds.), *Handbook of positive psychology* (pp. 45–59). New York: Oxford University Press.

Keyes, C. L. M., & Martin, C. C. (2017). The complete state model of mental health. In M. Slade, L. Oades, & A. Jarden (Eds.), *Wellbeing, recovery and mental health* (pp. 86–97. Cambridge, UK: Cambridge University Press.

Kirkeby, O. F. (2009). *The New Protreptics – The Concept and the Art.* Copenhagen: Copenhagen Business School Press.

Lacan, J. (2007). *Ecrits* (Bruce Fink, trans.). New York: Norton.

Lambert, M. J. (Ed.). (2013). *Bergin and Garfield's handbook of psychotherapy and behaviour change* (6th ed.). Hoboken, NJ: Wiley.

Leamy, M., Bird, V., Le Boutillier, C., Williams, J., & Slade, M. (2011). Conceptual framework for personal recovery in mental health: Systematic review and narrative synthesis. *The British Journal of Psychiatry, 199,* 445–452.

Levinas, E. (1981). *Otherwise than Being: Or, beyond essence.* The Hague: Netherlands: M. Nijhoff.

Levy, K. N., Meehan, K. B., Weber, M., & Reynoso Clarkin, J. F. (2005). Attachment and borderline personality disorder: Implications for psychotherapy. *Psychopathology, 38,* 64–74.

Linehan, M. M. (1993). *Cognitive behavioral treatment of borderline personality disorder.* New York, USA: The Guilford Press.

Linehan, M. M. (2020). *Building a life worth living: A memoir.* New York, USA: Random House.

Livesley, W. J. (2012). Moving beyond specialized therapies for borderline personality disorder: The importance of integrated domain-focused treatment. *Psychodynamic Psychiatry, 40*(1), 47–74.

Livesley, W. J. (2017). *Integrated modular treatment for borderline personality disorder: A practical guide to combining effective treatment methods.* Cambridge, UK: Cambridge University Press.

Lomas, T., & Ivtzan, I. (2016). Second wave positive psychology: Exploring the positive-negative dialectics of wellbeing. *Journal of Happiness Studies, 17*(4), 1753–1768.

Lomas, T., Waters, L., Williams, P., Oades, L.G., & Kern, M.L. (2020). Third wave positive psychology: Broadening towards complexity. *The Journal of Positive Psychology,* DOI: 10.1080/17439760.2020.1805501

Madigan, S. (2011). *Narrative therapy. Theories of psychotherapy series.* New York: American Psychological Association.

McAdams, D. P. (2001). The psychology of life stories. *Review of General Psychology, 5*(2), 100–122.

Marsh, A., Smith, L., Piek, J., & Saunders, B. (2003). The purpose in life scale: Psychometric properties for social drinkers in alcohol treatment. *Educational and Psychological Measurements, 63,* 859.

Mental Health Commission. (2005). *A vision for a recovery model in Irish mental health services.* Dublin: Mental Health Commission.

Mohi, S. R., Deane, F. P., Bailey, A., Mooney-Reh, D., & Ciaglia, D. (2018). An exploration of values among consumers seeking treatment for borderline personality disorder. *Borderline Personality Disorder and Emotion Regulation, 5*(8), 1–10.

Morgan, A., Felton, A., Fulford, K. W. M., Kalathil, J., & Stacey, G. (2016). *Values and ethics in mental health: An exploration for practice.* London, UK: Palgrave-MacMillan.

Mussey, C. (2016). Foreward. In M. Watts, & A. Higgins, *Narratives of recovery from mental illness.* London, UK: Routledge.

Myers, N. L. (2015). *Recovery's edge: An ethnography of mental health care and moral agency.* Nashville, USA: Vanderbilt University Press.

National Institute for Mental Health in England. (2004). *Emerging best practices in mental health recovery.* London, UK: NIMHE.

Nussbaum, M.C. (2004). *Emotions as judgments of value and importance.* Oxford, UK: Oxford University Press.

Orange, D. M. (2011). *The suffering stranger: Hermeneutics for everyday clinical practice.* London, UK: Routledge.

Paris, J. (2020). *Treatment of borderline personality disorder: A guide to evidence-based practice* (2nd ed.). New York: Guilford Press.

Pazzagli, A., & Monti, M. (2000). Dysphoria and aloneness in borderline personality disorder. *Psychopathology, 33,* 220–226.

Ralph, R. O. (2000). Recovery. *Psychiatric Rehabilitation Skills, 4,* 480–517.

Resnick, S. G., & R. A. Rosenheck (2006). Recovery and positive psychology: Parallel themes and potential synergies. *Psychiatric Services, 57*(1), 120–122.

Rhodes, P., & De Jager, A. (2014). Narrative studies of recovery: A critical resource for clinicians. *Clinical Psychologist, 18,* 99–107.

Rilke, R. M. (2002). *Letters to a young poet.* Dover Publications.

Rosfort, R. (2019). Personhood. In G. Stanghellini, M. R. Broome, A. V. Fernandez, P. Fusar-Poli, A. Rabello, & R. Rosfort (pp. 335–343). *The Oxford handbook of phenomenological psychopathology.* London, UK: Oxford University Press.

Schon, D. A. (1983). *The reflective practitioner: How professionals think in action.* New York, NY: Basic Books.

Schrank, B. & Slade, M. (2007). Recovery in psychiatry, *Psychiatric Bulletin, 31*(9), 321–325.

Schrank, B., Brownell, T., & Slade, M. (2014). Positive psychology: An approach to supporting recovery in mental illness. *East Asian Archives of Psychiatry, 24,* 95–103.

Seligman, M. (2002). *Authentic happiness: Using the new positive psychology to realize your potential for lasting fulfilment.* New York: Free Press.

Seligman, M., & Csikszentmihalyi, M. (2000). Positive psychology: An introduction. *American Psychologist, 55,* 5–14.

Sims, C. (2017). Second wave positive psychology coaching with difficult emotions: Introducing the mnemonic of 'TEARS HOPE'. *The Coaching Psychologist, 13*(12), 66–78.

Slade, M. (2010). Mental illness and wellbeing: The central importance of positive psychology and recovery approaches. *BMC Health Services Research, 10,* 26, pp. 1–14.

Slade, M. (2014). *Personal recovery and mental illness: A guide for mental health professionals.* Cambridge, UK: Cambridge University Press.

Slade, M., Amering, M., & Oades, L. (2008). Recovery: An international perspective. *Epidemiologia e Psichiatria Sociale, 17*(2), 128–137.

Snyder, C. R. (Ed.). (2000). *Handbook of hope: Theory, measures, and applications.* San Diego, CA: Academic Press.

Spaniol, L., Wewiorski, N., Gagne, C., & Anthony, W. (2002). The process of recovery from schizophrenia. *International Review of Psychiatry, 14,* 327–336.

Stanghellini, G., & Rosfort, R. (2013). *Emotions and personhood: Exploring fragility – Making sense of vulnerability.* Oxford, UK: Oxford University Press.

Stanghellini, G., & Mancini, M. (2019). The life-world of persons with borderline personality disorder. In G. Stanghellini, M. R. Broome, A. V. Fernandez, P. Fusar-Poli, A. Raballo, & R. Rosfort (Eds.), *The Oxford handbook of phenomenological psychopathology*(pp. 665–681).Oxford, UK: Oxford University Press.

Stelter, R. (2018). *The art of dialogue in coaching: Towards transformative exchange.* London, UK: Routledge.

Substance Abuse and Mental Health Services Administration. (2005). *National Consensus conference on mental health recovery and systems transformation.* Rockville, MD: Department of Health and Human Services.

Tondora, J., & Davidson, L. (2006). *Practice guidelines for recovery-oriented behavioral health care.* Connecticut: Connecticut Department of Mental Health and Addiction Services.

Vaughan-Smith, J. (2019). *Coaching and trauma: From surviving to thriving.* London, UK: Open University Press.

Watts, M., & Higgins, A. (2017). *Narratives of recovery from mental illness: The role of peer support.* London, UK; Routledge.

Welman, P., & Bachkirova, T. (2010). Power in the coaching relationship. In S. Palmer, & A. McDowall (Eds.), *The coaching relationship: Putting people first* (pp. 139–158). London, UK: Routledge.

Western, S. (2012). *Coaching and mentoring: A critical text.* London, UK: Sage.

Western, S. (2019). *Leadership: A critical text* (3rd ed.). London, UK: Sage.

Whittington, J. (2020). *Systemic coaching & constellations: The principles, practices and application for individuals, teams and groups* (3rd ed.). London, UK: KoganPage.

Wilson, K. G., Sandoz, E. K., Kitchens, J., & Roberts, M. E. (2010). The valued living questionnaire: Defining and measuring valued action within a behavioural framework. *The Psychological Record, 60,* 249–272.

World Health Organisation. (1993). *The ICD-10 classification of mental and behavioural disorders: diagnostic criteria for research* (vol. 2). Geneva: World Health Organisation.

Zanarini, M. C. (2008). Reasons for change in borderline personality disorder (and other axis 11 disorders). *Psychiatric Clinics of North America, 31*(3), 505–515.

Zanarini, M. C. (2019). *In the fullness of time: Recovery from borderline personality disorder.* New York: Oxford University Press.

Chapter 7

Self-understanding of the coaching psychologist and ways of knowing about recovery

In this chapter, we explore perspectives on self-understanding and 'ways of knowing' that may assist the critical reflection of coaching psychologists interested in interacting with people with BPD, inclusive of critical reflection on assumptions about mental illness and what constitutes recovery. We strongly believe that coaches/coaching psychologists need to be informed not only about understanding mental ill health in terms of approaches to identifying and understanding mental illness (Cavanagh & Buckley, 2018) but also in terms of the philosophical worldviews and ways of knowing that profoundly influence practice. Frameworks and perspectives are presented under different headings and we hope that the order of presentation will read as a golden thread narrative that speaks to heart and mind. We will also try to situate our coaching practice in GLOW11 related to the frameworks presented.

Self-understanding and levels of coaching

Hawkins and Turner (2020) offer an integrative summary of the different levels of coaching based on a review of various coaching approaches and paradigm shifts:

Level 1:

Traditional individual centred coaching – 'attempts to objectively focus on enabling the individual or team as a separate entity to develop itself using tried and tested methods' (p. 27).

Level 2:

Relational, dialogic, and intersubjective coaching – 'recognises that the coach is an engaged partner in a collaborative inquiry with the coachee' (p. 27).

DOI: 10.4324/9781003048978-7

Level 3:

Systemic coaching – 'recognises that learning and development happens not inside the individual but in dynamic engagement with the wider systems they are part of and relate with; it reflects that we are part of communities and cultures that shape our language, ways of being, thinking and doing' (p. 27).

Level 4:

Eco-systemic and ecological coaching – Hawkins and Turner (2020) state that as yet there is very little written about this level and address it in their text.

On reflection, GLOW11 leaned towards a relational, dialogic and inter-subjective approach to coaching. Cavicchia and Gilbert (2019) refer to inter-subjectivity (a core element of the relational orientation in coaching) as the reciprocal process of influencing that occurs, moment by moment, in every relationship and conversation (citing Stolorow & Attwood, 1992), inclusive of the need to be able to hold different perspectives in mind simultaneously, with meaning arising in the process of relating. These authors describe a coaching scenario which reflects elements of the coaching dynamics experienced in GLOW11 – for example, that a coachee who is anxious facing into a significant challenge, in part by how she/he is making meaning about their situation and role in it, will be influenced not just by the coach's support in reframing the narrative at a cognitive level, 'but in large part by the coach's welcoming, calm, attuned, responsive and reflective manner' (p. 94). Equally, if the coach is prone to anxiety and moving quickly to finding solutions, the coachee may implicitly pick this up as a sign of danger, hinting that anxiety 'cannot be tolerated, contained and thought about, but has to be expelled into activity and finding a quick fix' (p. 94). There were no quick fixes in GLOW11, thankfully! GLOW11 also contained some elements of systemic coaching, at least in the sense of recognition that each participant interacted of necessity with for example, the mental health system, family of origin and/or current family, work, leisure activities, and finding a satisfactory balance between being solitary and being connected to community.

While participants in GLOW11 were cognisant to varying degrees of the impacts of globalisation and climate change in wider society, of more immediate impact was their own daily strivings, struggles and achievements of a very grounded, ordinary and personal dimension. This prompts a question as to how coaching can become something more than an organisational adjunct and have greater presence in communities, in particular among people who are most vulnerable to marginalisation, alienation and dislocation?

Much coaching theory is positioned in a postmodern context. Elliott (2020) in questioning the postmodern perspective regarding self, states that 'it is not hard to find in this whole discourse an academic distaste for ordinary human experience; and indeed, it is my view that such anti-self discourses are unlikely to speak directly to (or energize) contemporary women and men in their daily strivings and struggles in today's world' (p. 208).

Levels of self-understanding as a coach/coaching psychologist

Here we look at a chapter article by Bachkirova (2020) on the topic of understanding oneself as a coach, as a sounding board for critical self-reflection.

There are varying views about whether it is possible at all to engage in helpful reflection on understanding self. Holmes (2020) states that 'deprived of a mirroring, triangulating, a borrowed-brain other, self-knowledge is at best inherently elusive, at worst a narcissistic illusion' (p. 111). Frith (2012) advises that our access to the underlying processes involved in reflecting on and justifying our behaviour to others is quite limited and that our reports on our own intentions and the intentions of others can be quite inaccurate. In this context, Frith (2012) highlights the importance of metacognition as the cognitive process involved in thinking about thinking and that 'through discussions of our perceptual experiences with others, we can detect sensory signals more accurately, even in the absence of objective feedback' (p. 2213).

Bachkirova (2020) discusses the complexity involved in trying to define 'self,' mentioning a range of disciplines that grapple with this – philosophy, psychology, neuroscience, phenomenology, education, and others. She writes that her purpose is not to engage in a highly theoretical discussion about self and is motivated to try to arrive at an understanding that can be useful to coaching practitioners.

Bachkirova (2020) states that when thinking about the self, we ordinarily mean one of the following ways:

- 'How we experience things – a very unique first-person perspective, like a personal window on the world' (p. 1)
- 'How we act – what allows us to respond to challenges, make decisions and engage with things, supporting our sense of agency' (p. 1)
- 'How we describe ourselves – a narrative about oneself, the description of who we think we are, creating a sense of identity' (p. 1)

Bachkirova (2020) writes that the desire to understand oneself is an important prerequisite towards being a good professional coach. Self-appraisal is inherently a difficult undertaking. It can be helpful to at least have an awareness of the possibility if not the likelihood of self-deception. Bachkirova (2015) states that 'coaches themselves are not immune from self-deception and may be missing many signs of their own self-deception involved in self-evaluation and their actions in coaching practice' (p. 2) and that coaching supervision is one way to engage with the task.

Bachkirova (2020) makes a case for three levels of self-understanding for coaches, self-inventory, self as instrument and fully professional self. She adds that in recognising the complexity of our own nature, we need to become much more thoughtful and tentative regarding how we understand our clients' selves and to avoid imposing on clients' excessive expectations for an 'objective and accurate' evaluation of self (Bachkirova, 2020).

Level 1: Self-inventory

'...self-inventory as a level of self-understanding as a coach is important because it is necessary simply in order to identify oneself as a professional coach ... this level of self-understanding is a prerequisite for starting your practice' (p. 4).

Self-inventory requires an honest appraisal of one's professional capabilities, focusing on strengths, weaknesses and addressing the gaps, inclusive of considering whether one has the necessary knowledge and skills necessary for the work and how one's experience impacts on practice over time. Regular reviews of these elements are recommended inclusive of coaching supervision and continuing professional development (CPD). During one's training to become a coach and ongoing CPD, one may also become familiar with coaching tools and exercises that help to enhance psychological preferences, values, and attitudes relevant to coaching practice (Bachkirova, 2020).

Level 2: Self as an instrument

This level of self-understanding typically emerges as a coach becomes more experienced, along with a realisation that one is much more than just a 'bag of tools' however useful these may be.

Building effective relationships require the coach to be trustworthy in the eyes of clients and such relationship – building requires more than one's knowledge and skills as a coach. Coaching clients want to connect with a person, not just a coach in role, however professionally this is carried out. The 'coach as a main instrument of coaching' (Bachkirova, 2016) is inclusive of the coach's life experiences, current perspectives and feelings, all expressed in the 'right now' of coaching sessions, and not simply recalling the 'right thing to say.'

This level of self-understanding requires a significantly higher degree of self-awareness in that it implies a double focus by the coach during the session – paying a great deal of attention not only to the content of the client's story, what is happening to the client during coaching, but also to the client's internal states (their feelings, thoughts, and intuitions).

At this level, coaches feel more confident in bringing an appropriate level of self-disclosure (citing Jourard, 1971), rather than a compulsive 'sharing' of their experiences or a passive holding back of information in fear of interfering with the client's agenda. In this process, the coach is able to pay 'sufficient and non-judgmental attention to the impulse to share something personal with the client' (p. 5) taking account of the client's receptivity, timing, importance of the message intended, which is then regulated in terms of the form and length of sharing.

Seeing oneself as instrument of coaching also brings benefits to coaches, for example, enabling them to act in ways congruent to current thoughts, feelings and beliefs. Coaching becomes more liberating, involves less emotional labour and is less tiring. The process of seeing oneself as instrument of coaching usually begins from 'a genuine curiosity about oneself, not just strengths and weaknesses, but emotions, physical states and fleeting thoughts' (p. 6). Supervision also contributes to developing this level of self-understanding in terms of explicit work with the self-awareness of the coach.

Level 3: Fully professional self

This level of self-understanding 'implies a wider focus of attention expanding further from self-inventory and even the self as an instrument' (p. 6). At this level of self-understanding, the coach's focus of attention includes the unfolding of the client's story in the session, the coach's own internal states and processes, and the complex interaction of the many different relationships in the interdependent environment of which both client and coach are part (citing Stacey, 2003).

Coaching at this level of self-understanding involves having 'system intelligence' (citing Hamalainen and Saarinen 2008), understanding oneself as an intrinsic part of such systems and having awareness of the influence of the system on them and their influence on the system.

Bachkirova (2020) (citing Martela & Saarinen, 2013) adapted the elements of systems intelligence from a coaching perspective:

In the coaching session
- Awareness of the changing situation in the session that includes variation in states and actions of both client and coach and the session dynamics.
- Tuning into this dynamic by sharing observations and emotions to facilitate an intersubjective perception of the process.
- Agency as the ability to adapt and act in different situations in the coaching session.

Outside the coaching session
- Reflexivity as the ability to reflect on one's motives, behaviours, ways of thinking and values that influence coaching practice.

- Perspective-taking as the ability to adopt new perspectives and interpretations of coaching practice.
- Long-term systemic orientation as an ability to recognise and attend to the
cumulative and long-term effects of changes in the coaching profession.

All of these abilities need to be understood in the context of the wider influences
on coaches, for example, two dominant worldviews or ways of knowing that
co-exist – modernism and postmodernism. We refer to Bachkirova (2020) regarding this topic in the next section of this chapter within the broader context
of 'ways of knowing' and recovery in mental illness/BPD.

Influences of ways of knowing on self-understanding of coaches/coaching psychologists and their perspectives on recovery

In writing about the self-understanding of the coach Bachkirova (2020)
refers to the worldviews of modernism and postmodernism as ways of
knowing that influence self-understanding as a coach. The influence of
modernist and postmodernist worldviews and ways of knowing is also referred to by a number of authors and researchers in the context of mental
illness and recovery. In considering coaching with people with BPD and
indeed any form of significant mental distress, it is necessary to have an
awareness and understanding of the modernist and postmodernist worldviews, inclusive of critical reflection on assumptions about mental illness and
what constitutes recovery, as the stated aim of this chapter.

Bachkirova (2020) writes that self-understanding at the level of fully
professional self brings awareness of modernism and postmodernism as two
dominant worldviews of influence. Coaches influenced by the modernist
science-centred perspective will aspire that their coaching interventions be
evidence-based and supported by theories and knowledge from core disciplines, for example, psychology. Coaches influenced by the postmodern
perspective that views the world as socially constructed, aim for interventions that focus on meaning-making conversations (Bachkirova, 2020).
Bachkirova (2020) states that coaches with self-understanding at the level of
fully professional self will likely recognise that modernist and postmodernist
influences 'work at the same time and create various incompatible beliefs
about our practice ... for example, we, as coaches, believe in the unique self-
expression of individuals, but create uniform competences frameworks ...
we may hate hierarchies, but create categories of professionalism' (p. 7), for
example, master-coach (citing Bachkirova, 2017).

Bachkirova (2020) advocates philosophical pragmatism as a more appropriate philosophy of coaching (citing Bachkirova & Borrington, 2019). She
distinguishes pragmatism from modernism and postmodernism in the sense
that 'it avoids reducing strategic action to a single model and allows greater

flexibility for the role of the coach relevant to the task at hand' and 'is compatible with complexity theories and with an understanding of self as a network of different mini-selves' described in Bachkirova (2011). Bachkirova (2020) offers a helpful comparison framework regarding competent self (modernist), dialogic self (postmodernist), and pragmatic self (pragmatist).

Bachkirova (2020) advises that it is not possible to become fully independent from the discourses and ideas that influence coaches and that what is important is that one's awareness of these influences allows for more flexibility and space for manoeuvre in actions in the context of also contributing to the professional world as another complex and dynamic social system. She recommends that in order to develop the level of self-understanding of fully professional self, coaches need to invest in further education, or re-visit a wide range of theories and conceptual perspectives; develop a good level of criticality in relation to various influences (especially to the flood of popular ideas that might otherwise be taken on board without discernment (citing Bachkirova, Jackson, Gannon, Iordanou, & Myers, 2017); and learn to observe oneself in one's practice and actions in a similar way to observing others (Bachkirova, 2020).

Bachkirova (2020) concludes that the level of self-understanding of fully professional self 'depends nearly entirely on our reflexivity as a unique human capacity of paying attention to our own actions, thoughts, feelings and their effect in the interplay with the events in our environment' and that 'good supervision for this work is simply invaluable' (p. 9).

In the context of relating one's level of self-understanding as a coach to a consideration of engaging with mental illness and recovery, Bracken and Thomas (2013) situate mainstream psychiatry as essentially a modernist enterprise that is at odds with the type of medical engagement required by individuals in the mental health services system. Bracken and Thomas (2013) lay out in explicit language the modernist worldview which underpins the assessment, diagnosis and service delivery model that is still dominant in terms of people with a mental illness – the perspective that 'mental problems can be scientifically investigated and modelled. They can be measured and counted. Experts exist who can organise treatments and interventions. Progress is to be understood in terms of new scientific discoveries in neuroscience, psychology, or psychopharmacology. Such discoveries happen in university departments and research laboratories' (p. 124).

One of the primary reasons for our including a chapter devoted to self-understanding and ways of knowing is to highlight that coaching/coaching psychology may, knowingly or unknowingly adopt the dominant modernist worldview and way of knowing with regard to mental illness and to individuals encountered in coaching who are experiencing significant emotional distress. Self-awareness about one's philosophical worldview is important. In such a scenario, it may be appropriate that a referral be made to counselling or psychotherapy when one is assured that the professional concerned has relevant experience, expertise and capabilities, rather than making a referral based on unexamined assumptions. A key question to ask in such a scenario may be 'is my coaching in the best interest of the coachee?' (Cavanagh & Buckley, 2018, p. 462). In this context, Cavanagh and Buckley (2018) make the important points that for the coach, understanding when not to coach is a vital skill (just as understanding when one might coach is an important skill) and that just as it is important for a coach to be aware of the categorical approach to diagnosis (e.g. ICD-10, 2010; DSM-5, 2013), a psychosocial understanding of mental health is especially important. Obviously, GLOW11 happened in a post-diagnosis context and in a post-DBT context. However, now that GLOW11 has happened, we believe it is timely to continue with and broaden the conversation within coaching/coaching psychology to be cognisant of the different worldviews and ways of knowing as they pertain to the mental health service system and recovery. This should be inclusive of the elements of systemic intelligence referred to by Bachkirova (2020) above, for example, reflexivity as the ability to reflect on one's motives, behaviours, ways of thinking and values that influence coaching practice; perspective-taking as the ability to adopt new perspectives and interpretations of coaching practice; and a long-term systemic orientation as an ability to recognise and attend to the cumulative and long-term effects of changes in the coaching profession.

The worldviews and ways of knowing that influence the different professional disciplines involved in mental health systems are not simply de-contextualized matters. Ways of knowing (e.g. modernist, postmodernist, pragmatic, etc.) significantly impact on professional theorising and practice and consequently on the lives of individuals seeking support. In this context, Jackson (2019) writes that 'our understanding of mental illness is informed by different disciplinary practices and attitudes. General social attitudes, while not necessarily held by a mentally ill individual, still directly affect their day-to-day life in trying to navigate and understand their lives' (p. 989). Importantly, Jackson (2019) concludes that individuals experiencing significant mental distress frequently face into 'a cacophony of different competing disciplinary approaches to mental health' (p. 989) and in trying to navigate their own care and self-knowledge can become 'epistemically adrift,' in the sense that too many interdisciplinary disagreements about the nature and existence of mental illness prevents those living with it be able to determine how to live flourishing lives.

Similar to the view of Bracken and Thomas (2013) that situates mainstream psychiatry as a modernist enterprise, Jackson (2019) describes DSM-5 as existing in the form of a long, general laundry list of mental health conditions, disorders and states, because of conflicting ideas about the nature of mental illness. Jackson (2019) states that instead of engaging directly with individuals themselves and their valid subjective experience, professionals are frequently more concerned with filling out checklists. He cites Potter (2016) writing that 'the DSM works together with other epistemic practices that constrict many clinicians' access to knowing well. Thus, clinicians shape themselves into, and are shaped into, a privileged way of knowing that elides many crucial factors that influence the experiences and needs of the person in front of them' (p. 160).

While the context here is that of the existing dominant practice within mental health service delivery systems and has specific reference to the practices of psychiatry, we refer to it here simply to highlight that different worldviews and ways of knowing are both pervasive and widely influential across and within many other professions and disciplines. Coaching/ coaching psychology is not immune from these influences and it is important to at least be aware of which worldviews and ways of knowing one is working from. Critical reflection matters in this regard because we are in the privileged if at times risky position of making decisions that significantly affect the lives of others, for example, whether to coach or not to coach a person who is experiencing significant mental distress.

In conclusion here, it is interesting to examine the comparison framework above (Bachkirova, 2020) from the perspective of GLOW11. Our overview is that the work of coaching psychologists in GLOW11 hovered primarily between dialogic self (postmodernist) and pragmatic self (pragmatist). The reader may discern differently! Assuming that a basic competency in coaching already existed, the role of coaching psychologists in GLOW11 varied between partnership in dialogue and co-experimenting, with working via values intrinsic to the coaching conversation and allowing space for experimenting as regards how different participants wished to proceed (e.g. towards actions/ behaviours in relationships that were more congruent with chosen values or opting for a more broadly based sense of life direction and purpose informed by values). The actions identified by participants, while committed to in sessions, invariably did not lead to a resolution, in the main due to the complexity of individuals' relational lives (e.g. concerning family of origin and experiences of trauma; employment relationships and trying to manage emotions). Key to the experience, process, and psychological flexibility of GLOW11 was the work on self-knowing that each coaching psychologist was already engaged in and which continued throughout GLOW11, inclusive of peer supervision. In this context, we agree with Western (2012) that 'a coach who hasn't done the work on themselves, cannot do the work on others. Self-knowing is about personal insight and also relational insight (i.e. how you relate to others and how they relate to you' (p. 270).

Epistemological basis of mental health services and implications for recovery practice

The primary source here regarding the epistemological basis of personal recovery is Slade (2012) who makes a central distinction between personal recovery and clinical recovery, with clinical recovery focused on symptom remission and relatively independent functioning and personal recovery as 'a deeply personal, unique process of changing one's attitudes, values, feelings, goals, skills, and/or roles. It is a way of living a satisfying, hopeful and contributing life even within the limitations caused by illness' (citing Anthony, 1993).

Epistemology is the aspect of philosophy that relates to knowledge and belief, 'including the nature of knowledge itself, how it is obtained, what people know, and how knowledge relates to related concepts such as truth and belief' (Slade, 2012, p. 78). Slade (2012) makes a distinction between nomothetic and idiographic knowledge. Nomothetic knowledge is concerned with a tendency to generalise, with the study of groups which represent populations and typically using quantitative methodologies (Slade, 2012). Idiographic knowledge, in contrast, in concerned with the study of the subjective experiences of individuals and what sets them apart from other individuals, typically using qualitative methodologies (Slade, 2012). Research based on the development of nomothetic knowledge involves a type of reductionism – 'squeezing all the subjectivity or meaning or perspective out of a situation, so that the truth can be revealed' (Slade, 2012, p. 79). Slade (2012) writes that reductionism in the natural sciences is an advantage, allowing reproducibility of a theory through experimentation. Slade (2012) then states that the nomothetic worldview 'is the cultural and scientific context in which clinical research has developed and accounts for why evidence from the randomised controlled trial has become dominant' (p. 79) (the evidence-based medicine movement). He adds that randomised controlled trials as the gold standard of research methodology undoubtedly has benefits, for example, that poorly controlled or uncontrolled studies are given less weight (Slade, 2012). However, Slade (2012) asks 'how applicable to mental illness are scientific methods based on Enlightenment principles?' (p. 80) (nomothetic knowledge) and asserts that the starting point for understanding mental illness is or should be the experience of the individual concerned and that 'the *emphasis* in understanding mental illness should be on the subjective experience' (p. 80).

Consequently, Slade (2012) states that the primary challenge for any science of mental illness is to accommodate knowledge from both observation and the individual's subjective experience, but that such an integration has been problematic because two broad and opposing philosophies have dominated thinking. These philosophies are idealism (subjectivism) and objectivism. Subjectivism holds that the existence of any object is dependent on a person's subjective awareness of it and this implies that in a clinical context, if clinical insights are no more than perceptions 'and therefore of no greater intrinsic worth than the patient's perception, what is the justification for perception – independent labelling of experiences such as "paranoia" and "hallucinations"?' (Slade, 2012, p. 81). On the other hand, objectivism (the end point of an emphasis on observable reality) holds that there is a mind-independent reality, contactable through sensory perception 'and that objective knowledge is obtained from this perception by measurement' (p. 81). Slade (2012) concludes here that in terms of mental illness, the problem with a purely objectivist approach (allied to descriptive taxonomies) is that the person can become an object of enquiry, a case rather than a person.

The current position in mental illness research and practice is that the science of mental illness remains slanted towards the objectivist position; clinical guidelines and research are focused on diagnostic groups; evidence-based practice uses nomothetic knowledge developed using RCT methodology; and interventions are evaluated with the purpose of identifying generalisable rules expressed as NNT (numbers-needed-to-treat) statistics (Slade, 2012).

So, what is the issue here? Slade (2012) states that the central problem is that nomothetic knowledge only provides half the story, because mental illness research is a human science, not just a natural science and the mental health system values nomothetic knowledge more than idiographic knowledge.

Because there is a fundamental tension between nomothetic and idiographic knowledge, which ultimately impacts negatively on individuals with a diagnosed mental illness, Slade (2012) outlines this tension in relation to mental health professionals, science, and people who access mental health services.

Mental health professionals
(i) Emphasising nomothetic knowledge results in the job of mental health professionals being understood in terms of 'technical rationality' (citing Schon, 1987, pp. 3–4) – 'Technical rationality holds that practitioners are instrumental problem solvers who select technical means best suited to particular purposes. Rigorous professional practitioners solve well-formed instrumental problems by applying theory and technique derived from systematic scientific knowledge.'
(ii) Technical rationality is an inadequate approach for addressing human problems (citing Schon, 1983, p. 49). 'If the model of Technical Rationality is incomplete, in that it fails to account for practical competence in 'divergent' situations, so much the worse for the model. Let us search instead for an epistemology of practice implicit in the artistic, intuitive processes which some practitioners do bring to situations of uncertainty, instability, uniqueness, and value conflict.' Slade (2012) also cites Grimmett and Erikson (1988, p. 25) who refer to 'the unmindful aping of natural science paradigms in the social sciences (sometimes referred to as scientism) that seems so pervasive in the professional schools of universities.'

Science
  (i) Giving primacy to nomothetic knowledge impoverishes scientific discourse.
 (ii) Assumptions about what really matters in the course of investigating the experience of recovery, for example Leamy, Bird, Le Boutillier, Williams, and Slade (2011) in a systematic review identified 97 published descriptions and models of personal recovery and narrative synthesis, used to develop a conceptual framework for personal recovery. Characteristics (e.g. recovery is gradual, non-linear, a struggle, and multidimensional) and stages in the recovery journey were identified, in addition to five key Recovery Processes (connectedness; hope and optimism; identity; meaning and purpose; and empowerment).
(iii) Two key points emerge from this research: firstly, personal recovery is very different from clinical preoccupations with symptom reduction, risk management and crisis containment; secondly, personal recovery is positive and forward looking, not all about getting rid of symptoms or social disability (approach rather than avoidance motivation) and points to a completely different way of envisaging the job of mental health professionals.

People who access mental health services
  (i) Individuals who use services give primacy to idiographic knowledge. They have detailed self-knowledge about what makes them the person who they are and the emphasis on group membership (e.g. diagnostic categories) over individual difference, implicit in nomothetic knowledge, does not value this self-knowledge.
 (ii) While evidence-based medicine approaches can incorporate values like autonomy and self-determination, the orientation is around evidence rather than values.
(iii) There is a close association between nomothetic knowledge and clinical practice, with some people experiencing services as aversive and unhelpful, and consequently reject the evidence base that underpins the service (Slade, 2012).

Slade (2012) is not arguing for abandonment of nomothetic knowledge, but is arguing that 'we can and must do better than simply relying on clinical anecdote (in which care depends on the intuition of the clinician), historical precedent (since the treatment of mental illness has not been an auspicious success), or even consumer demand – the person is seeking help precisely because they are stuck and do not know the way forward' (p. 87). Bracken and Thomas (2005) echo this perspective, arguing that the theories and models created by professionals, and defended by them, are the means through which the experiences of people experiencing mental distress are structured. They add that the 'way in which we have come to discuss our states of distress and alienation through a language of psychology, psychiatry and therapy is not neutral but based on certain values, assumptions and priorities' (p. 105). If coaching/coaching psychology wishes to enter and be of service to individuals experiencing mental distress/BPD, it is incumbent that we at least critically reflect on how our language and discourses reflect our values, assumptions, and priorities. More broadly, does coaching/coaching psychology thinking and practice about people experiencing significant mental distress (mental illness) lean more towards nomothetic or towards idiographic knowledge as a primary orientation point?

Epistemological and personal recovery

Personal recovery addresses the epistemological challenges just outlined, in that it puts value on nomothetic data and on idiographic knowledge (the subjective experience that only the person concerned can access (Slade, 2012). While both types of knowledge are necessary types of evidence, with each telling us something valid and meaningful in a balanced perspective of the world, Slade (2012) proposes constructivism as a more helpful epistemological basis. A key assumption underpinning constructivism is that everyone and everything is connected and that an 'emphasis on intrapsychic and interpersonal process, and the dynamic, changing nature of development, provides a more helpful model of self when applied to mental illness' (p. 89)...opening up 'the possibility of adaptation, reorientation, integration, and the other responses to the experience by the individual' (p. 89). Slade (2012) makes the following important points regarding the value of constructivism as a knowledge basis for supporting people with a mental illness:

(i) It recognises the dynamic nature of social role negotiation – 'if everyone treats the person as being mentally ill, this inexorably influences the self-image of that individual, just as the behaviour of the person influences how others respond to them' and 'in particular, the *way* that mental health staff work with people in the 'patient' role may be as important as *what* they do' (p. 89).

(ii) Mental health professionals 'who are insensitive to the negotiated nature of knowledge inadvertently hinder the development of a coherent personal narrative – my story of how I came to be and what my future may hold' (p. 90).

(iii) In clinical interactions, 'engagement as partners is only possible when there are two experts in the room – the clinician who has expertise in translating nomothetic knowledge, and the service user who has expertise in assessing that fit with their idiographic knowledge' (p. 90). Slade (2012) states that all clinicians have this interpersonal skill, however development of these skills is frequently not a focus of professional training.

(iv) Slade (2012) advocates for 'the need for philosophical training to be more present in professional training courses, to equip clinicians with the skills to recognise the limits of their own world view as a necessary prerequisite for fostering partnership relationships' (p. 90) and that 'this goes beyond interpersonal skills training, and involves supporting the development of specific personal values in the clinician...' (p. 90).

(v) A constructivist epistemology emphasises the importance of both professional knowledge and the self-knowledge of the person concerned. Therefore, the role of the professional is significantly more than a technical role implementing treatments defined by clinical guidelines – it is to be 'an active and influential person working in partnership with the consumer, bringing nomothetic expertise-by-training to complement the person's idiographic expertise-by-experience' (citing Slade, 2009).

Slade (2012) concludes by saying that the critical advantage offered by a constructivist perspective is its focus on utility. The question is asked, does the clinical model being used help the person concerned? If the clinical model does not help the person, then the model needs to be changed, as opposed to trying to change the person! (Slade, 2012). We argue that this perspective resonates with Bachkirova (2020) pragmatic level of self-understanding as a coach's ability to create a rationale of their approach to practice, 'their individual model of coaching as a unique professional offer to their clients' (p. 8), requiring 'a sophisticated analysis of their knowledge, skills, their own values and principles examined through the lens of a good number of theories and perspectives that have been influencing their view on human nature, change and development' (p. 8).

In a similar vein to Slade (2012), Bracken et al. (2012) highlight that a move away from a technological paradigm strongly resonates with critical insights from the recovery approach to mental healthcare (citing Slade, 2009), adding that 'a therapeutic context that promotes empowerment and connectedness and helps rebuild a positive self-identity is of great significance' (p. 432; citing Mancini, Hardiman, & Lawson, 2005; Tew et al., 2012). Bracken et al. (2012) stress that they are not trying to replace one paradigm with another and that 'a post-technological psychiatry will not abandon the tools of empirical science or reject medical and psychotherapeutic techniques but will start to position the ethical and hermeneutic aspects of our work as primary, thereby highlighting the importance of examining values, relationships, politics and the ethical basis of care and caring' (p. 432). Bracken and Thomas (2013) state that while many individuals using mental health services do have concerns about the system, some are satisfied to define themselves and their difficulties through the concepts given to them by psychiatry. However, they also highlight that while there is a wide variety of opinions within the recovery movement, they are broadly united by the rejection of the technological framework and how mental health problems are defined in it through an expert vocabulary and logic.

Bracken and Thomas (2013) highlight how personal accounts of recovery from serious mental health problems moves the discussion away from a medical and technical focus on issues such as assessment, diagnosis, classification, prognosis, and treatment to the importance of discussion on the central importance of the non-technical, non-specific aspects of care, prioritising questions such as: how hope is generated and sustained; how dignity can be maintained even in the midst of crisis; and how a sense of personal empowerment is frequently the driving force behind a person's journey towards mental health. They cite consumer-led research exploring what people wanted from mental health services, prioritised as:

- Acceptance
- Shared experience and shared identity (e.g. meeting with others who have had similar experiences).
- Emotional support
- A reason for living
- Finding meaning and purpose in life
- Peace of mind, relaxation (Faulkner & Lazyell, 2000).

The issues that mattered most to GLOW11 participants closely mirror with these priorities. Also, the opportunities for participants to meet with others diagnosed with BPD was an invaluable element of the process.

Hope

Hope has been identified as a critical element in personal recovery (Bracken & Thomas, 2005; Andresen, Oades, & Caputi, 2011; Schrank, Hayward, Stanghellini, & Davidson, 2011; Slade, 2009; Watts & Higgins, 2017). There are many perspectives on the meaning of hope. The poet, Emily Dickinson wrote: 'Hope is the thing with feathers, that perches in the soul, and sings the tune without words, and never stops at all...' Eagleton (2015) writes that for there to be genuine hope, 'the future must be anchored in the present. It cannot simply irrupt into it from some metaphysical outer space... A future that could be adequately captured in the language of the present would be too complicit with the status quo, and so would scarcely count as a genuine future at all' (p. 38). In the context of mental health and recovery, Schrank, Stanghellini, and Slade (2008) define hope as a mainly future-orientated expectation that one will attain personally valued goals that will give or restore meaning to one's experiences.

Andresen, Pades, and Caputi (2003) state that the importance of hope is pervasive in the self-narrative literature on recovery. In a context of personal recovery, Deegan (1995) states that 'hope is not just a nice sounding euphemism, it is a matter of life and death' (p. 3). In the context of people with BPD, Livesley (2017) writes that while discontent is a powerful motivator for change, it is often not sufficient – 'it is also necessary to build the hope that change is possible' (p. 127). Andresen et al. (2011) write that 'if hopelessness is a cause of chronicity, then hope has been identified as both the catalyst and the linchpin of recovery' (p. 67). Watts and Higgins (2017) describe hope as the emotional essence of recovery, referring to 'the centrality of people having a belief in themselves and a belief that they can and will overcome obstacles, as well as other people believing in their recovery potential' (p. 21). Rosfort (2019) writes that our ideas about a good life have significant impact on our mental health and 'our hope for the good life can help us through disturbances of our mental health and alleviate our mental suffering' (p. 976).

Slade (2009) writes however, that hope is a problem in mental health services. While the rhetoric is clear that mental health services should work in ways that foster hope, the reality for many people is quite the opposite and the possibility of a good future is all too infrequently communicated by mental health professionals (Slade, 2009). Lack of hope has toxic consequences and 'a focus on clinical recovery, with its emphasis on engendering realistic (e.g. low) expectations, can destroy hope' (Slade, 2009, p. 41). Watts and Higgins (2017), citing Stuart (2010), state that despite the centrality of hope to recovery, it is 'the most absent ingredient in contemporary mental health care' (p. 361). Hobbs and Baker (2012), citing Turner-Crowson and Wallcraft (2002) refer to 'the devastating effects of having been told by mental health professionals that prospects for recovery were slim or even non-existent' (p. 246). Davidson (2011) refers to an individual who experienced significant improvements in his mental health, who when asked what he found was the most helpful element of the therapeutic work said 'you believed in me, even when I didn't believe in myself' (p. 232). Davidson (2011) comments that he has heard a similar response from many individuals who describe it as one of the foundations of their recovery. We heard similar comments from participants in GLOW11. The coming into being and awareness of hope may take time. Watts and Higgins (2017) write that it 'takes time for deeply felt physical sensations, such as terror or hope, which are spontaneous responses to the behaviour of other people, to be translated into meaningful thoughts which can then direct behaviour' (p. 76).

Schrank et al., 2011 asks a question about the evidence to support a pivotal role for hope in recovery? He refers to Snyder's hope theory being used to guide interventions aimed at enhancing hope, describing it as a highly linear understanding of the therapeutic benefits of hope, with clearly defined stages, pathways and goals (Schrank et al 2011). Schrank et al. (2011) states that the resulting interventions can be, in principle, applicable to every person, and, importantly, measurable. However, Schrank et al. (2011) also refers to another story about hope – that engaging qualitatively with the narratives of individuals 'enables us to respect the differences between people's definition of hope, their respective emphasis on process and goal, and their temporal and cultural orientation to these' (p. 230).

Hope is different to optimism (Slade, 2009). Slade (2009) writes that hope 'involves not only positive expectancies and specific goals of agency, but also the flexibility to respond to obstacles by changing goals or methods' (p. 129) and 'people with high hope are more likely to have positive expectations that they can cope with future adversity (citing Snyder, Feldman, Taylor, Schroeder, & Adams, 2000), and indeed hopefulness moderates the relationship between unanticipated stressors and successful coping (citing Snyder and Pulvers, 2001). Eagleton (2015) writes that optimism is 'based on an opinion that things tend to work out well, not on the strenuous commitment that hope involves' (p. 1) and that authentic hope needs to be underpinned by reasons – 'it must be able to pick out the features of a situation that render it credible, otherwise it is just a gut feeling' ... 'hope must be fallible, as temperamental cheerfulness is not' (p. 3).

The professional relationship as a source of hope in personal recovery and implications for coaching/coaching psychology

Slade (2009) emphasises the importance of promoting hope through the professional relationship with individuals as one context in which hope can grow. Slade (2009) also stresses that the relationship itself can be insufficient and that action is required (for example, recovery goals as an individual's aspirations and dreams, influenced by personality and values, that are unique and often idiosyncratic, are forward-looking, create approach rather than avoidance motivation, are strengths-based and oriented towards reinforcing positive identity and developing valued social roles). In the context of the professional relationship, Slade (2009) strongly advocates for a partnership relationship, where there is a welcoming attitude to the individual with listening to understand what the person wants, where the person is the ultimate decision-maker (other than where legal issues over-ride) and the professional's basic orientation 'is towards actively seeking to be led by the individual and their own wishes, goals, and dreams (citing Bracken & Thomas, 2005). Slade (2009) states that a partnership relationship will involve a professional acting in accordance with three key principles:

(i) **The experience of mental illness is normally meaningful** – meaninglessness enhances stigma and alienation, the sense of being 'other'; an expectation of meaningfulness will lead the professional to look for meaning.

(ii) **A clinical model provides one of many ways to make sense of experience** – human experience cannot be grasped using a technical idiom; the claims of any theory as universally valid or foundational is rejected; a partnership relationship requires that the professional is modest in relation to the universality of their own theory; the person's experience of being treated with respect and involved in decision-making is more predictive of good outcomes than mental health professionals' ratings.

(iii) **Only the individual can define their own interests** – expertise-by-experience is strongly valued in a partnership relationship as it comes closest to the essence of mental illness, subjective experience. 'What the person says may of course not accurately reflect their inner world: the experiences may not be expressible in words; they may not yet have processed the experiences sufficiently to be able to reflect on and describe them; or they may not trust the person asking them. But what people say, or otherwise communicate such as through art or poems, provides the best available approximation to their inner world. Lived experience is necessary because individuals with mental illness, just like individuals without a mental illness, are the experts on the topic of their own experiences, needs, and preferences, and consequently are best able to identify what would be helpful, or not, in promoting their own recovery (citing Davidson et al., 2005).

In fulfilling a professional relationship founded on a partnership approach, Slade (2009) highlights the advantages of a coaching approach:

(a) 'It assumes the person is or will be competent to manage their life. The capacity for personal responsibility is a given' (p. 123).

(b) 'The focus is on facilitating the process of recovery to happen, rather than on the person. Coaching is about how the person can live with mental illness, and differs from a clinical focus on treating the mental illness' (p. 123).

(c) 'The role of the coach is to enable this self-righting capacity to become active, rather than to fix the problem. This leads to amplification of strengths and natural supports, rather than of deficits' (p. 123).

(d) Effort in the coaching relationship is directed towards the goals of the coachee, not the coach. The skills of the coach are a resource to be offered. Using these skills is *not* an end in itself' (p. 123).

(e) Both participants must make an active contribution for the relationship to work' (p. 123).

In keeping with the purpose of this particular chapter on the self-understanding of the coaching psychologist and reflecting on ways of knowing about recovery, Slade (2009) states that 'the uncomfortable reality is that working to promote recovery will often require professionals to reflect on their own values, boundaries and beliefs' (p. 123). In the context of therapy with individuals with BPD (and we suggest also applicable to coaching with individuals with BPD), Linehan (2020) asserts that 'the therapist has to accept the client – this means not just accepting but radically accepting. Accepting the client has to come from the depths of the therapist's soul. That isn't always easy' (p. 251). Hope is a two-way street in the helping relationship. Reflection on values and beliefs needs to include one's disposition regarding hopefulness, in particular in the act of engaging with the individual concerned. Do I convey an attitude of authentic hopefulness? Am I overly optimistic and prone to feelings of defeat when faced with challenges or thoughts of everything will work out no matter what? Can I work with a person who seems to veer from hope to hopelessness and back again as a recurring pattern? Do I coach from who I am?

Discussion points

1. Using the framework by Hawkins and Turner (2020) as a guide, have you a personal model of coaching and an underpinning knowledge base?
2. Is there something that triggers anxiety in you when coaching that you have never seriously addressed?
3. On the basis that the desire to understand oneself is an important prerequisite toward being a good professional coach, how much time do you give to this topic in your professional supervision?
4. What do you know about the epistemological basis underpinning mental health services and implications for mental health practice?

Suggested reading

Bachkirova, T. (2020, in press). Understanding yourself as a coach (Chap 4), In J. Passmore (Ed.). *The coaches handbook*: *The complete practitioner's guide for professional coaches*(1st ed.). London, UK: Routledge. (This chapter provides a very comprehensive and challenging argument about the importance of understanding oneself as a coach and implications for practice).

Cavicchia, S., & Gilbert, M. (2019). *Thetheory and practice of relational coaching*: *Complexity, paradox and integration*. London, UK: Routledge. (Chapters 6 and 7 have an excellent overview of understanding relational dynamics from a developmental perspective and co-creating the coaching relationship. pp. 93–123).

Hawkins, P., & Turner, E. (2020). *Systemic coaching: Delivering value beyond the individual*. London, UK: Routledge. (While the book itself is recommended reading, chapters 1, 2 and 3 are particularly important as regards the need for a new approach to coaching and related issues).

Jackson, J. (2019). Phenomenological psychopathology and America's social lifeworld. In G. Stanghellini, M. R. Broome, A. V. Fernandez, P. Fusar-Poli, A. Raballo, & R. Rosfort (Eds.), *The Oxford handbook of phenomenological psychopathology* (pp. 987–1003). Oxford, UK: Oxford University Press. (While primarily addressing important issues in psychiatric practice, this chapter is recommended because its underlying thesis that psychiatry and mental illness do not exist in a vacuum, but in a complicated world, is also highly relevant to thinking about coaching psychology).

Linehan, M. M. (2020). *Building a life worth living: A* memoir. New York: Random House. (An excellent and indeed inspiring book, both personally and professionally, by the developer of Dialectical Behaviour Therapy).

Slade, M. (2012). The epistemological basis of personal recovery. In A. Rudnick (Ed.), *Recovery of people with mental illness: Philosophical and related perspectives* (pp. 78–94). Oxford, UK: Oxford University press. (Provides an excellent overview of the epistemological basis of the mental health services system and implications for recovery practice).

References

Andresen, R., Oades, L. G., & Caputi, P. (2011). *Psychological recovery: Beyond mental illness*. Chichester, UK: Wiley-Blackwell.

Andresen, R., Pades, L. G., & Caputi, P. (2003). The experience of recovery from schizophrenia: Towards an empirically validated stage model. *Australian and New Zealand Journal of Psychiatry, 37*, 586–594.

Anthony, W. A. (1993). Recovery from mental illness: The guiding vision of the mental health system in the 1990's. *Innovations and Research, 2*, 17–24.

Bachkirova, T. (2011). *Developmental coaching: Working with the self*. Maidenhead, UK: Open University Press.

Bachkirova, T. (2015). Self-deception in coaches: An issue in principle and a challenge for supervision. *Coaching: An International Journal of Theory, Research and Practice.* http://dx.doi.org/10.1080/17521882.2014.998692

Bachkirova, T. (2016). The self of the coach: Conceptualisation, issues, and opportunities for practitioner development. *Consulting Psychology Journal: Practice and Research, 68*(2), 143–156.

Bachkirova, T. (2017). Developing a knowledge base of coaching: Questions to explore. In T. Bachkirova, G. Spence, & D. Drake (Eds.), *The Sage handbook of coaching* (pp. 23–41). London, UK: Sage.

Bachkirova, T. (2020, in press). Understanding yourself as a coach (Chap 4). In J. Passmore (Ed.), *The* (1st ed.). London, UK: Routledge.

Bachkirova, T., & Borrington, S. (2019). Old wine in new bottles: Exploring pragmatism as a philosophical framework for the discipline of coaching. *Academy of Management Learning and Education, 18*(3), 337–360.

Bachkirova, T., Jackson, P., Gannon, J., Iordanou, I., and Myers, A. (2017). Reconceptualizing coach education from the perspectives of pragmatism and constructivism. *Philosophy of Coaching: An International Journal, 2*(2), 29–50.

Bracken, P., & Thomas, P. (2005). *Postpsychiatry: Mental health in a postmodern world*. Oxford, UK: Oxford University Press.

Bracken, P., & Thomas, P. (2013). Challenges to the modernist identity of psychiatry: User empowerment and recovery. In K. W. M. Fulford, M. Davies, R. G. T. Gipps, G. Graham, J. Z. Sadler, G., Stanghellini, & T. Thornton. *The Oxford handbook of philosophy and psychiatry*. Oxford, UK: Oxford University Press.

Bracken, P., Thomas, P., Timimi, S., Asen, E., Behr, G., Beuster, C., ...Yeomans, D. (2012). Psychiatry beyond the current paradigm. *The British Journal of Psychiatry, 201*, 430–434.

Cavanagh, M., & Buckley, A. (2018). Coaching and mental health. In E. Cox, T. Bachkirova, & D. Clutterbuck (Eds.), *The complete handbook of coaching* (3rd ed., pp. 450–464). London, UK: Sage.

Cavicchia, S., & Gilbert, M. (2019). *The theory and practice of relational coaching: Complexity, paradox and integration.* London, UK: Routledge.

Davidson, L., Sells, D., Sangster, S., & O' Connell, M. (2005). Qualitative studies of recovery what can we learn from the person? In R. O. Ralph, & P. W. Corrigan (Eds.), *Recovery in mental illness. Broadening our understanding of wellness* (pp. 147–170). Washington, DC: American Psychological Association

Deegan, P. (1995). Coping with recovery as a journey of the heart. *Psychiatric Rehabilitation Journal, 19,* 91–97.

Dickinson, E. (2019). *Hope is the thing with feathers: The complete poems of Emily Dickinson.* USA: Gibbs Smith.

DSM-5 (2013). *American psychiatric association. Diagnostic and statistical manual of mental disorders.* American Psychiatric Pub.

Eagleton, T. (2015). *Hope without optimism.* London, UK: Yale University Press.

Elliott, A. (2020). *Concepts of the self* (4th ed.), Cambridge, UK: Polity Press.

Faulkner, A., & Lazyell, S. (2000). *Strategies for living: A report of user-led research into people's strategies for living with mental distress.* London, UK: Mental Health Foundation.

Frith, C. D. (2012). The role of metacognition in human social interactions. *Philosophical Transactions of the Royal Society B, 367,* 2213–2223.

Grimmett, P., & Erikson, G. (1988). *Reflection in teacher education.* New York: Teachers College Press.

Hamalainen, R. P., & Saarinen, E. (2008). Systems intelligence – the way forward? A not on Ackoff's why few organisations adopt systems thinking. *Systems Research and Behavioural Science, 24*(6), 821–825.

Hawkins, P., & Turner, E. (2020). *Systemic coaching: Delivering value beyond the individual.* London, UK: Routledge.

Hobbs, M., & Baker, M. (2012). Hope for recovery – how clinicians may facilitate this in their work. *Journal of Mental Health, 21*(2), 144–153.

Holmes, J. (2020). *The Brain has a mind of its own: Attachment, neurobiology, and the new science of psychotherapy.* London, UK: Confer Books.

Jackson, J. (2019). Phenomenological psychopathology and America's social life-world. In G. Stanghellini, M. R. Broome, A. V. Fernandez, P. Fusar-Poli, A. Raballo, & R. Rosfort (Eds.), *The Oxford handbook of phenomenological psychopathology.* Oxford, UK: Oxford University Press.

Jourard, S. (1971). *The transparent self.* Van Nostrand Reinhold Inc.

Leamy, M., Bird, V., Le Boutillier, C., Williams, J., & Slade, M. (2011). Conceptual framework for personal recovery in mental health: Systematic review and narrative synthesis. *The British Journal of Psychiatry, 199,* 445–452.

Linehan, M. (2020). *Building a life worth living: A memoir.* New York: Random House.

Livesley, W. J. (2017). *Integrated modular treatment for borderline personality disorder: A practical guide to combining effective treatment methods.* Cambridge, UK: Cambridge University Press.

Mancini, M. A., Hardiman, E. R., & Lawson, H. A. (2005). Making sense of it all: Consumer providers' theories about factors facilitating and impeding recovery from psychiatric disabilities. *Psychiatric Rehabilitation Journal, 29*, 48–55.

Martela, F., & Saarinen, E. (2013). The systems metaphor in therapy discourse: Introducing systems intelligence. *Psychoanalytic Dialogues: The International Journal of Relational Perspectives, 23*(1), 80–101.

Potter, N. N. (2016). *The virtue of defiance and psychiatric engagement.* Oxford, UK: Oxford University Press.

Rosfort, R. (2019). Phenomenological psychopathology and psychiatric ethics. In G. Stanghellini, M. R. Broome, A. V. Fernandez, P. Fusar-Poli, A. Rabalo, & R. Rosfort (Eds.), *The Oxford handbook of phenomenological psychopathology* (pp. 972–986). Oxford, UK: Oxford University Press.

Schon, D. (1983). *The reflective practitioner.* New York: Basic Books.

Schon, D. (1987). *Educating the reflective practitioner.* New York: Basic Books.

Schrank, B., Hayward, M., Stanghellini., G., & Davidson, L. (2011). Hope in psychiatry. *Advances in Psychiatric Treatment, 17*, 227–235.

Schrank, R., Stanghellini, G., & Slade, M. (2008). Hope in psychiatry: A review of the literature. *Acta Psychiatrica Scandinavica, 118*, 421–433.

Slade, M. (2009). *Personal recovery and mental illness: A guide for mental health professionals.* Cambridge, UK; Cambridge University Press.

Slade, M. (2012). The epistemological basis of personal recovery. In A. Rudnick (Ed.), *Recovery of people with mental illness: Philosophical and related perspectives* (pp. 78–94). Oxford, UK: Oxford University press.

Snyder, C. R., Feldman, D. B., Taylor, J. D., Schroeder, L. L., & Adams, V. (2000). The roles of helpful thinking in preventing problems and enhancing strengths. *Applied and Preventive Psychology, 15*, 262–295.

Snyder, C. R., & Pulvers, K. (2001). Dr. Seuss, the coping machine, and "Oh, the places you will go." In C. R. Snyder (Ed.), *Coping with stress: Effective people and places* (pp. 3–19). New York: Oxford University Press.

Stacey, R. D. (2003). *Complexity and group processes: A radically social understanding of individuals.* Hove, UK: Brunner-Routledge.

Stolorow, R., & Attwood, G. (1992). *Contexts of being – The intersubjective foundations of psychological life.* Hillsdale, NJ: Analytic Press.

Stuart, G. W. (2010). Mind to care and a future of hope. *Journal of the American Psychiatric Nurses Association, 16*, 360–365.

Tew, J., Ramon, S., Slade, M., Bird, V., Melton, J., & Le Boutillier, C. (2012). Social factors and recovery from mental health difficulties: A review of the evidence. *British Journal of Social Work, 42*, 443–460.

Turner-Crowson, J., & Wallcraft, J. (2002). The recovery vision for mental health services and research: A British perspective. *Psychiatric Rehabilitation Journal, 25*(3), 245–254.

Watts, M., & Higgins, A. (2017). *Narratives of recovery from mental illness: The role of peer support.* London, UK: Routledge.

Western, S. (2012). *Coaching and mentoring: A critical text.* London, UK: Sage.

World Health Organisation (WHO). (2010). *International classification of diseases* (ICD-10). Geneva: WHO.

Chapter 8

Education, training, and continuing professional development of coaching psychologists

In this chapter, we identify particular issues related to interaction with people with Borderline Personality Disorder (BPD) which we believe are important to consider in the context of the education, training, continuing professional development and supervision of coaches/coaching psychologists. In addition, we believe that the issues identified also transcend interaction with people with BPD only and apply to a wider consideration of coaching/coaching psychology at this time.

We do not intend to explore in any explicit detail the usual normative questions that arise regarding coaching psychology education and practice, for example, regulation, standards, accreditation/certification, qualifications, examinations, and quality assurance (O'Riordan & Palmer, 2019). We acknowledge the statement by Gannon and Myers (2018) that there is a scarcity of research regarding coach education, training and development and 'a very limited evidence base on the education, training and development choices coaches make...' (p. 479).

Coaching formation

It is challenging at this time to conceptualise how best to address the issue of coaching formation. We will attempt to create a cogent synthesis of elements from different perspectives on coach education and training that we believe offers a helpful context for critical reflection, in particular for coaches/coaching psychologists considering interaction with individuals with BPD. We believe that this attempted synthesis may also be of assistance to coaches-in-training, coaches-in-practice, and coaching educators. Our references place a strong emphasis on what we see as the importance of the development of the coaching practitioner as a person and a professional congruent with greater insight and understanding regarding the body of knowledge and theory or theories that inform practice. Without this development, insight and understanding or at least there being a genuine commitment towards, the risk of doing harm increases. We identify with the idea advocated by Western (2012) about 'communities of practice'

DOI: 10.4324/9781003048978-8

consisting of coaching practitioners, academics, trainers, coachees, and other coaching stakeholders coming together to formally and informally contribute to developing a coaching meta-theory. In particular, we view the 'community of practice' idea as being a potentially significant approach towards broadening out the space where the potential of coaching/coaching psychology to bring value to the lived experience of individuals with BPD (and other forms of significant mental distress) can be shared and discussed with the intention to formulate a coherent perspective. Based both on our experience of GLOW11 and the advent of new mental health challenges arising from COVID-19, we believe this to be an opportune time for such critical reflection and dialogue among coaching practitioners and other stakeholders.

Einzig (2017) states that all coaching training should include basic knowledge of psychological and personality disorders, along with familiarity with common diagnostic tools. This appears to be a more or less normative perspective with regards to how coaches/coaching psychologists should engage with people who are experiencing significant mental distress. However, Einzig (2017) also advocates that coaches/coaching psychologists need also to be asking particular questions of potential coachees, for example, how well is the person sleeping, questions about appetite, about what brings joy and pleasure, about relationships and sex, and about thoughts of suicide. Einzig (2017) writes that these are questions not asked by the majority of coaches. In this we agree with Einzig (2017) and in Chapter 5 we have outlined elements of our own coaching approach with GLOW11 participants, with a particular reference to the coaching process undertaken at an ecology centre with the whole group.

We have adopted the term 'coaching formation' from Western (2012) as it sits accurately with our sense of the importance of ongoing and applied learning from GLOW11. Western (2012) reframes coaching education, training and development as coaching formation, with an emphasis 'on life-long learning, learning through contexts and practice and from other coaches, and focuses on the coaches forming themselves, rather than becoming coaches through learning skills and techniques' (p. 264). We believe that an emphasis on coaches forming themselves rather than an over-emphasis on learning skills and techniques (coaching competencies) is both desirable and appropriate given that anecdotally at least, the majority of individuals who apply for admission to third-level coaching programmes have significant life and work experiences already and therefore should be presented with coaching education and training that is both supportive and personally challenging (Table 8.1).

In our opinion, the emphasis by Western (2012) on coaches forming themselves rather than over emphasis on coaching skills and techniques has echoes to the case made by Bachkirova and Lawton Smith (2015) for a capabilities rather than a competencies approach to the assessment of

Table 8.1 (Bachkirova & Lawton Smith, 2015, p. 132)

What coaching competencies imply	What coaching capabilities imply
A checklist approach that seeks to identify specific behaviours as indicators of professional practice.	A holistic process that can assess the relational factors that often determine coaching success.
A process that assesses past performance and from that infers future performance.	A way of evaluating meaning making of the hypothetical situations that the coach may face on the basis of learning.
A reductive process that seeks to simplify effective coaching into specific activities.	An expansive process that acknowledges the complexity of coaching and can give credit for the knowledge and understanding required to evaluate and respond to that complexity.
An assessment that focuses on explicit knowledge of the assessment criteria and the ability of the coach to demonstrate those competencies explicitly.	A way to expose the tacit knowledge that the coach holds that will be applied appropriately when relevant.
An individualistic process to assess a collaborative activity.	A systemic perspective that allows for contextual factors in the collaborative coaching process.
A system for evaluating only outputs from the coach as a 'black box.'	A system for evaluating the process taking place within the coach as an instrument of coaching.
The intention to seek universality.	The appreciation of diversity and uniqueness.

coaches, as more effectively reflecting the view of coaching/coaching psychology as a complex adaptive system. The implications arising are summarised by Bachkirova and Lawton Smith (2015) in the table.

Bachkirova and Lawton Smith (2015) draw a helpful distinction between a competencies approach and a capabilities approach as highlighting a tension between modernist and postmodernist worldviews respectively, as two dominant worldviews. They acknowledge that an element of a competencies approach may be unavoidable in coaching assessment, but that the capabilities approach builds on this by providing a more complete picture of the role of the coach (Bachkirova & Lawton Smith, 2015; Bachkirova 2015). In similar vein, while postmodern thinking has developed as a challenge to modernist thinking, it also builds on it 'and offers a theoretical shift that might be necessary if we wish to align our practice with a more expansive view of the world that acknowledges complexity, unpredictability, and the inter-subjectivity of meaning that we create' (Bachkirova & Lawton Smith, 2015; Bachkirova 2015, p. 136). Bachkirova and Lawton Smith (2015) conclude that a shift towards a capabilities approach in coaching education and training allied to greater emphasis on postmodern thinking 'would require more focus on the development of the coach as a person and a professional, aiming for congruence between the person and their particular model of practice' (p. 136), inclusive of more specific attention to developing critical reflection and reflexivity as generic skills.

The perspective of Cavicchia and Gilbert (2019) on coaching training frameworks also echoes some of the main points made by both Western (2012) and Bachkirova and Lawton Smith (2015) above. They highlight how different professional paths, academic histories, teaching approaches, and their embedded philosophical approaches will all contribute to shaping coach and coachee orientation to knowledge and the facilitation of learning and change (Cavicchia & Gilbert, 2019). More particularly, Cavicchia and Gilbert (2019) state that while positivist scientific disciplines and research frameworks (modernist thinking) will likely orient both coach and coachee toward objectivity and logic, 'postmodern and relational ideas about the nature of reality, meaning and experience may orient coach and coachee more towards intersubjectivity and meaning as a negotiated and socially co-constructed phenomenon' (p. 89).

In a related context, Hawkins and Turner (2020) refer to the development journey of the systemic coach in the context of describing coaching as being relational and dialogic by its nature, 'where two or more people discover new meaning and co-create new thinking and ways of being and doing in the world between them' (p. 1). Hawkins and Turner (2020) state that coaching education and training is only partially about learning new skills and acquiring new knowledge and that at the heart of all coach training is the individual developing themselves in terms of their own cognitive, emotional and ethical maturity (citing Hawkins, 2011). We agree in particular with Hawkins and Turner (2020) that it is essential to receive coaching and/or counselling and psychotherapy for oneself as a means towards being able to understand the work from the perspective of the coachee, 'as well as growing one's own self-awareness, emotional regulation, and relational and emotional intelligence' (p. 201).

Many coaching practitioners have experienced and/or experience significant mental health challenges. This is simply a fact of life. Suffering and resilience are not nor should be considered the preserve of individuals labelled as clients or coachees only. To adopt or internalise this mode of assumption increases the risk of considering and relating to individuals who experience significant mental distress as 'other.' One of the authors has a coach mentoring role with students involved in a third-level coaching education and training programme. Of particular interest in the context of this chapter is the frequency with which students bring previous or co-occurring mental health issues to the fore in their coach mentoring topics. Mental health issues are likely to continue intermittently or otherwise to be life challenges for students post-qualifying. It is important that a culture of acceptance of and practical support for students is available within coaching education and training programmes. The answer is not always a referral to student counselling. The development journeys of coaching practitioners should include active destigmatising of latent taboos regarding acknowledgment of mental health challenges. This is not unrelated to how students as post-qualifying coaching practitioners find themselves able to empathically relate or otherwise to coachees who experience mental distress.

Hawkins and Turner (2020) also highlight the importance of the development of collaborative intelligence, which includes the capacity 'to move beyond seeing individuals and individual perspectives, to perceiving the connections between individuals, between teams, and between organisations and their stakeholders and finally between the human and 'more-than-human' worlds' (pp. 202–203). In the context of the development journey of the systemic coach, Hawkins and Turner (2020) emphasise the critical importance for the coach/coaching psychologist of intentional commitment to growing one's self-awareness, emotional regulation and relational and emotional intelligence. We would regard these qualities as being essential prerequisites for *all* committed coaching practitioners and qualities that should be integral to all bona fide third-level coaching education and training programmes. Collaborative intelligence was a necessary element in the planning and operation of GLOW11, as regards perceiving, building and working with both helpful and conflictual connections between participants in GLOW11 group coaching sessions, the connections between GLOW11 participants and the DBT therapists and clinical psychologists with whom they had already formed supportive relationships, and the connections between the clinical psychologists in the mental health team concerned and ourselves as coaching psychologists. Collaborative intelligence was central to our capacity to coach safely and creatively with individuals who on the one hand were embedded in the mental health service system and who on the other hand expressly desired to move beyond the system towards greater degrees of autonomy and responsibility.

Referring to coaching psychology in particular, O'Riordan and Palmer (2019) note that psychologists bring with them to coaching psychology elements such as 'professional training, understanding the importance of theory, ingrained ethics, professionalism, the scientist-practitioner approach and core micro skills (citing Palmer & O'Riordan, 2014) and that consequently it is important that such factors are included within any future coaching psychology educational process or framework' (p. 580). In this context, we also agree with Palmer (2008) regarding the inclusion of coaching psychology in undergraduate psychology programmes, and indeed, we would add that it is also timely for coaching psychology to feature in third level clinical psychology doctoral programmes.

In the field of positive psychology, Lomas, Oades, Williams, and Kern (2020) refer to a third wave in positive psychology scholarship that advocates going beyond the individual person as the main focus of enquiry and looking more deeply at the groups and systems in which people are embedded, thus acknowledging greater complexity. Lomas et al. (2020) write that this scholarship in various ways 'embraces complexity and goes beyond the boundaries of psychology to incorporate knowledge and re-search methodologies from a broad range of fields to look deeply at the groups, organisations, cultures, and systems in which people – and their wellbeing – are embedded' (p. 21). In their paper, Lomas et al. (2020) pro-vide a broad but helpful sweep of the first, second, and third 'waves' of coaching psychology. They (Lomas et al., 2020) describe the first wave as essentially characterised by a focus on positive phenomena (including emotions, traits, behaviours, cognitions, and organisations) and acknowl-edge that 'in accentuating the positive, positive psychology could be seen as generating a polarising rhetoric, in which apparently positive qualities are regarded as necessarily beneficial and to be pursued, while negative phe-nomena as undesirable and to be avoided' (p. 6, citing Ehrenreich, 2009). Lomas et al. (2020) acknowledge that while the second wave of positive psychology remains focused on the concepts that underpinned the first wave, for example flourishing and wellbeing, the second wave is characterised by a more nuanced to concepts of negative and positive, 'an appreciation of the ambivalent nature of the good life, and an understanding of the funda-mentally dialectical nature of wellbeing' (p. 7; citing Lomas & Ivtzan, 2016). The third wave of positive psychology that may be forming is described by Lomas et al. (2020) as a general movement towards greater *complexity* (Lomas et al., 2020 emphasis). Implicit within a move towards greater complexity, Lomas et al. (2020) specify complexity in terms of 'focus of enquiry (becoming more interested in super-individual processes and phe-nomena); disciplines (becoming more interdisciplinary); culture (becoming more multicultural and global); and methodologies (embracing other ways of knowing)' (p. 8). The latter development is a helpful factor in the context of this chapter and our focus on the importance of 'ways of knowing' and the need for clarity and insight into the epistemological and theoretical underpinnings of coaching practice. Lomas et al. (2020) emphasise a broadening out and openness within third wave positive psychology to different epistemologies, such as 'interpretivist/hermeneutic, constructionist, phenomenological, and action-praxis' (p. 17; citing Hefferon, Ashfield, Waters, & Synard, 2017).

We view the development of positive psychology as structured by Lomas et al. (2020) as especially important from the perspective of how positive psychology is contextualised in third-level coaching education and training. In our experience, there can sometimes be a simplistic version of positive psy-chology (for example, positive thinking and positive emotions as a 'fix' re-gardless of context) that attracts some prospective students to third-level coaching programmes, in particular where 'positive psychology' is flagged as a major element of the programme. Lomas et al. (2020) importantly refer to a particular issue arising from the ever-expanding Masters of Applied Positive

Psychology programmes which has ethical implications, where graduates subsequently describe themselves as 'positive psychology practitioners' or 'positive psychologists' the latter label referred to as legally contentious.

Contingent to reflection on the perspectives mentioned previously, their similarities and constructive tensions are questions asked by Lane (2017) about the importance of clarity regarding the discourses underpinning professional practice in coaching and underpinning coaching education – 'Given that most trainees are asked to build their own model of practice what is the evidence base that supports a personal model of practice? '... what scientific discourse and what discourse of the practitioner underpins the way we train coaches?' 'How are these discourses related? Are they complementary or contradictory and how do they emerge in practitioner accounts?' 'What might a practitioner say they use to inform their work?' and critically, 'What are the responsibilities of education providers for promoting such an approach to professional practice?' (p. 655). Being involved in the education and training of coaching practitioners the authors fully endorse the importance of these questions. In this context, we would strongly advocate for inclusion in third-level coaching education and training programmes a module focused on the philosophical underpinnings of coaching theories, concepts, approaches and practice frameworks. We regard this issue as being of high importance both ethically and professionally. In the areas of counselling and psychotherapy, Raabe (2013) makes the following argument, which we regard as equally applicable to coaching education and training – 'unfortunately, most clinical psychologists, psychotherapists, and counsellors receive little if any formal training in philosophy before they offer their techniques as a service to the public. This leaves them inadequately prepared to deal with issues such as ethical decision-making, sorting out confused reasoning, coming to terms with religious beliefs, defining reality, determining what it means to be a 'normal' person within society, defining one's true self, and generally helping individuals to overcome the problems which cause emotional suffering, cognitive distress, and so on. Unfortunately, while the heart of all talk therapies is the practice of philosophy, most students and professionals have no idea that this is the case. Students are taught the methods or techniques of the various psychotherapies without ever gaining a solid understanding of the content or practice of philosophy' (pp. 3–4).

In this section, we have tried to highlight our view about the pivotal importance of the lifelong development of the coaching practitioner and the requisite need for clarity about and understanding of one's epistemological perspectives underpinning practice. These are topics that need to be explicit as content and process in third-level coaching education and training, and ongoing towards quality supervision and mentoring. Our emphasis on the epistemological underpinnings of coaching practice also dovetails into earlier considerations about the various epistemological underpinnings at work within the mental health system which translate into professional interactions with individuals with a diagnosis of BPD and other mental health challenges (for example, interactions that are informed by modernist/clinical or postmodernist/recovery-based ways of thinking). In our considerations of epistemologies or ways of knowing in both coaching/coaching psychology (for example, Western, 2012; Bachkirova & Lawton Smith, 2015; Cavicchia & Gilbert, 2019; Hawkins & Turner, 2020) and the mental health system in the western world in particular (Slade, 2009, 2012; Bracken & Thomas, 2009, 2013) there is a common theme of some complementarity, clear elements of tension and differences between modernist and postmodernist ways of thinking.

We have tried to make a case that coaching education and training third-level programmes need to incorporate methodologies that will both support and challenge students to actively engage with critical reflection and reflexivity to intentionally engage with coach development, appreciating, and understanding the importance of how different philosophical perspectives inform and guide ethical behaviour, decision-making, practice, and critically the inner working model one has of the other as person or otherwise. In our respective roles in third-level coaching education and training, we meet with student coaches from many backgrounds and varied levels of life experience. Initially, the majority are looking for *the* technique, *the* approach, *the* model, *the* 'killer' question, or insight that will 'fix' the problem (which is invariably not *the* problem but symptoms of). We have not offered any solutions in this book. We do not have any universal truth. Hopefully this will not disappoint the reader. Hopefully it will excite the reader. In constructing GLOW11 as an overarching framework, we learned to ease with some degree of comfort and a greater degree of challenge into not-knowing as an attitude and an approach, with a growing curiosity about what really mattered to each participant, what each really cared about, which we refer to as values. Such an attitude, we discovered, brings one into interesting and important experiences of aloneness and belonging, disconnection and connection, not-knowing and understanding, not so much as opposites but more as co-occurring. We experienced the invitation implicit in the challenge referred to by Stelter (2012) that 'coaching should be understood as a dialogue form that focuses especially on the coachee as a fellow human being … a partner in a shared process of learning and development' (p. viii) where coaching constitutes interaction and dialogue, not intervention, 'where shared meaning-making and reflections on essential life values carry special importance in the conversation' (pp. viii–ix).

States of mental distress and recovery in a time of COVID-19

We have mentioned the already-changing parameters in coaching/coaching psychology when considering the traditional boundary between interacting with clinical and non-clinical populations and that coaches/coaching psychologists are likely to be faced regularly with coachees showing some type of mental health difficulty (Cavanagh & Buckley, 2018). The advent of COVID-19 as a global and contagious pandemic is also perhaps influencing our perceptions of boundaries between clinical and non-clinical populations. In effect, the terms *clinical* and *non-clinical* are perhaps becoming redundant as regards usefulness.

As a result of COVID-19 and possibly in a way not previously experienced, to varying degrees, every human being is confronted on a daily basis with a profound uncertainty. We are not ultimately in charge or in control of nature, as the assumptions of unremitting globalisation, illusions of endless resources, and instant artificial connectivity might have led us to believe. The living interconnected organism that we are supposed to co-exist with and belong in has taken on a threatening and questioning visage. The physical and mental health of billions of people is threatened. Wellbeing is no longer the desired preserve of the heretofore comfortable middle and professional classes and upwards in the socio-economic pyramid. We are located within a profoundly unsettled and unsettling experience that has significantly dislocated our sense of any certainty about life, the present, and the future. Rettie and Daniels (2020) in the first study to examine health anxiety and coping responses in the general population (UK) identified the following initial emerging issues as significant – findings support emerging research that suggests the general public is struggling with uncertainty, more than normal; that quarantine can have a negative and potentially long-lasting impact on psychological health and this can be amplified by stressors within and after quarantine (e.g. duration of quarantine, lack of information, financial loss' (citing Brooks et al., 2020); that for people who are significantly challenged 'by the uncertain time frame of restricted movement, reduced social contact for extended periods, and illness of self or close others, the psychological effects are likely to be very pronounced' (p. 2); and that many people had significant concerns about the impact COVID-19 will have on their psychological health, more than physical health concerns (citing Holmes et al., 2020). Many of these individuals will previously have been described as the category of the 'worried well.'

The existential uncertainty triggered by COVID-19 has significant implications for the education, training, continuing professional development, and supervision of coaches/coaching psychologists, with particular reference to changing parameters and boundaries regarding mental distress. It is very likely that coaches/coaching psychologists will encounter an increasing number of potential clients experiencing elevated levels of anxiety, depression, and indeed varieties of emotional dysregulation. It is also likely that many coaches/coaching psychologists themselves will be experiencing elevated levels of anxiety, depression and varieties of emotional dysregulation. The need to bring third-level coaching education, training, and development online will pose critical challenges, with perhaps technological challenges being the least of these. Mental health challenges of coaching/coaching psychology students and practitioners will require something more than a competencies/coaching skills approach to education and training.

We agree with Clutterbuck (2007) that coaches need to be aware of the boundaries that it is unsafe, indeed dangerous to cross, and that this stipulation should remain the case. We agree also with Cavanagh and Buckley (2018) that coaches with a background in psychology or the psychological therapies may have the training, skills, and experience to come to an informed decision about the mental health issue at hand and may well be able to offer effective 'therapy,' but should still ask the question 'Can my coaching help?' rather than 'Can I help?' and that ability to recognise unusual signs and relate these to an individual's circumstances is the primary task when deciding how to answer the question 'Is my coaching appropriate?' (p. 455). And we agree with Buckley (2007) that the coach also needs to have the capability to explore signs of a possible mental health issue with the individual concerned to avoid making premature judgements. However, we believe that something more is now required in order to help coaches/coaching psychologists be more equipped to interact in ways that can bring value to individuals, groups, or teams experiencing elevated levels of mental distress.

Our view is that immersion in the recovery frameworks and related issues around ways of knowing, as explored in this book, hold much promise in contributing to coaching psychology education and practice at this time. While these recovery frameworks have emerged mainly through the subjective narratives of individuals in recovery (experts by experience) and unfolding research from the 'world' of mental illness, we believe that these frameworks also offer both a significant existential communication of grounded hope and a practical methodology for research and practice to coaching practitioners and to coaching education and training. We believe that based on the experience of GLOW11 and the reflections outlined in this book that the opportunity exists to bring a 'coaching for recovery' philosophy and practice into coaching psychology education and practice curricula, not simply as a specialist area, but as a framework that offers much in the context of coach development as a person and a professional, as well as to critical reflection and reflexivity on models of coaching practice.

It may be helpful here to refer again to the most commonly cited definition of personal recovery. 'Recovery is a deeply personal, unique process of changing one's attitudes, values, feelings, goals, skills, and/or roles. It is a way of living a satisfying, hopeful, and contributing life even within the limitations caused by illness. Recovery involves the development of new meaning and purpose in one's life as one grows beyond the catastrophic effects of mental illness' (Anthony, 1993). At this point we want also to position another previously mentioned perspective that helps to broaden out the meaning and applicability of recovery as a human need and experience.

Mussey (2016) writes about the recovery process 'revealing a human journey that is not unique to those who have been diagnosed with a 'mental-illness.' Who among us has not struggled to recover from some form of distress – like the loss of a loved one, a debilitating illness or accident, abandonment, betrayal, war, trauma, violence, abuse, or addiction? During dark times, haven't we too needed someone to listen with compassion to our story, inspire hopefulness and remind us of our resilience?' (p. viii). Every human being who experiences a disorienting mental distress is potentially subject to having their distress medicalised, classified, and diagnosed. However, the perspective we want to highlight is the degree to which coaching practitioners and coaching education and training providers may, without critical reflection, lean towards the medicalisation of human distress as normative practice. Watts and Higgins (2017) write that human beings are not simply physical objects, are not devoid of agency, choice, reason, and sense-making potential and 'they actively engage with, interpret and respond to the world' (p. 14) and conclude, citing Slade (2009), that 'filtering human experience through the medical or psychopathological sieve results in an impoverished and decontextualized version of meaning' (p. 14).

The philosophy and frameworks of personal or psychological recovery (for example, CHIME (Leamy, Bird, Le Boutillier, Williams, & Slade, 2011); CRM (Andresen, Oades, & Caputi, 2011) has the potential to be of intrinsic value *both* to people with a diagnosed mental illness (for example, BPD) *and* to the wider population of people experiencing mental distress that coaching practitioners may encounter, thereby strengthening the case for inclusion of the recovery philosophy and frameworks in coaching education and training. For reasons of reminder to the reader we mention here again the core components of recovery identified by individuals with a diagnosed mental illness, which have been synthesised into an emergent framework by Schrank and Slade (2007) as: hope (the belief of the individual that recovery, or change, is possible); spirituality (an important source of hope and meaning when redefining one's life...); responsibility and control (re-assuming responsibility and control over one's life ... as an act of emancipation...); empowerment (as a corrective for lack of control and sense of helplessness...); connection (stresses the highly social aspect of recovery – the path from being isolated ... to re-joining the wider social world ... establishing and maintaining relationships, assuming social roles and having friends); purpose (to have meaning and purpose in life is a basic human need...); self-identity (the re-conceptualisation of the self in the face of...); symptom management; and (overcoming) stigma. Schrank and Slade (2007) describe the concept of recovery as defined through the narratives of people involved with mental health services as much more complex compared to the normative and dominant clinical recovery. Proponents of the recovery orientation call for its full implementation from policy rhetoric to reality in mental health services and in the community. We have highlighted the opportunity for the recovery orientation to be incorporated into coaching education and training so that coaching practitioners may be more fully equipped to humanly, professionally, and ethically have interactions of value with people experiencing various forms of mental distress. GLOW11 has demonstrated how such innovative and important practice can be supported, individually and systemically. We conclude this section with a reference by Einzig (2017) which captures the argument well – 'Let me be clear: I am not suggesting that coaches flout medical guidance or take on clients with clinical depression. Every one of us, coach, leader, doctor or teacher, needs to know our own limitations. However, if we only ever operate within these limitations, they become a self-imposed comfort zone that suppresses the new and remains fertile ground only for nurturing more self-limiting beliefs. Coaching is about challenging just this. We also need to challenge ourselves' (p. 129).

Personhood

In the hyper-artificially connected world of artificial intelligence, bio-technology, crisis management, digital revolution, global financial crisis, neuroscience, paradigm shifts, robotics, and systemic complexity, it is easy to overlook the fundamental notion of personhood and the interdependence of human beings in their social contexts and how social context impacts the way individuals see themselves and engage with the world (Shoukry, 2016). Rosfort (2019) writes that 'the notion of personhood plays a fundamental, but challenging role in contemporary mental health' and that 'to understand mental suffering we need to understand how the person experiences, thinks about, and deals with her or his suffering' (p. 335). Personal recovery is not a 'quick fix.' The person, while experiencing their own subjective sense of recovery built on hope will invariably also be experiencing an ongoing struggle with the effects of their mental distress, whatever the diagnosis. In order to constructively interact with individuals who, experience significant mental distress, such as BPD, the coaching practitioner needs to be open-minded in consideration of their own psychological or mental health history. High-quality supervision is essential in this context. A 'community of practice' approach among coaching practitioners and other stakeholders interested in exploring the meeting point between coaching/coaching psychology and significant mental could be helpful. Certainly, for students in third-level coaching education and training programmes, there is a need to consider how coach development personally and professionally can become a foundational and integral element. Rosfort (2019) writes that to understand a human being, oneself as well as another, as a person is a way of seeing and this means 'that seeing every human being as a person is a choice or – as some would argue – an ethical demand' (p. 335).

In coaching/coaching psychology, where there is now a multiplicity of approaches, contexts, genres, and some theoretical perspectives that are specific to coaching, it is easy to overlook the fundamental importance of the coaching relationship. Palmer and McDowall (2010) write that 'regardless of which techniques, frameworks or psychological underpinnings a coach might draw on, basic coaching processes all rest on interpersonal interaction in some way or another' (p. 1). De Haan and Gannon (2017) state that rapport – building, 'trust and transparency, commitment, collaboration and co-creation appear as evident in the literature now as the very earliest studies in the field' (pp. 212–213). In the coach mentoring work of one of the authors with students in a third-level coaching and training programme, it has been noted that one of the most frequent causes of students losing their way in coaching practice sessions is an over-focus on tools, techniques, and 'powerful questions' and a consequent losing sight of the importance of being present, attentive, building rapport, summarising, and striking a balance between support and challenge person to person, in other words, building a coaching relationship. When students are invited to critically reflect on the relationship-building process in their coaching sessions invariably it is as if a light is switched on. Implicit in such critical reflection is also invariably a reappraisal and reframing of the student's assumptions about coaching and sometimes a disrupting impact. Rosfort (2019) writes that when something disrupts our experience of the world, we become aware that that experience is *our* experience, we are not simply experiencing something, 'we are involved in our experience and that experience *matters* to us' (pp. 336–337). This is true whether one is a person with a diagnosis of BPD exploring how coaching psychology might be of value to their lived experience, a student in coaching education, and training or an experienced coaching practitioner.

In the course of time during third-level coaching education and training programmes, students build relationships, and invariably particular friendships that are critical to their mental health and wellbeing. It was noted that when the coach mentoring sessions mentioned above had to switch from face-to-face to virtual contact, how students spoke about a sense of loss resulting from having to leave university and return home, whether in Ireland or to other countries of origin. This highlights how our mental health is actively supported and nurtured by our relationships.

Relationship and relationship-building is not a 'quick fix.' Rosfort (2019) writes that 'persons are considerate, mean, passionate, dull, kind, reserved, good, melancholic, ambitious, shy, bad, obnoxious, outgoing, prying, invidious, cool, sincere, joyful, anxious, reticent, and so on. It is this interplay of normative universality and descriptive individuality that makes seeing a person – ourselves as well as other people – a challenging task' (p. 339). COVID-19 is bringing to the fore not only the human need for resilience but also the why such resilience matters, the factual existence of different forms of human suffering. Coaching practitioners will need to be open to the reality that human suffering is always personal suffering, in oneself and in others. Strivings and struggles around personhood and relationship are predicated on the reality that 'to be a person is more than our sense of self. The way other people see me, and my identity as a person depends on their recognition and respect' (Rosfort, 2019, p. 340).

From our experience of GLOW11 we find deep resonance with Einzig (2017) making a case for a positive role for coaching in circumstances where individuals struggle with their experience of 'darkness' – that it is primarily through talking with a trusted other, 'who has the patience and skill to give the right kind of attention and support, that we make sense of our darkness. It is through finding meaning and discovering purpose that despair and depression cease to overwhelm us. Suppose, then, we turned on its head the tendency in our culture to favour the light and view the darkness as the repository of all that is fearsome and bad? Suppose that in the darkness lay answers we seek and that to avoid travelling into the dark forest would be to miss out on that learning?' (p. 124).

An ethical stance to coaching with people with BPD

Hawkins and Turner (2020) describe a scenario from working in South Africa where individuals in charge of managing coaching were asked to present their 'coaching culture strategy' and suggested that every so often they would stop and receive feedback from different stakeholders speaking from their place in the wider ecosystem. They write that suddenly one of the young black frontline managers got up and said 'it sounds like the people with the big offices, big cars, big pay-checks, now get the big coaches. I think this is very expensive personal development for the already highly privileged' (p. 3). Hawkins (2020) describes beginning to question how much coaching is creating positive value for the wider human family and the 'more-than-human world' (citing Abrahms, 1996) – 'whether coaches were just feeding western individualistic narcissism and self-absorption, which may be part of the root causes of many 21st-century human problems' (p. 3).

In a related context, Shoukry (2016) notes that there is hardly any discussion on a possible role for coaching in responding to and addressing wider non-organisational social issues. GLOW11 was one such coaching psychology initiative.

GLOW11 was primarily a values-based approach to offering coaching psychology to individuals with a diagnosis of BPD. Slade (2009) writes that recovery begins with discomfort – for the person concerned, discomfort may be about experiencing a tension between professional expertise and one's own lived experience, and for the professional, 'the journey towards working in a way which supports discovery also involves discomfort, at the level of values' (p. 135) and that working in a recovery-focused way must begin with a consideration of values. Coaching in a recovery-focused way must also begin with a consideration and making explicit of one's own values, in order to invite critical discussion which is both supportive and challenging for all concerned. We advocate that the experience of such discomfort on a number of levels should also be at the core of personal and professional development in third-level coaching education and training programmes.

Western (2012, p. 303) sets out an emancipatory framework for his Analytic-Network Coaching approach below. Adapting the framework can be applied to mental health organisations in general and for coaching psychologists working with individuals with BPD in particular.

1. **Individual values and development:** To help each person discover their 'charism,' their unique gift to the world.
2. **Humanizing mental health organizations:** Striving for more humane organizations, accounting for human experience as well as for financial gain.
3. **Environmental sustainability:** To act responsibly towards our natural environment locally and globally.
4. **Speaking truth to power:** To counter the psycho-social patterns (often hidden) that reproduce power elites and perpetuate social disadvantage to any individual or group.
5. **Emancipation:** Ethics and freedom are symbiotic. Our coaching process aims to help individuals discover their creativity and autonomy, and to identify social patterns that promote conformity and totalizing social structures that entrap us.
6. **Good faith and the good society:** To commit ourselves to working from a place of 'good faith' to help create the 'good society.'

Discussion points

1. Has your coaching education and training helped to prepare for working with people experiencing significant levels of mental distress? What is your need now?
2. To what extent is the development of critical reflection and reflexivity skills a core element in your professional supervision?
3. What do you know about the different 'ways of knowing' that underpin coaching psychology theorising and practice?
4. When you experience times of 'darkness' in your life, do you have a trusted ally who can help you make some sense of it?

Suggested reading

Bachkirova, T., & Lawton Smith, C. (2015). From competencies to capabilities in the assessment and accreditation of coaches. *International Journal of Evidence Based Coaching and Mentoring, 13*(2), 123–140. (This is an important article in the context of coach education, training and continuing professional development).

Lomas, T., Oades, L. G., Williams, P., & Kern, M. L. (2020). Third wave positive psychology: Broadening towards complexity. *The Journal of Positive Psychology*, DOI: 10.1080/17439760.2020.1805501 (This is an important article which positions third-wave positive psychology as a movement toward greater complexity in terms of focus of enquiry, disciplines, culture and methodologies).

O'Riordan, S., & Palmer, S. (2019). Global activity in the education and practice of coaching psychology. In S. Palmer, & A. Whybrow (Eds.), *Handbook of coaching psychology: A guide for practitioners* (pp. 573–583). London, UK: Routledge. (The chapter provides a comprehensive overview of current and emerging international themes in the education and practice of coaching psychology).

Western, S. (2012). *Coaching and mentoring: A critical text*. London, UK: Sage. (Chapter 13 has a very interesting and challenging perspective on coach formation; p. 303 provides a concise framework for emancipatory ethics).

References

Abrahms, D. (1996). *The spell of the sensuous*. New York: Random House.

Andresen, R., Oades, L. G., & Caputi, P. (2011). *Psychological recovery: Beyond mental illness*. Chichester, UK: Wiley-Blackwell.

Anthony, W. (1993). Recovery from mental illness: The guiding vision of the mental health service system in the 1990s. *Psychosocial Rehabilitation Journal, 16*, 11023.

Bachkirova, T., & Lawton Smith, C. (2015). From competencies to capabilities in the assessment and accreditation of coaches. *International Journal of Evidence Based Coaching and Mentoring, 13*(2), 123–140.

Bracken, P., & Thomas, P. (2005). *Post-psychiatry: Mental health in a postmodern world*. Oxford, UK: Oxford University Press.

Bracken, P., & Thomas, P. (2013). Challenges to the modernist identity of psychiatry: User empowerment and recovery. In K. W. M. Fulford, M. Davies, R. G. T. Gipps, G. Graham, J. Z. Sadler, G. Stanghellini, & T. Thornton (Eds.), *The Oxford handbook of philosophy and psychiatry* (pp. 123–138). Oxford, UK: Oxford University Press.

Brooks, S. K., Webster, R. K., Smith, L. E., Woodland, L., Wessely, S., Greenberg, N., & Rubin, G. J. (2020). The psychological impact of quarantine and how to reduce it: Rapid review of the evidence. *Lancet, 395*, 912–920.

Buckley, A. (2007). The mental health boundary in relationship to coaching and other activities. *International Journal of Evidence-Based Coaching and Mentoring*, Special Issue, Summer: 17–23.

Cavanagh, M.J., & Buckley, A. (2018). Coaching and mental health. In E. Cox, T. Bachkirova, & D. Clutterbuck (Eds.), *The complete handbook of coaching* (3rd ed.). Sage.

Cavicchia, S., & Gilbert, M. (2019). *The theory and practice of relational coaching: Complexity, paradox and integration*. London, UK: Routledge.

Clutterbuck, D. (2007). *Coaching the team at work*. London, UK: Nicholas Brealey.

De Haan, E., & Gannon, J. (2017). The coaching relationship. In T. Bachkirova, G. Spence, & D. Drake (Eds.), *The Sage handbook of coaching* (pp. 195–217). London, UK: Sage Publications Ltd.

Ehrenreich, B. (2009). *Bright-sided: How the relentless promotion of positive thinking has undermined America*. New York: Metropolitan Books.

Einzig, H. (2017). *The future of coaching: Vision, leadership and responsibility in a transforming world*. London, UK: Routledge.

Gannon, J., & Myers, A. (2018). Coach education, training and development. In E. Cox, T. Bachkirova, & D. Clutterbuck (Eds.), *The complete handbook of coaching* (3rd ed., pp. 465–482). London, UK: Sage.

Hawkins, P. (2011). Building emotional, ethical and cognitive capacity in coaches – A development model of supervision. In J. Passmore (Ed.), *Supervision in coaching*. London, UK: Kogan Page.

Hawkins, P., & Turner, E. (2020). *Systemic coaching: Delivering value beyond the individual*. London, UK: Routledge.

Hefferon, K., Ashfield, A., Waters, L., & Synard, J. (2017). Understanding optimal human functioning – The 'call for qual' in exploring human flourishing and well-being. *The Journal of Positive Psychology*, *12*(3), 211–219. DOI: 10.1080/1743 9760.2016.1225120

Holmes, E. A., O'Connor, R. C., Perry, V. H., Tracey, L., Wessely, S., Arseneault, L., …Bullmore, E. (2020). Multidisciplinary research priorities for the COVID-19 pandemic: A call for action for mental health science. *The Lancet Psychiatry*, *7*, 547–560.

Lane, D. (2017). Trends in development of coaches (education and training): Is valid, is it rigorous and is it relevant? In T. Bachkirova, G. Spence, & D. Drake (Eds.), *The Sage handbook of coaching* (pp. 647–661). London, UK: Sage.

Leamy, M., Bird, V., Le Boutillier, C., Williams, J., & Slade, M. (2011). A conceptual framework for personal recovery in mental health: Systematic review and narrative synthesis. *British Journal of Psychiatry*, *199*, 445–452.

Lomas, T., & Ivtzan, I. (2016). Professionalising positive psychology: Developing guidelines for training and regulation. *International Journal of Wellbeing*, *6*(3), 96–112. DOI: 10.5502/ijw.v6i3.4

Lomas, T., Waters, L.E., Williams, P., Oades, L. G., & Kern, M. L. (2020). Third wave positive psychology: Broadening towards complexity. *The Journal of Positive Psychology* (August 2020 online), DOI: 10.1080/17439760.2020.1805501

McLean, J. J. (2018). People, planet and profit: Facilitating change through coaching. ICF Bengaluru Coaching Conclave. Conference keynote presentation, Bengaluru, India.

Mussey, C. (2016). Foreword. In M. Watts & A. Higgins, *Narratives of recovery from mental illness: The role of peer support*. London, UK: Routledge.

O'Riordan, S., & Palmer, S. (2019). Global activity in the education and practice of coaching psychology. In S. Palmer, & A. Whybrow (Eds.), *Handbook of coaching psychology: A guide for practitioners* (pp. 573–583). London, UK: Routledge.

Palmer, S. (2008). A coaching psychology perspective. *Psychology Teaching Review*, *14*(2), 40–42.

Palmer, S., & McDowall, A. (2010). The coaching relationship: Putting people first. An introduction. In S. Palmer, & A. McDowall (Eds.), *The coaching relationship: Putting people first* (pp. 1–8). Hove, UK: Routledge.

Palmer, S., & O'Riordan, S. (2014, December). *Developments in the education, practice and establishment of coaching psychology: An international perspective 2010*. Coaching Psychology: An International Perspective. Paper presented at the SGCP 4th International Congress of Coaching Psychology. British Psychological Society, London.

Raabe, P. B. (2013). *Philosophy's role in counselling and psychotherapy*. New York: Jason Aronson.

Rettie, H., & Daniels, J. (2020). Coping and tolerance of uncertainty: Predictors and mediators of mental health during the COVID-19 pandemic. *American Psychologist* (Advanced online publication).

Rosfort, R. (2019). Personhood. In G. Stanghellini, M. R. Broome, A. V. Fernandez, P. Fusar-Poli, A. Raballo, & R. Rosfort (Eds.), *The Oxford handbook of phenomenological psychopathology* (pp. 335–343). Oxford, UK: Oxford University Press.

Schrank, B., & Slade, M. (2007). Editorial. *Psychiatric Bulletin, 31*, 321–325, DOI: 10.1192/pb.bp.106.013425

Shoukry, H. (2016). Coaching for emancipation: A framework for coaching in oppressive environments. *International Journal of Evidence Based Coaching and Mentoring, 14*(2), 15–30.

Slade, M. (2009). *Personal recovery and mental illness: A guide for mental health professionals*. Cambridge, UK: Cambridge University Press.

Slade, M. (2012). The epistemological basis of personal recovery. In A. Rudnick (Ed.), *Recovery of people with mental illness: Philosophical and related perspectives* (pp. 78–94). Oxford, UK: Oxford University Press.

Stelter, R. (2012). *A guide to third generation coaching: Narrative-collaborative theory and practice*. London, UK: Springer.

Watts, M., & Higgins, A. (2017). *Narratives of recovery from mental illness: The role of peer support*. London, UK: Routledge.

Western, S. (2012). *Coaching and mentoring: A critical text*. London, UK: Sage.

Epilogue

In the spring of 2020, COVID-19 crashed onto the human shore, uncontained. A coaching psychologist living in Ireland who had been involved in GLOW11 in 2019 took a telephone call from a person residing about five hours away, also in Ireland. The caller was a person with a diagnosis of Borderline Personality Disorder (BPD) who had participated in GLOW11. The person was struggling, mentally and emotionally. The person was reaching out, for a word, for recognition, for connection, for help. Familiar negative thinking patterns had taken charge. Familiar painful emotions were back in their flow. The coaching psychologist listened as the caller spoke, a slow, almost whispered story of feeling too close to the cliff edge again.

The call posed an ethical and professional dilemma for the coaching psychologist. On the one hand, wanting to reach out and offer something that might help, though not sure about what would help. Just as the caller was feeling adrift mentally and emotionally, so the coaching psychologist felt uncertain, knowing that the caller was in need of specific help. The coaching psychologist experienced a sense of isolation and loss during the very moments when normally a helpful response would be forthcoming. As the caller spoke, there seemed to be no time to think, to consider, or reflect. The need expressed by the caller was urgent and immediate. The coaching psychologist experienced a surge of anxiety and an almost physically embodied panic.

Recovering a semblance of momentary balance, the coaching psychologist asked the caller for their phone number, asked that they wait for a call back and promised to phone back within 15 minutes at the most. The coaching psychologist was hoping against hope that that what needed to be arranged could be arranged in that time. The caller agreed. There followed a phone call seeking support and advice from a GLOW11 coaching psychologist colleague. This phone call provided necessary clarity. A referral of the person concerned back to the mental health services was immediately recommended. A further phone call to a personal number put that referral into operation.

The coaching psychologist phoned the person as promised. The person was informed that a particular mental health professional known to them, was waiting for their call and would take things from there to provide safety, care, and support. The specific steps that were recommended to the person were clear and sequential. The person who had phoned the coaching psychologist paused for a moment on receiving the information and then agreed to make the recommended phone call. The coaching psychologist waited for a call to confirm that the person concerned had contacted the recommended mental health professional. That call came.

The coaching psychologist then contacted their GLOW11 colleague again, for a longer phone conversation of grounding, support, and relocating a sense of perspective regarding what had just occurred.

This event is shared here with the reader to highlight an important point, which has already been alluded to earlier in the book. GLOW11 was not a standalone coaching psychology interaction with individuals with a diagnosis of BPD. GLOW11 functioned as a bridge for those individuals who had expressed a wish to mental health professionals who had supported them through a DBT programme that they wished to further build on their learning with a view to having a life worth living from their individual perspectives.

The purpose of this book is to invite a conversation between and across coaching psychologists, mental health professionals, and people with BPD regarding the concept of personal/psychological recovery and how to embody this in individuals' lived daily experience. We sincerely hope that this conversation can be had, especially at this time, when so many are in need of ethically important issues on which to focus attention.

Index